This Coloring Book Belongs to :

Candy

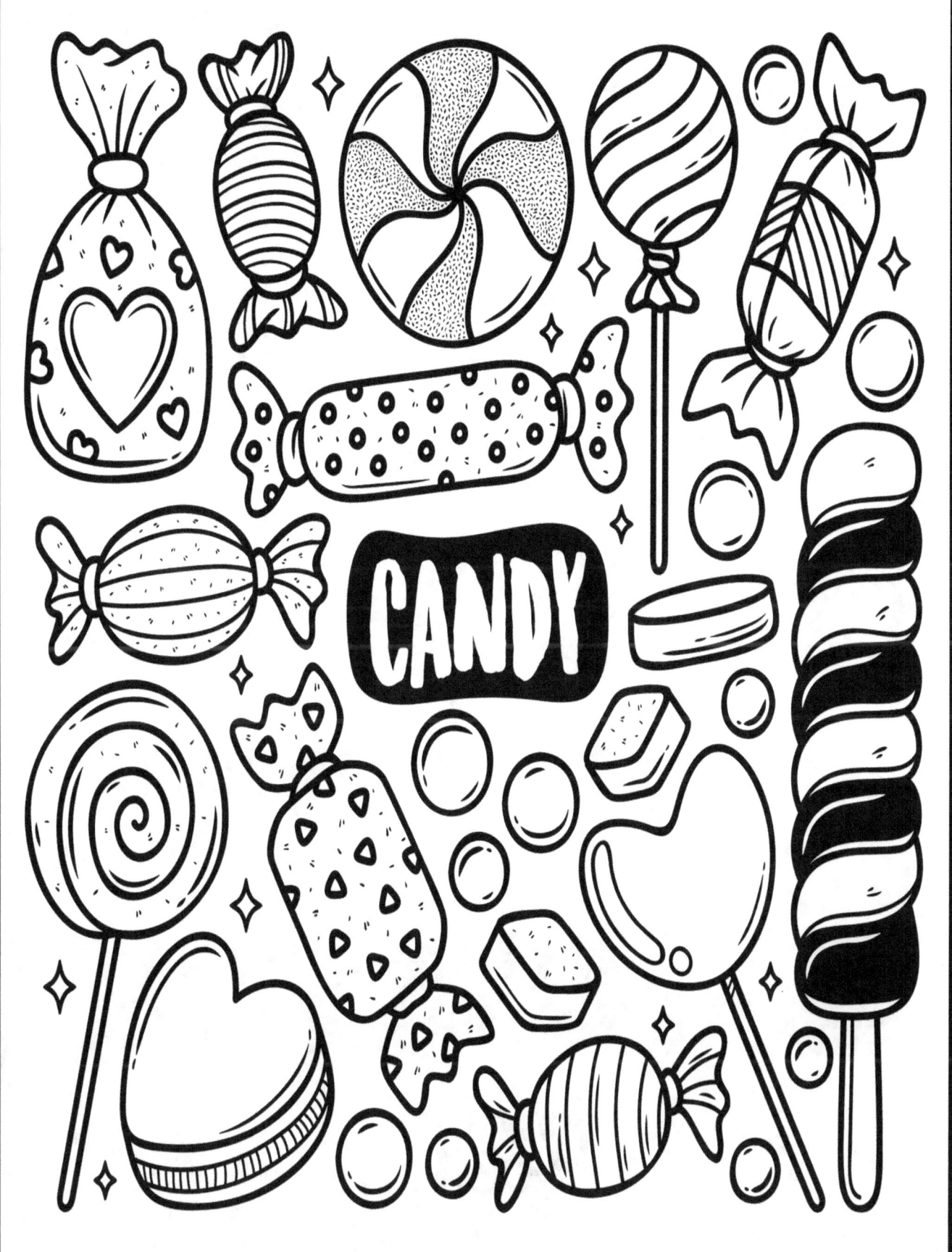

Yes...

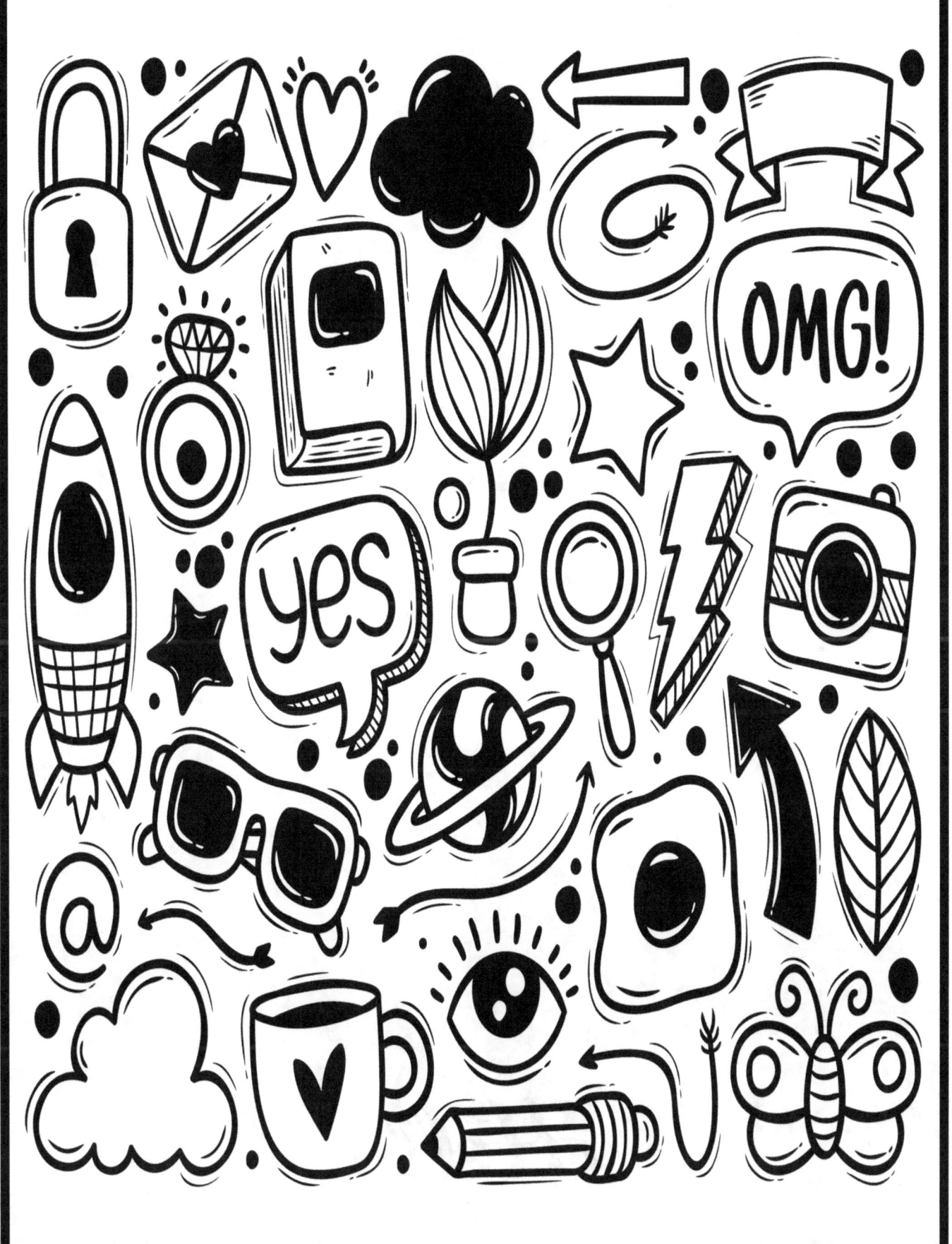

Hello

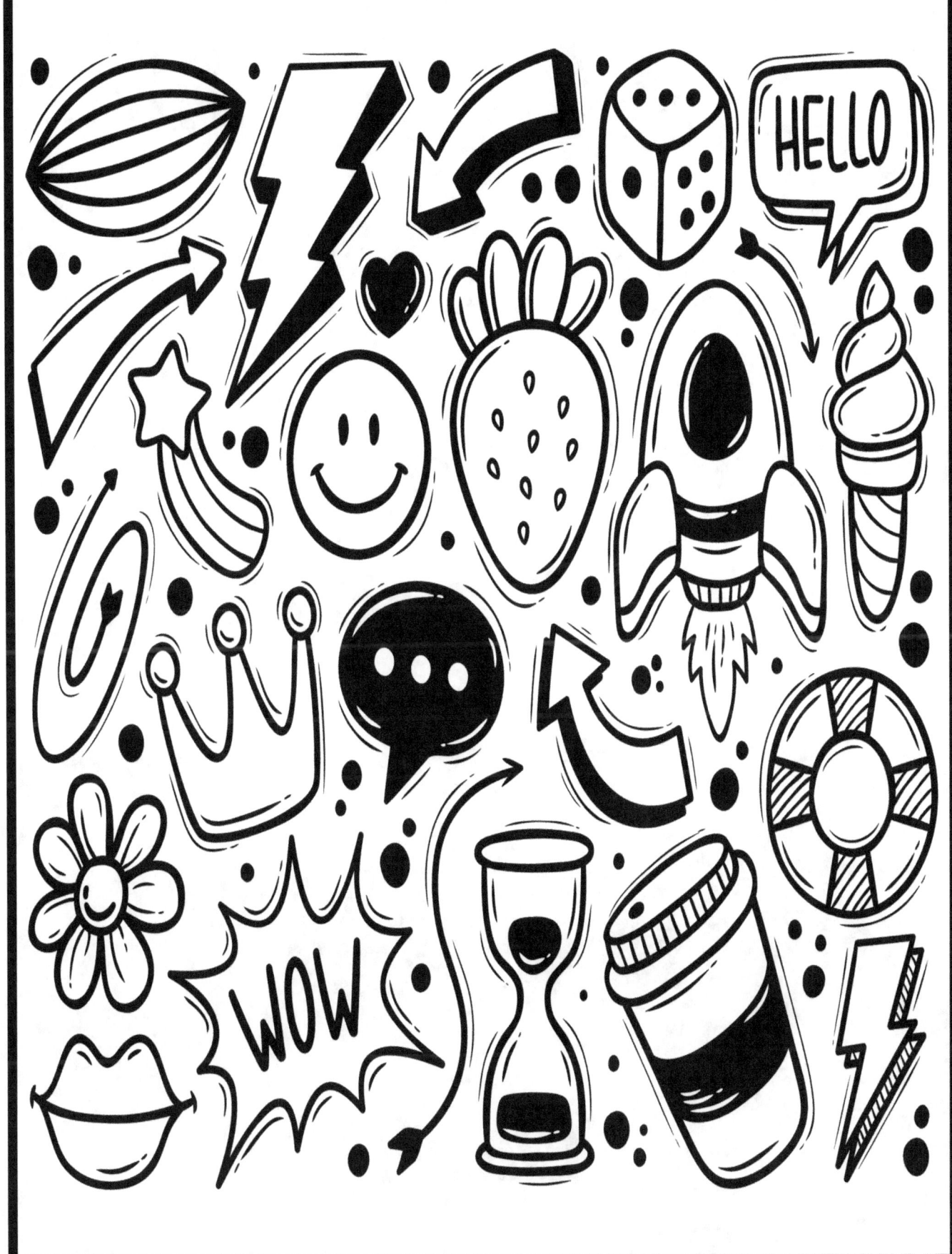

Ouch

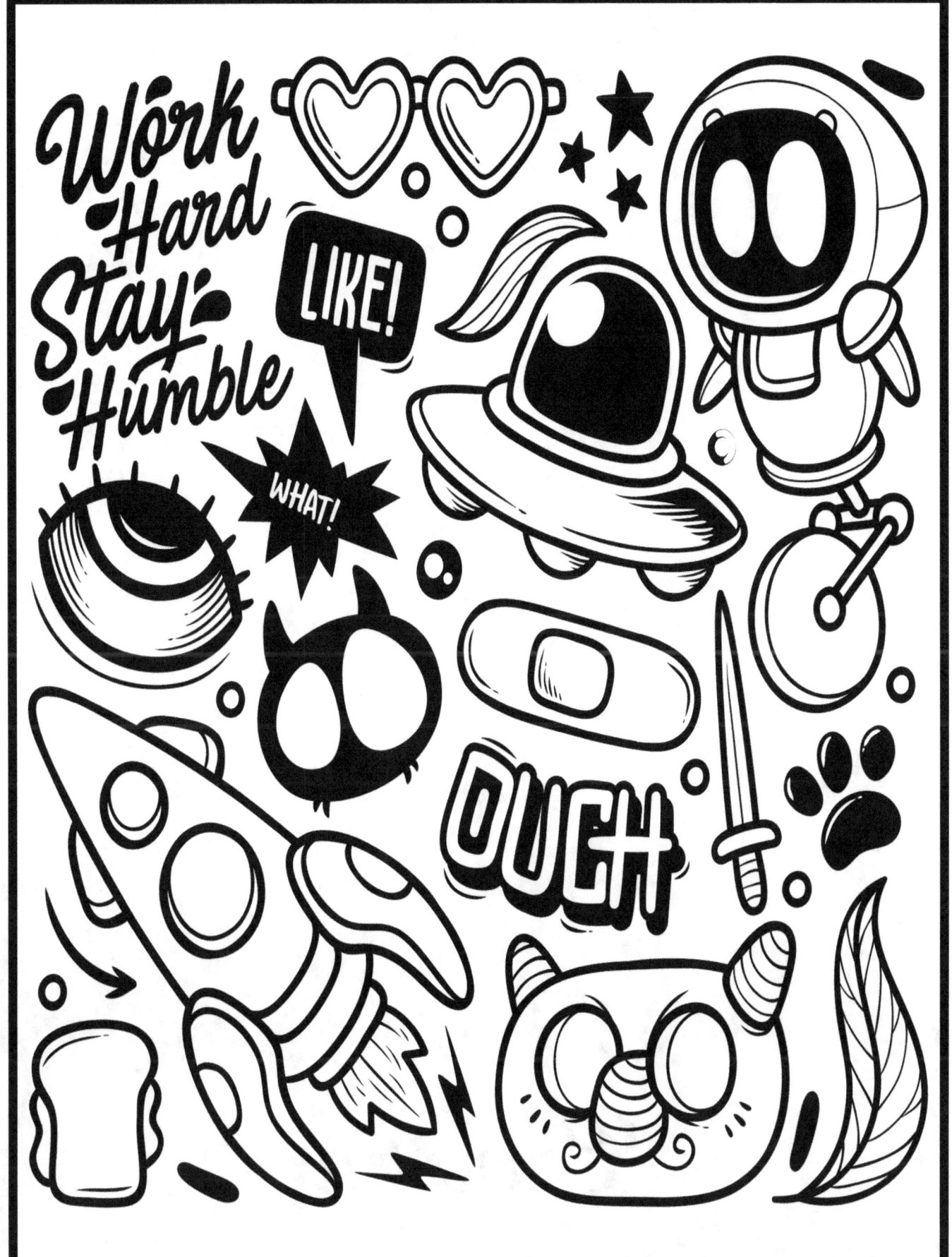

Camera

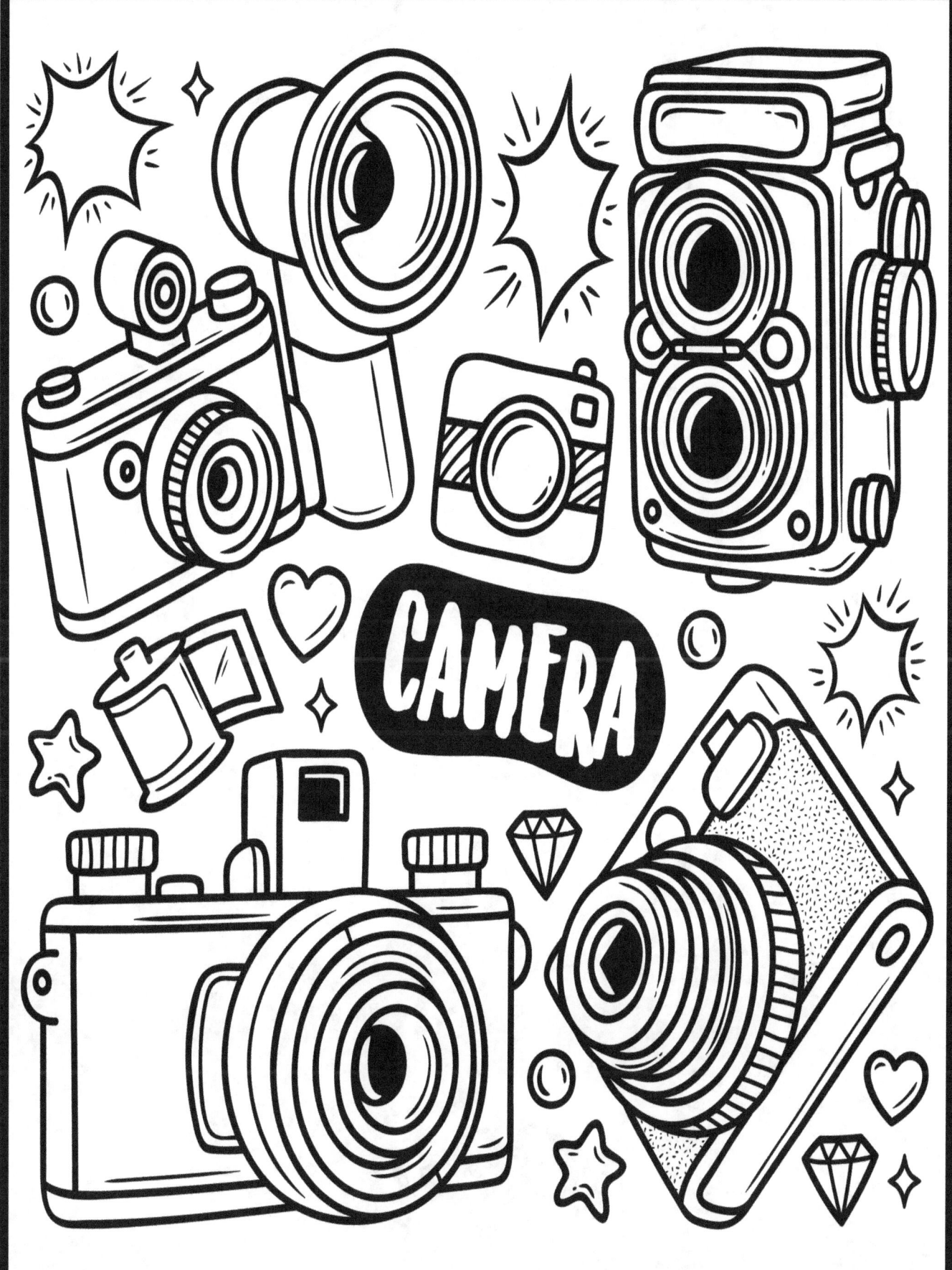

Okay

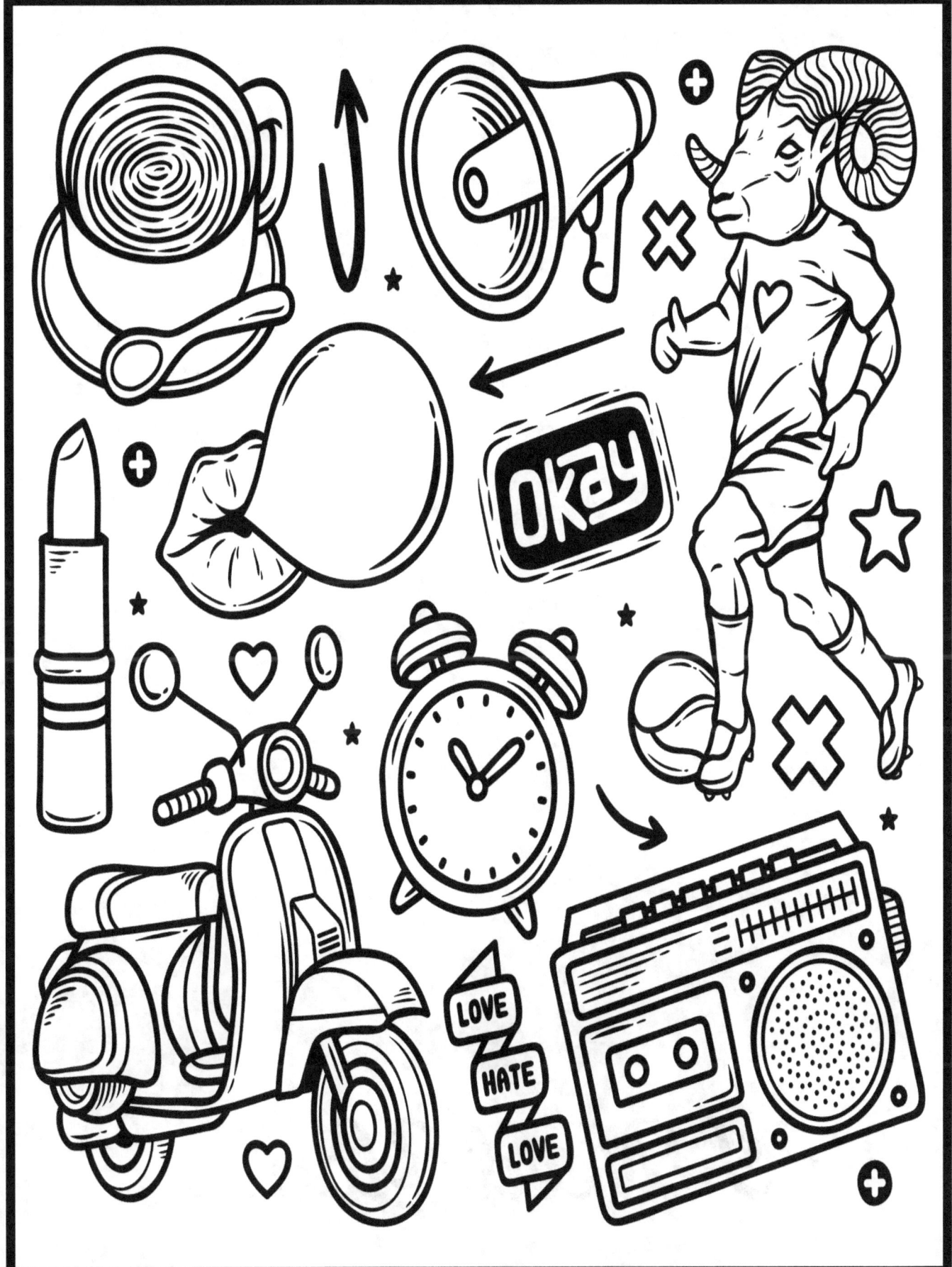

I Need You....

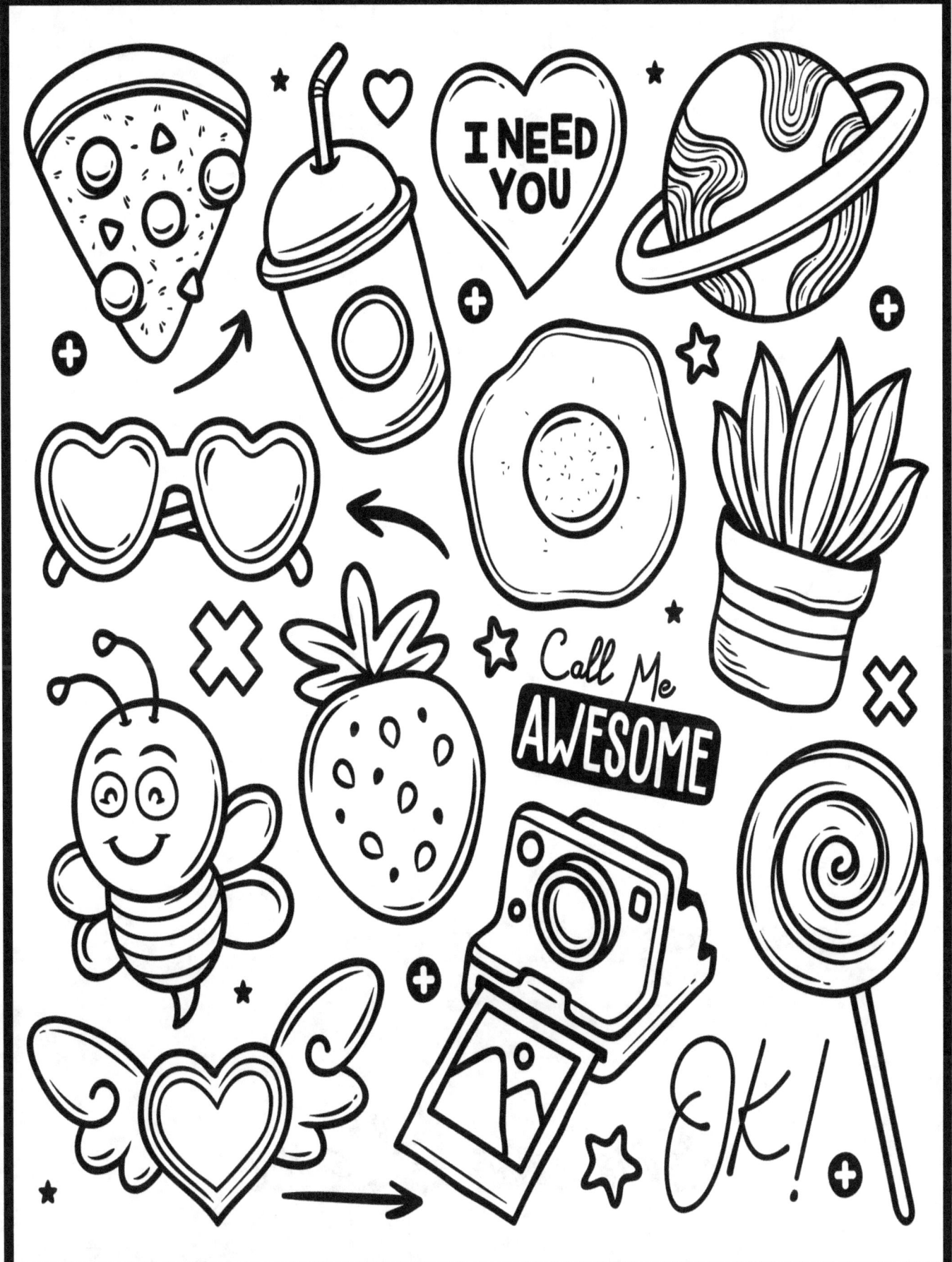

Stress Less

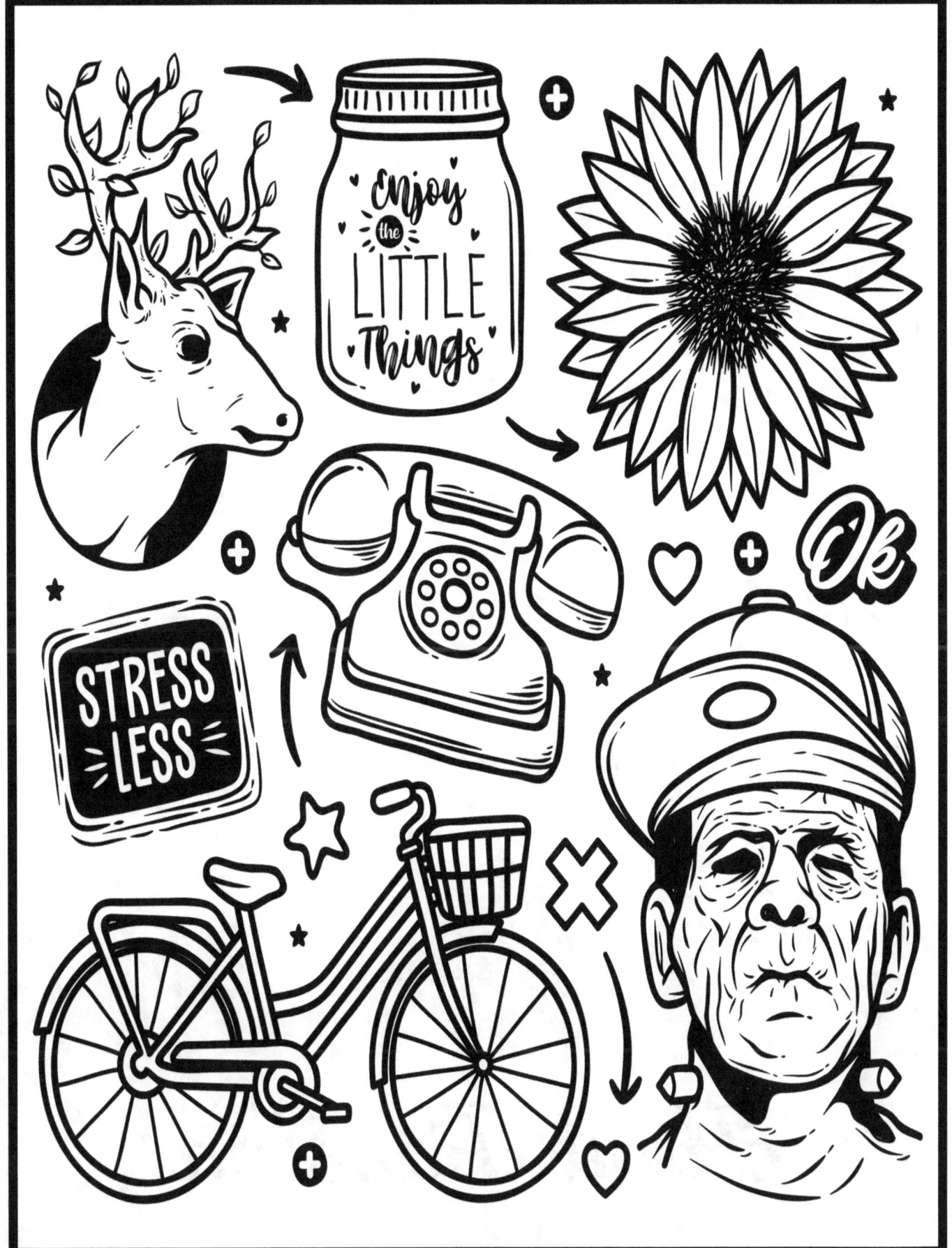

Have Passion

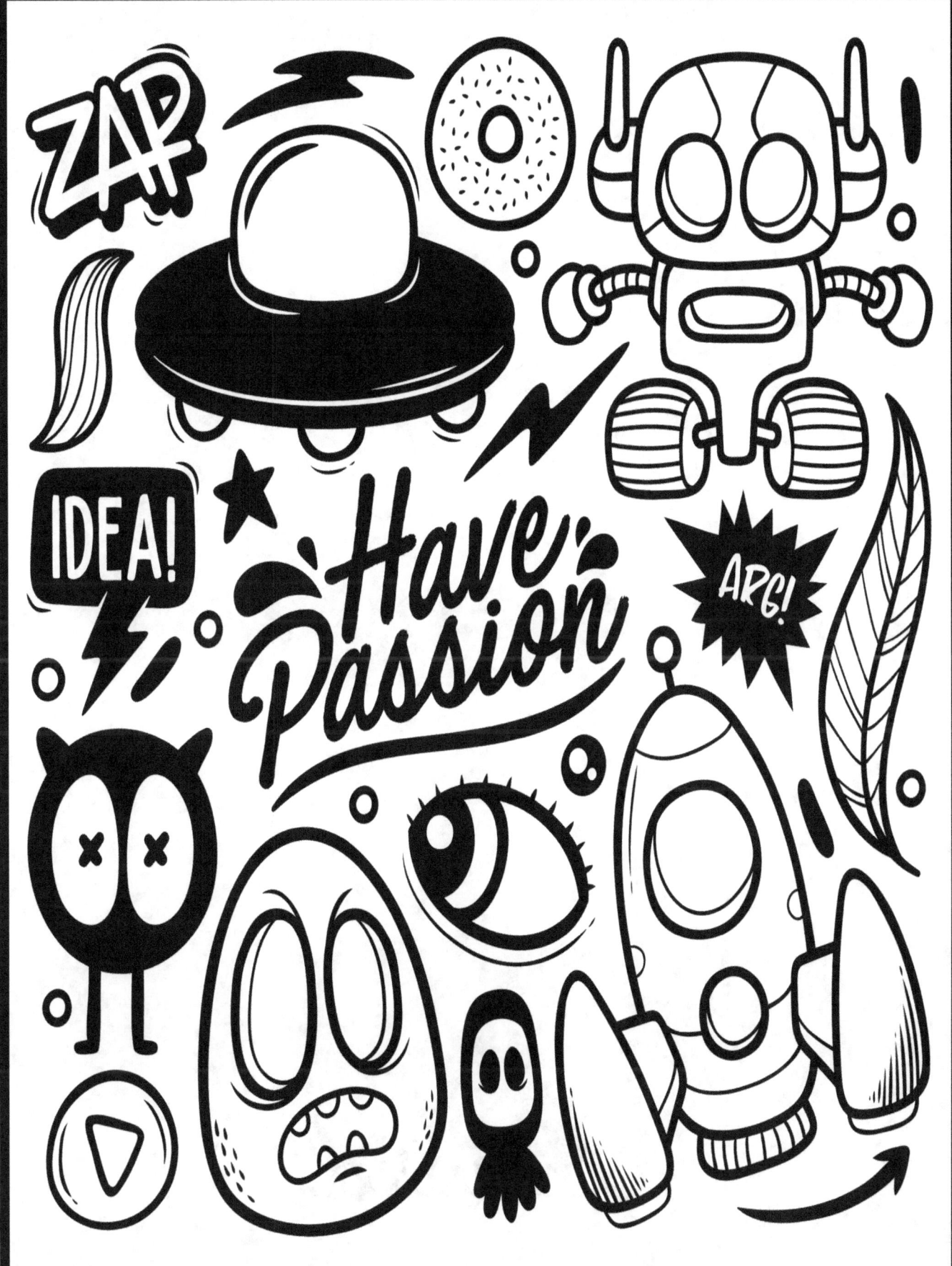

Award

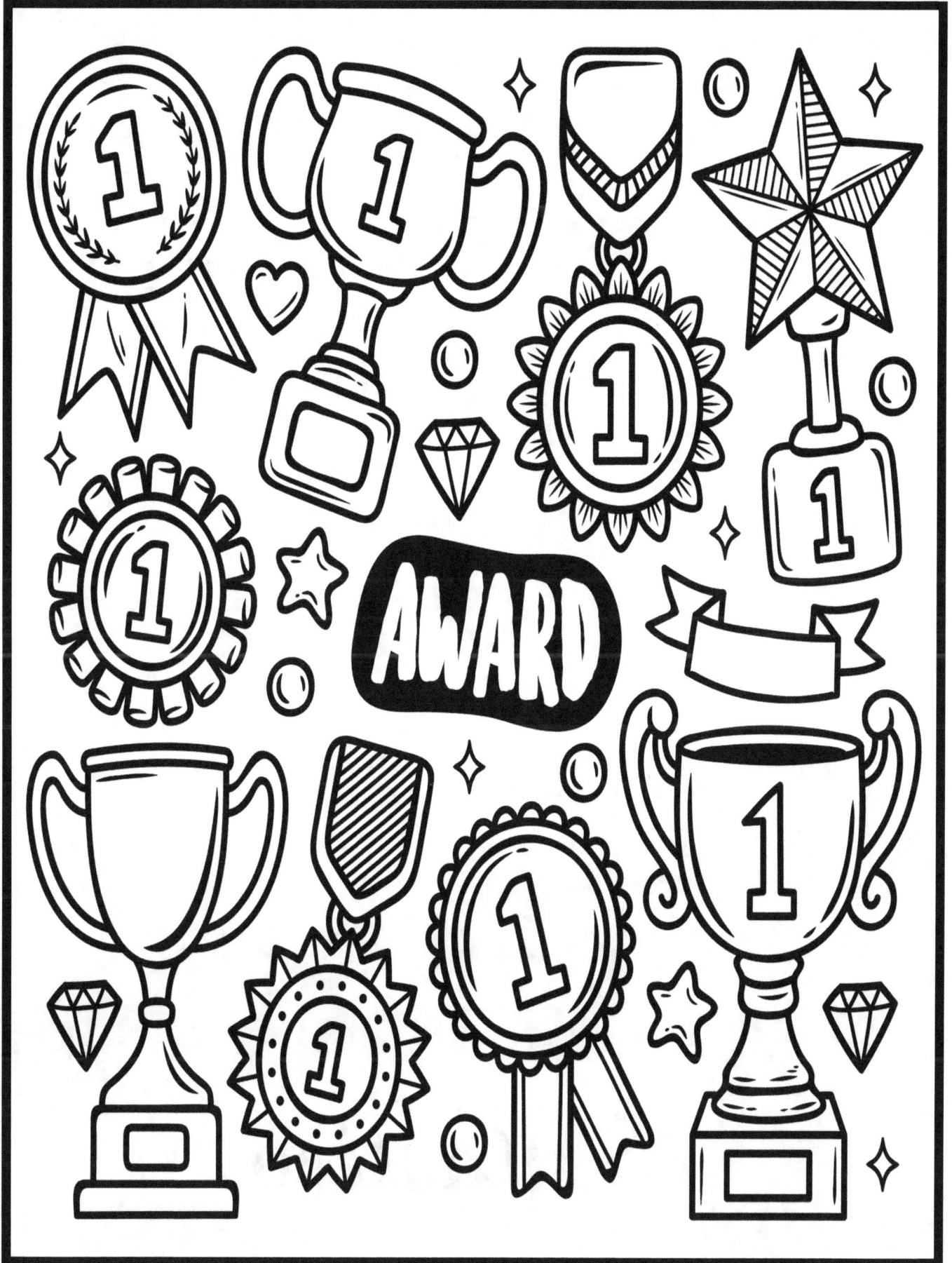

Fantastico

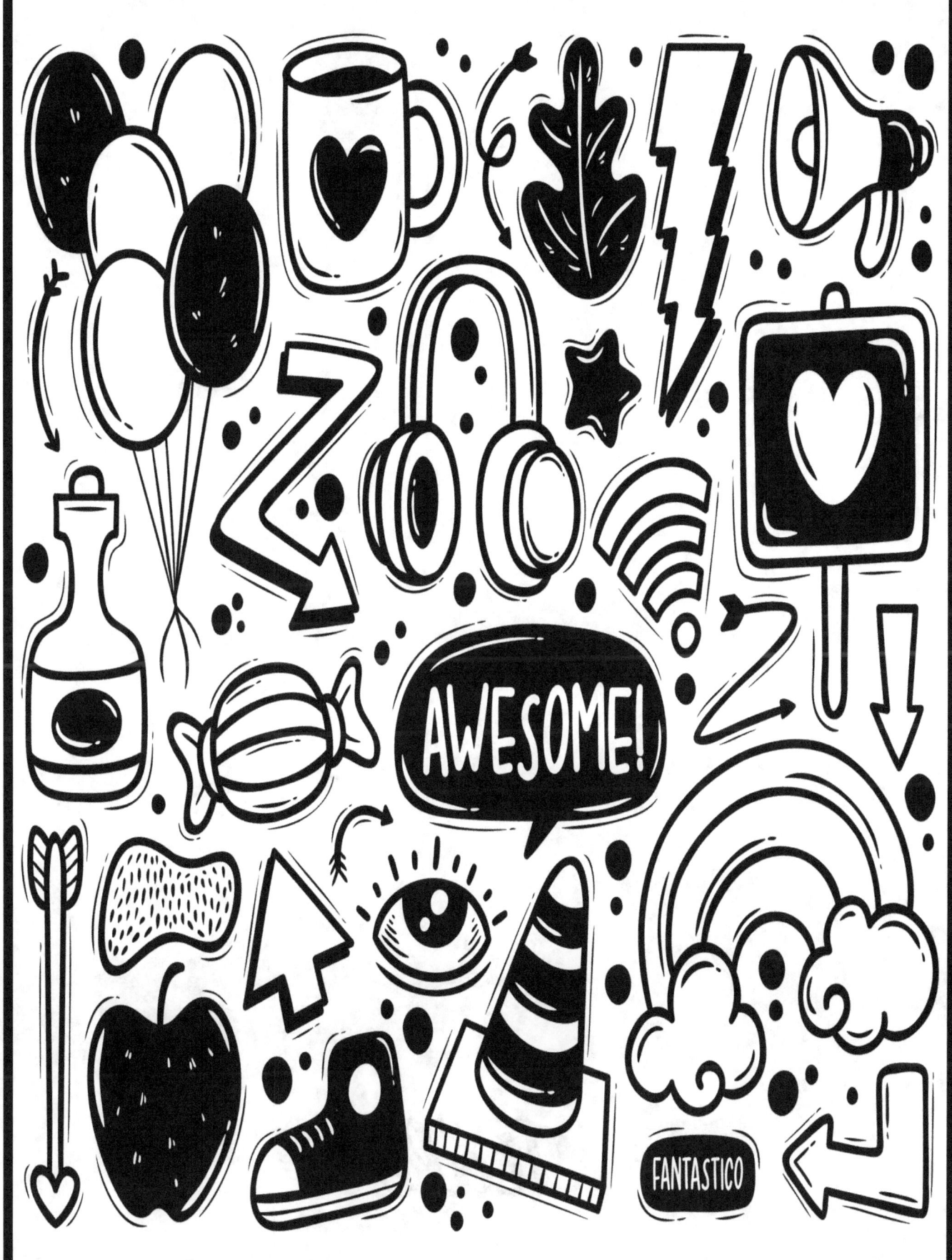

Italy

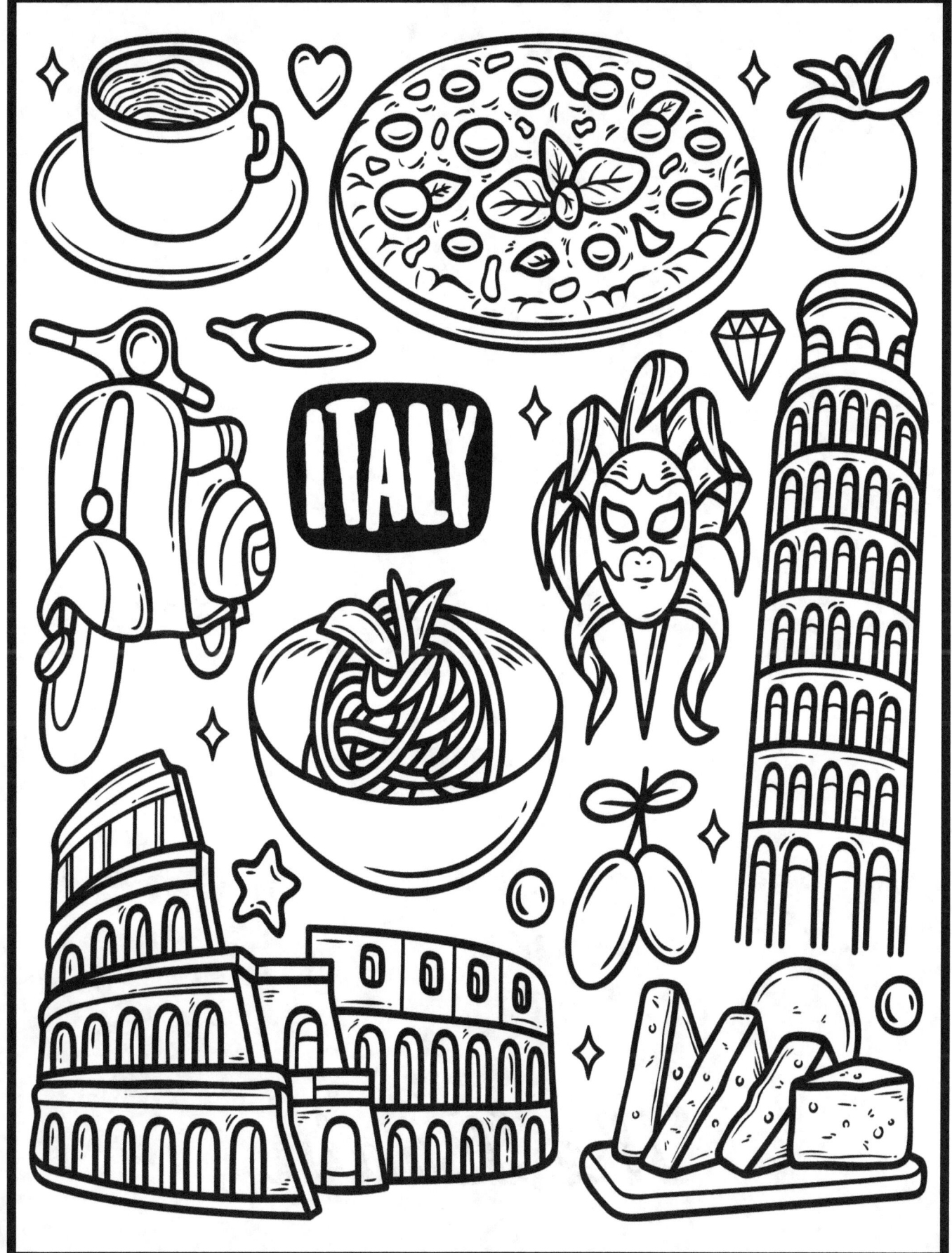

The Brain

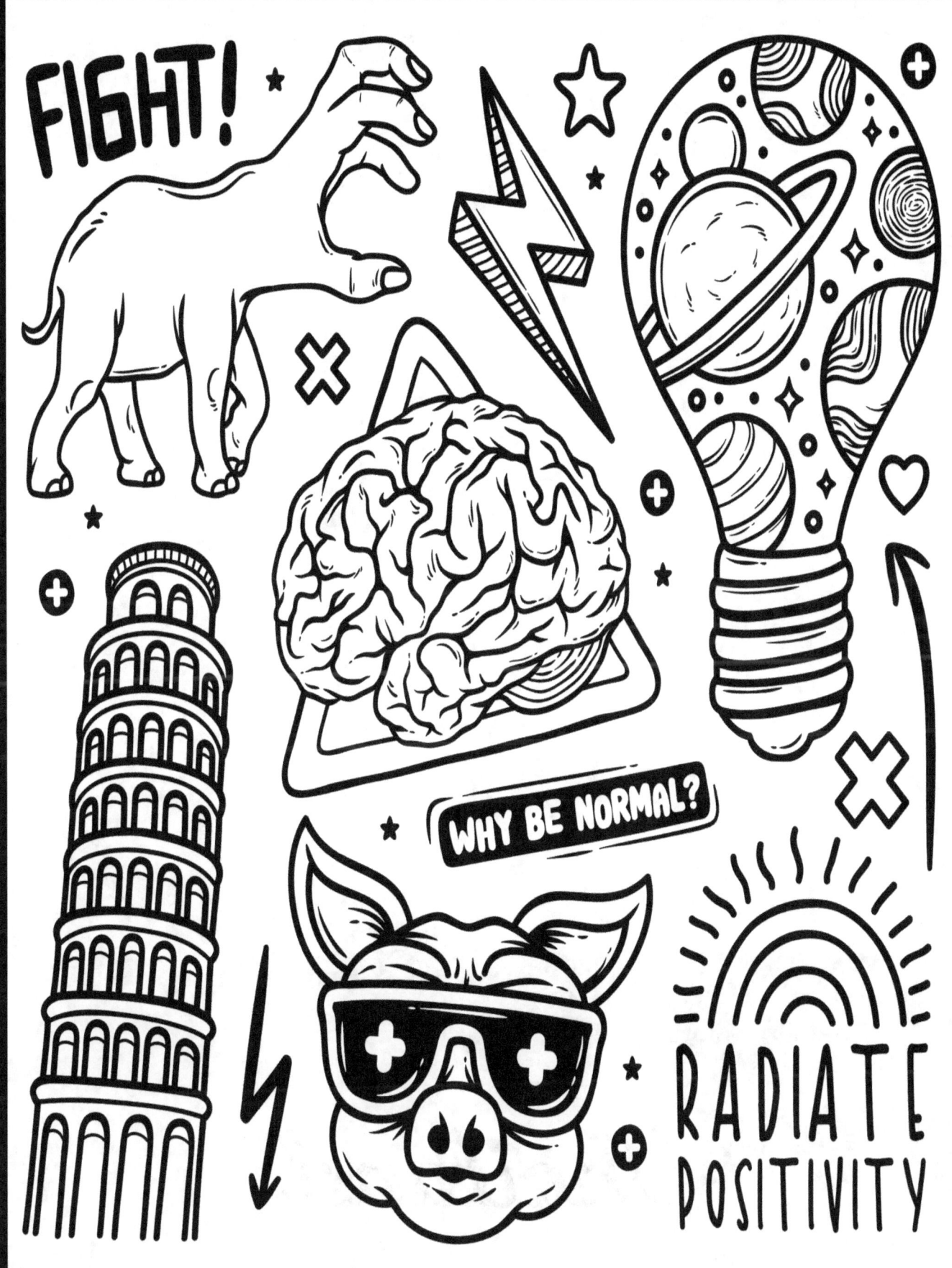

Thailand

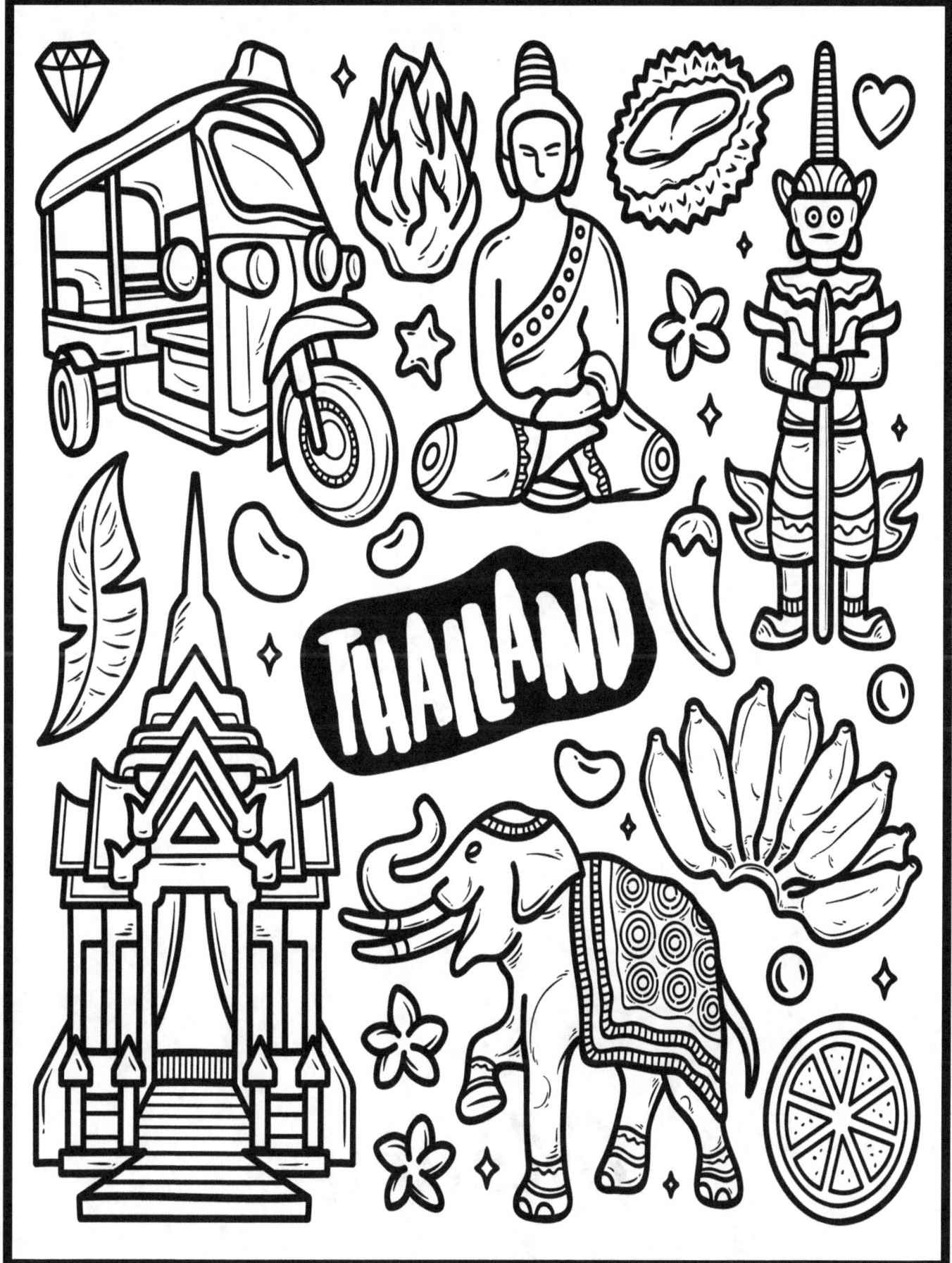

Money

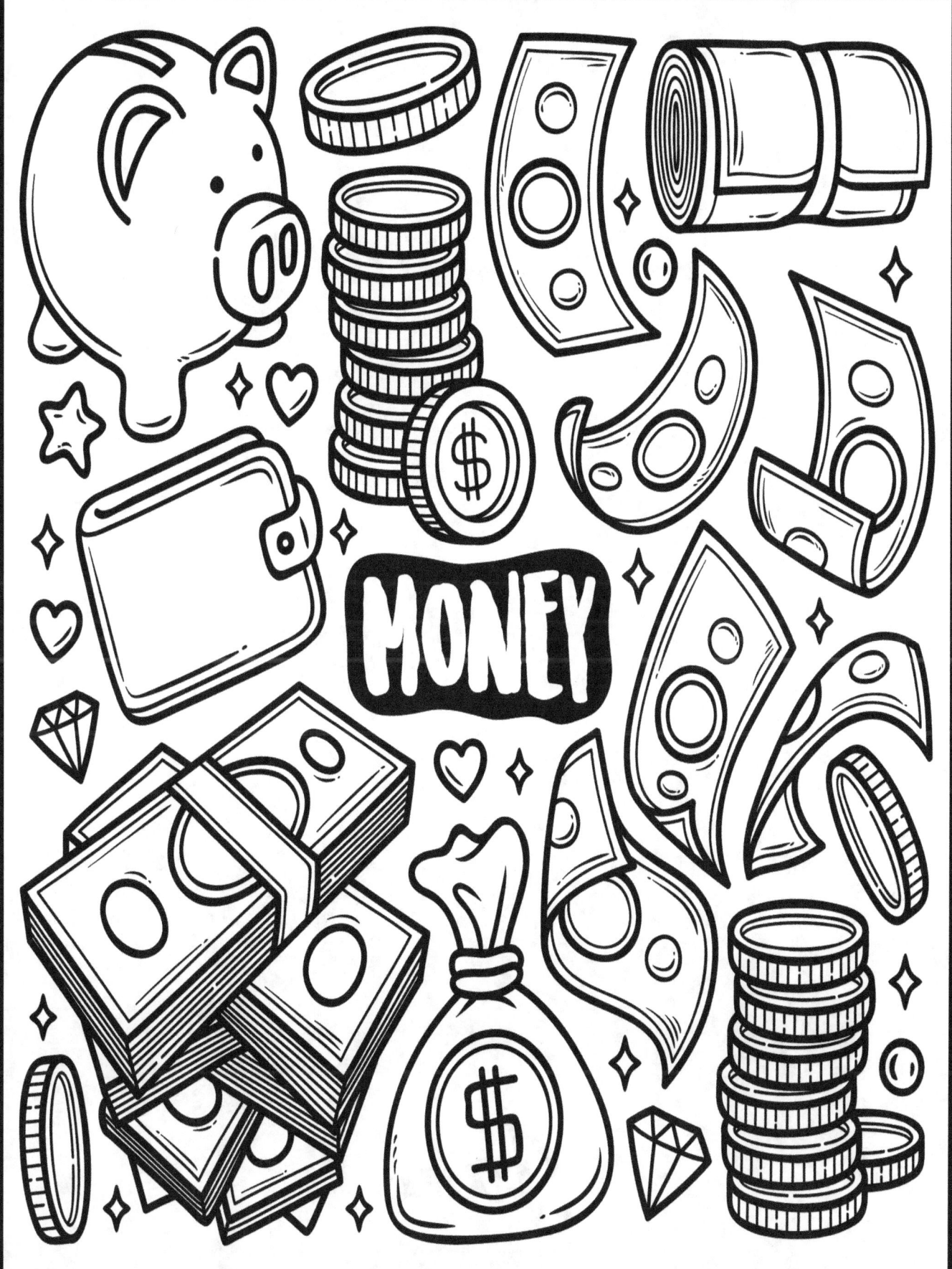

Jars

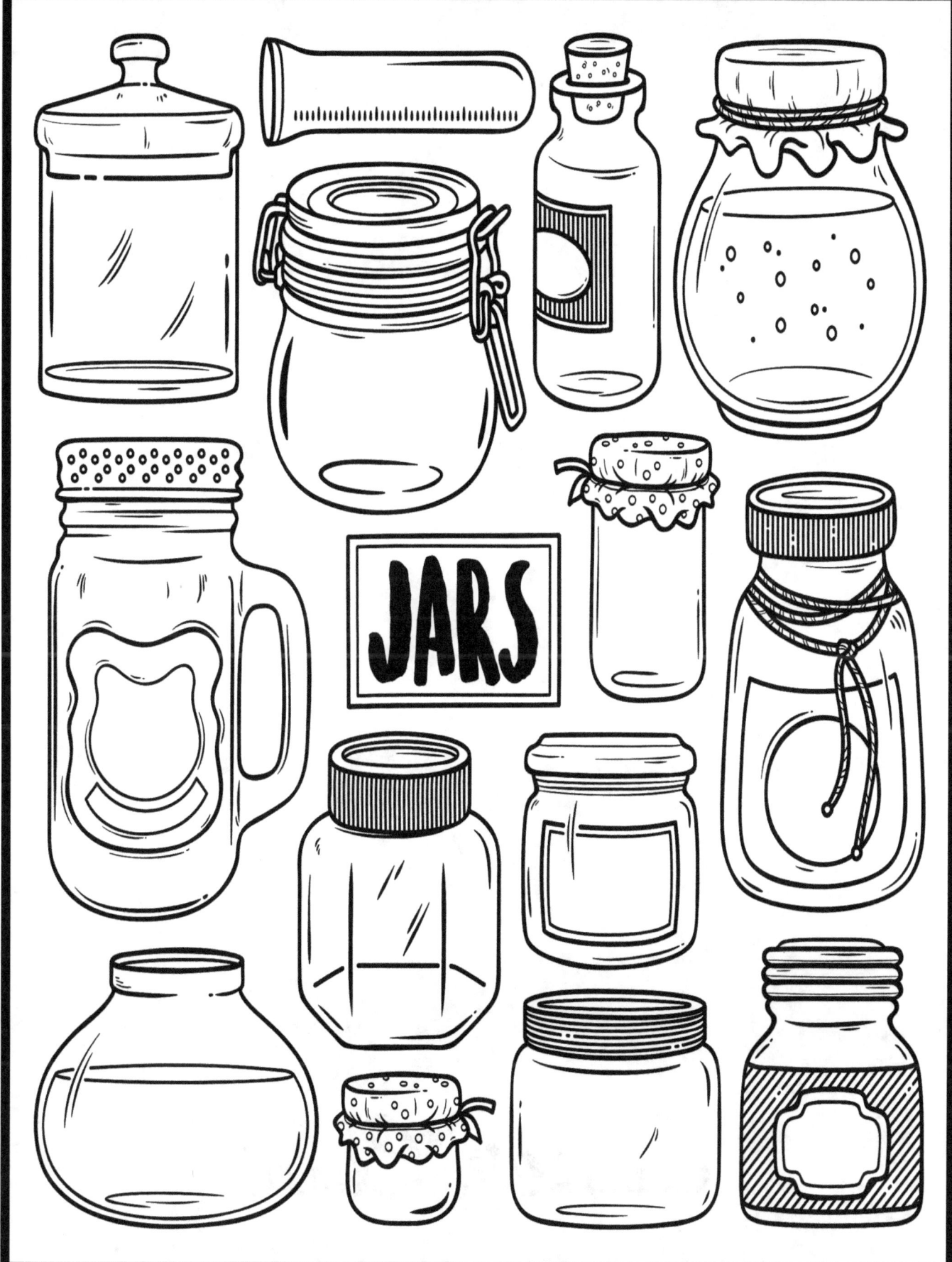

Super Cool

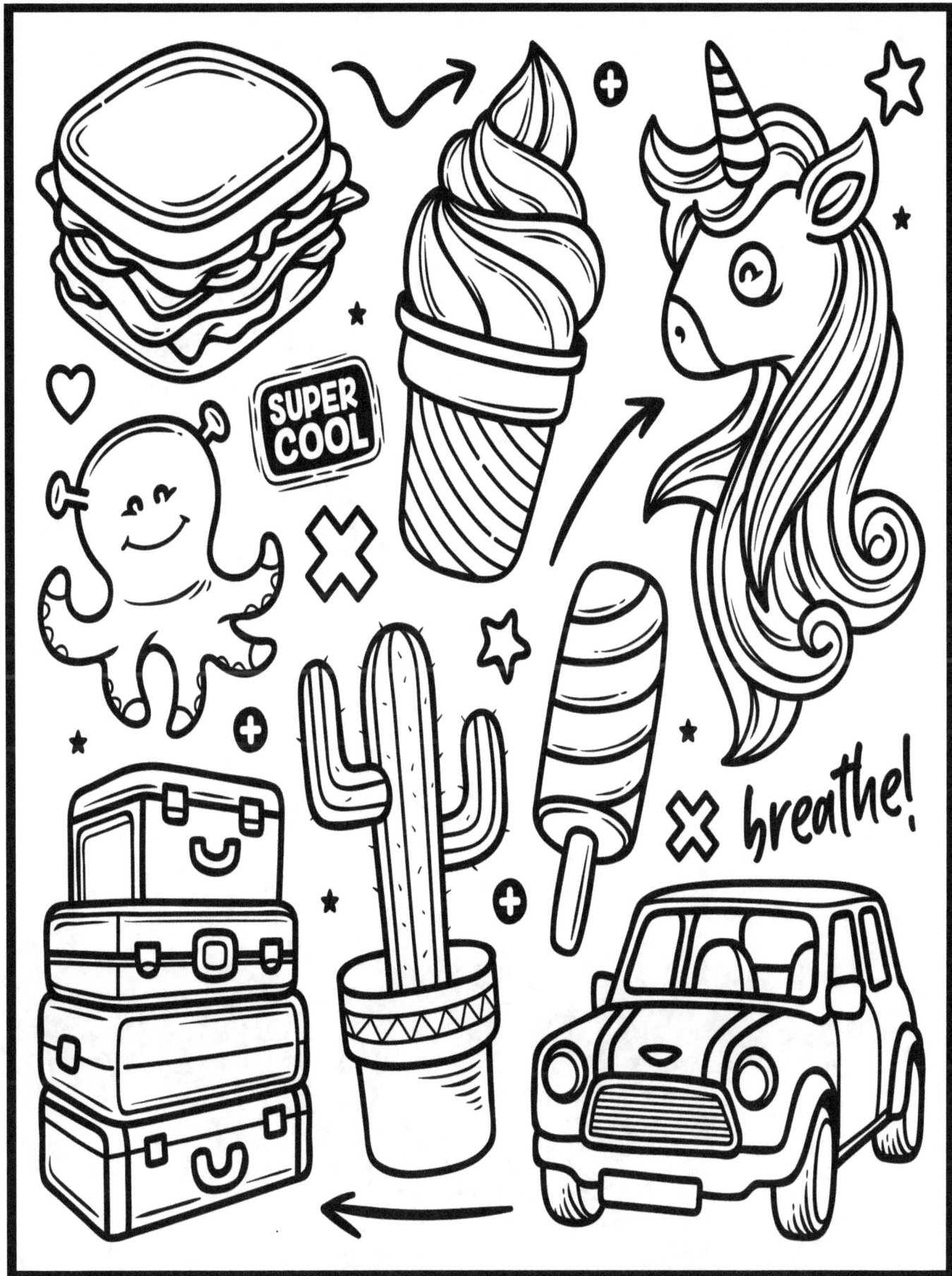

Graffiti

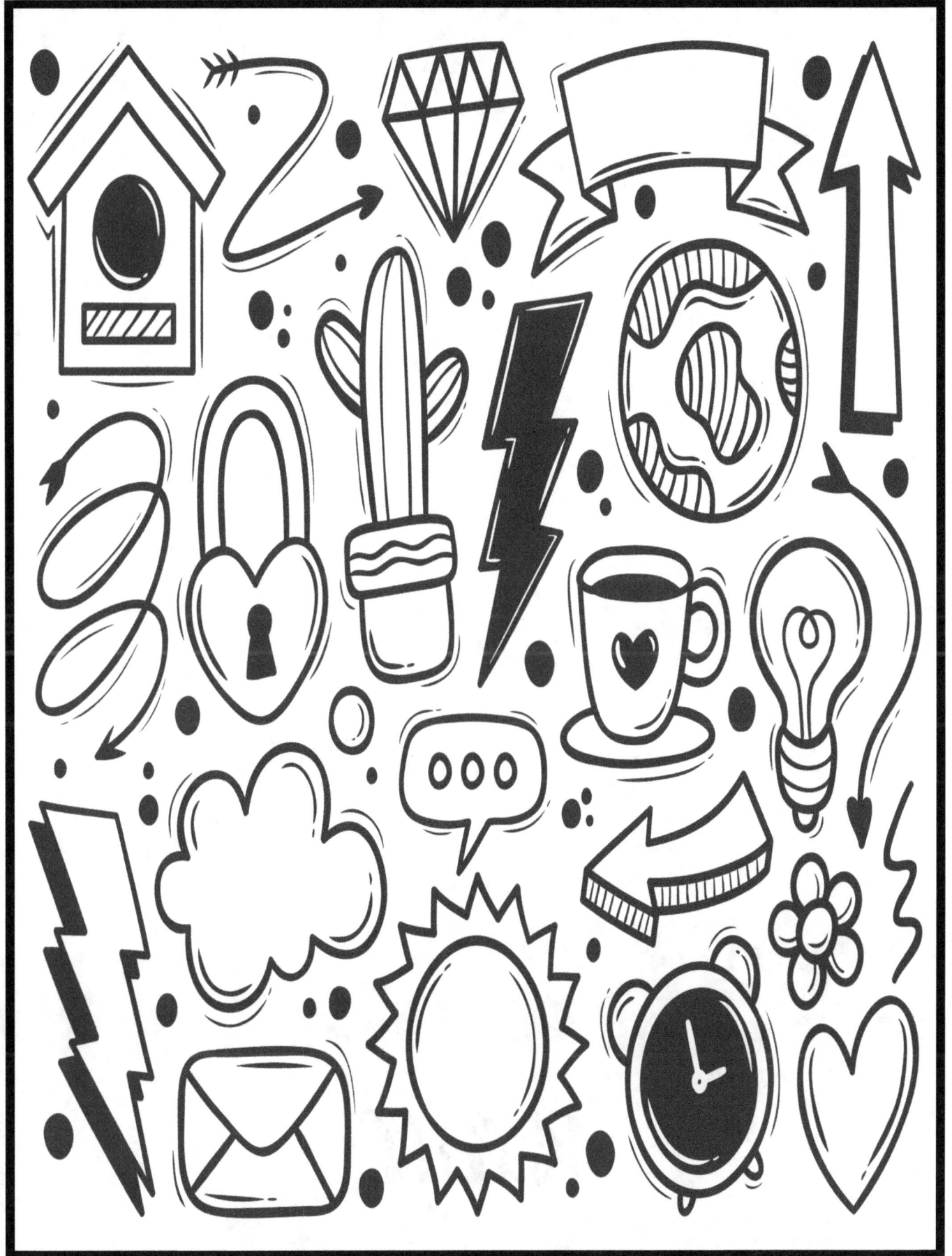

Chill

Crash

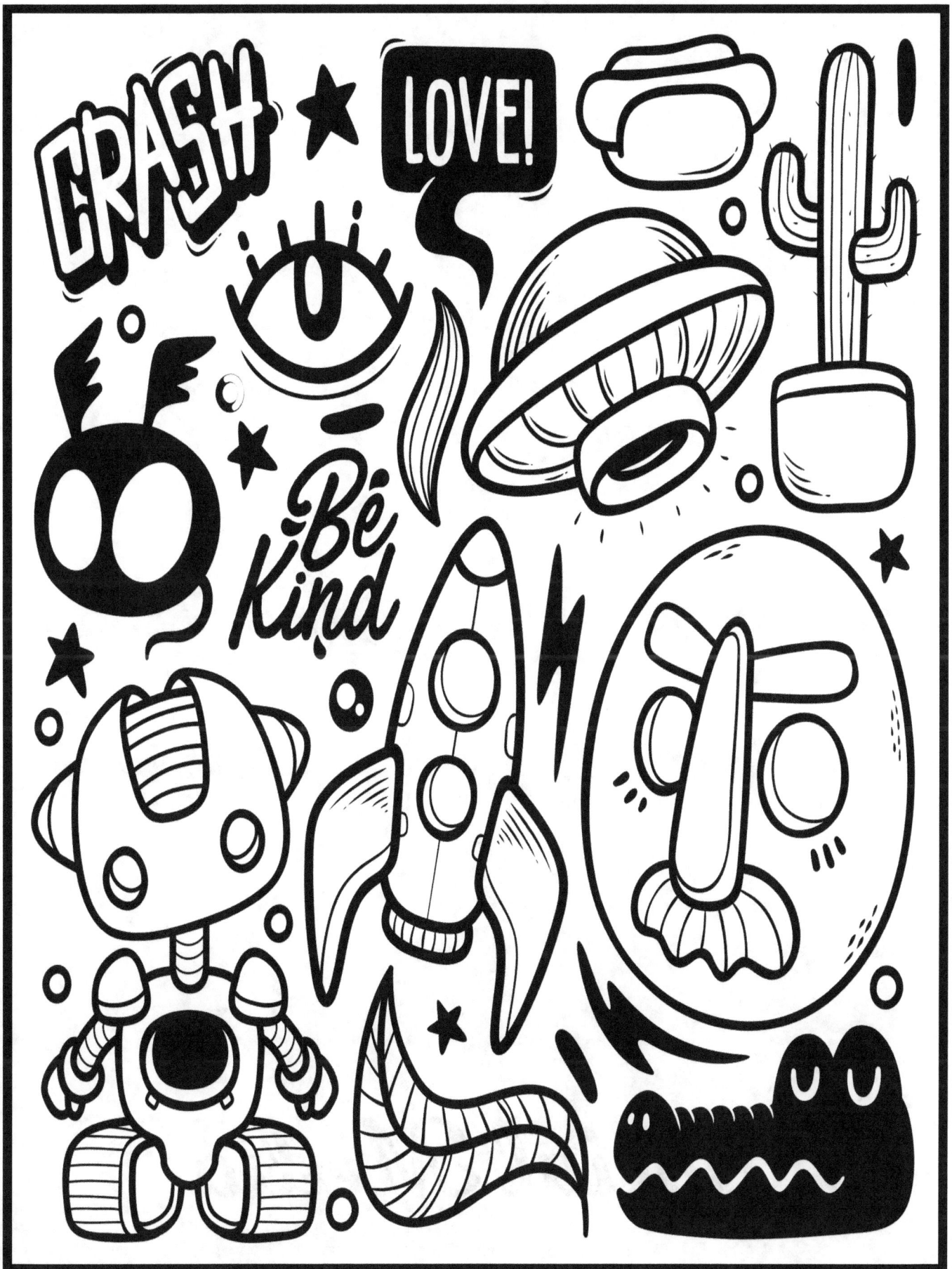

Social Media

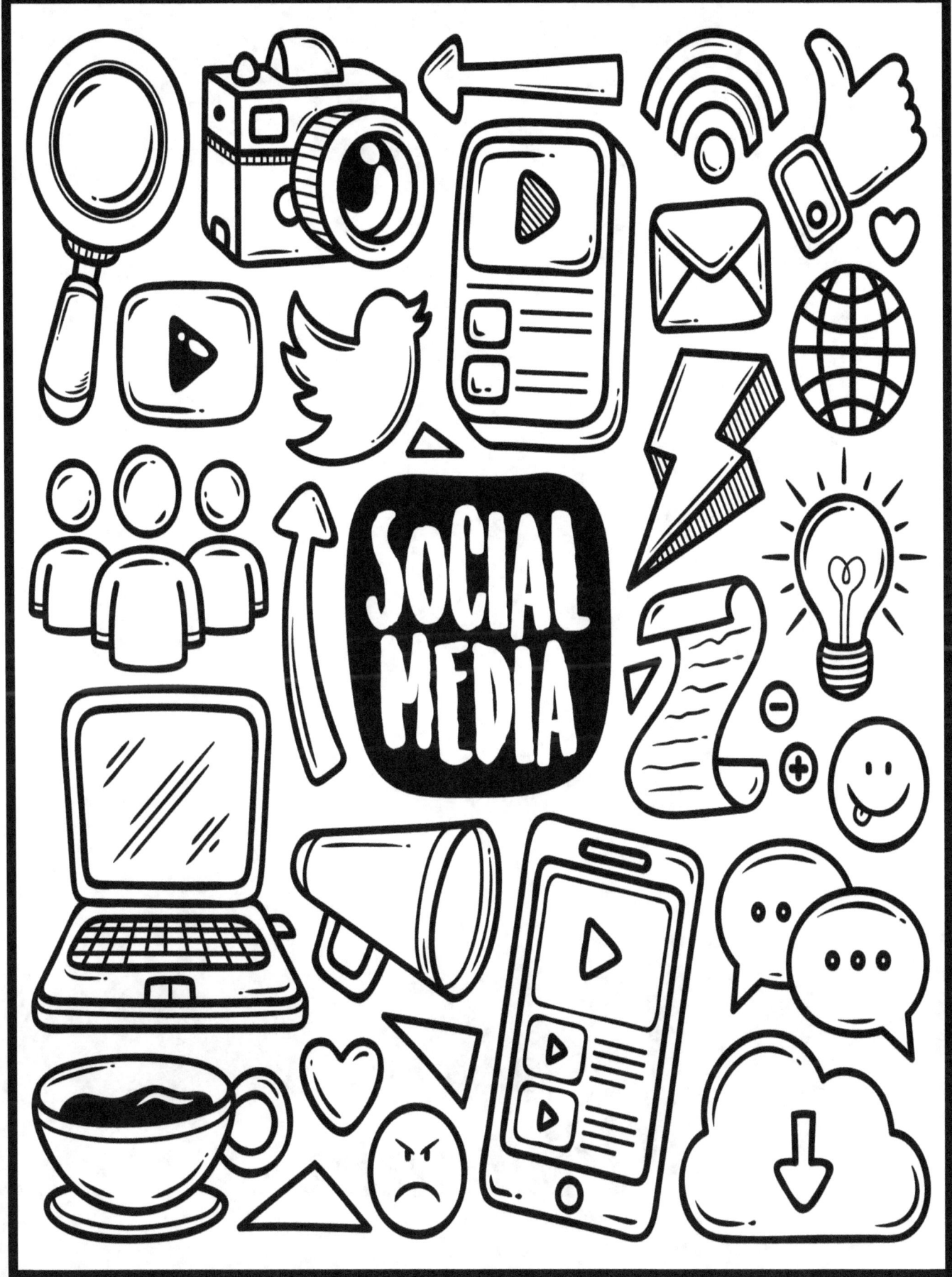

Vietnam

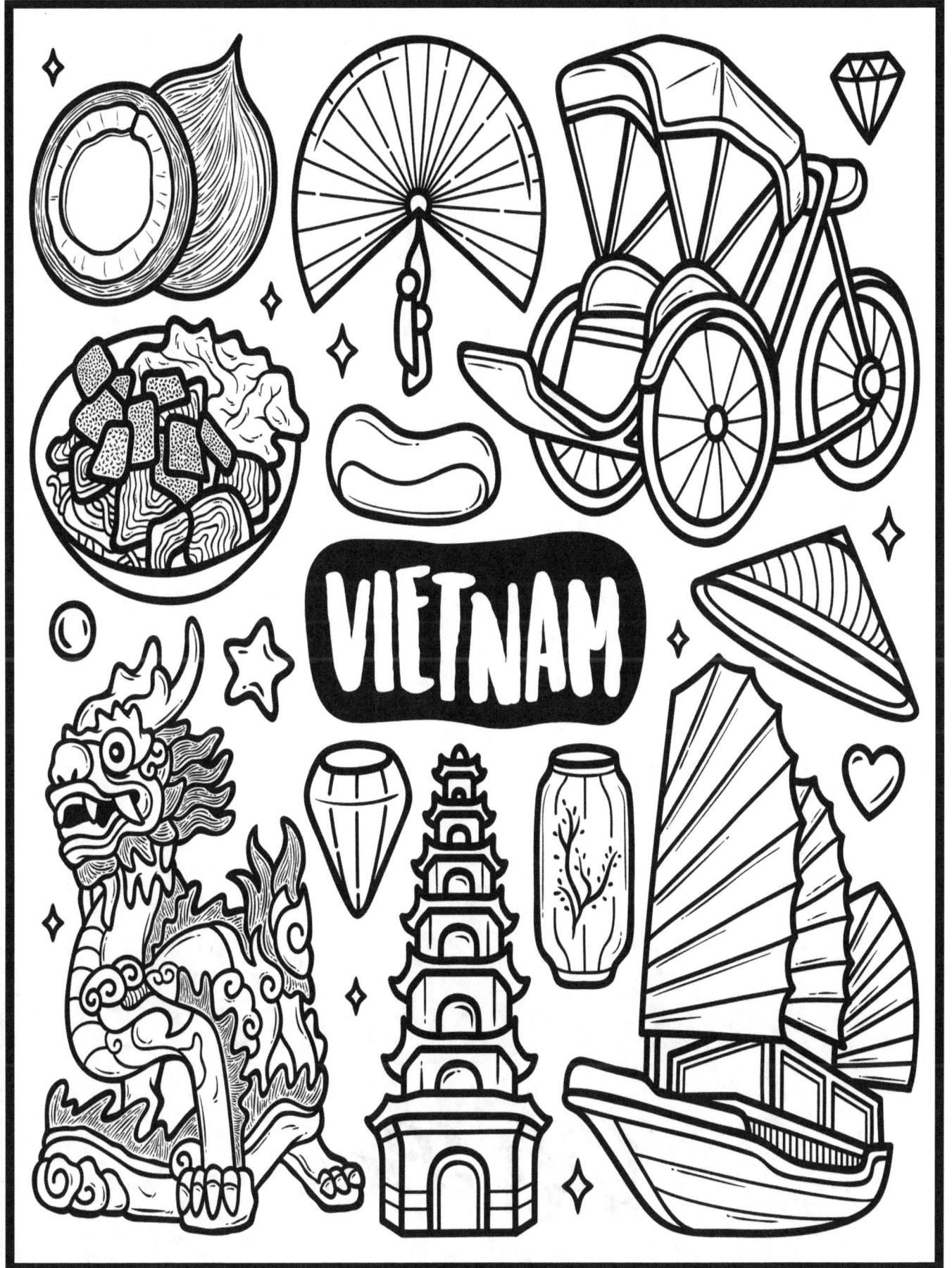

Gift Box

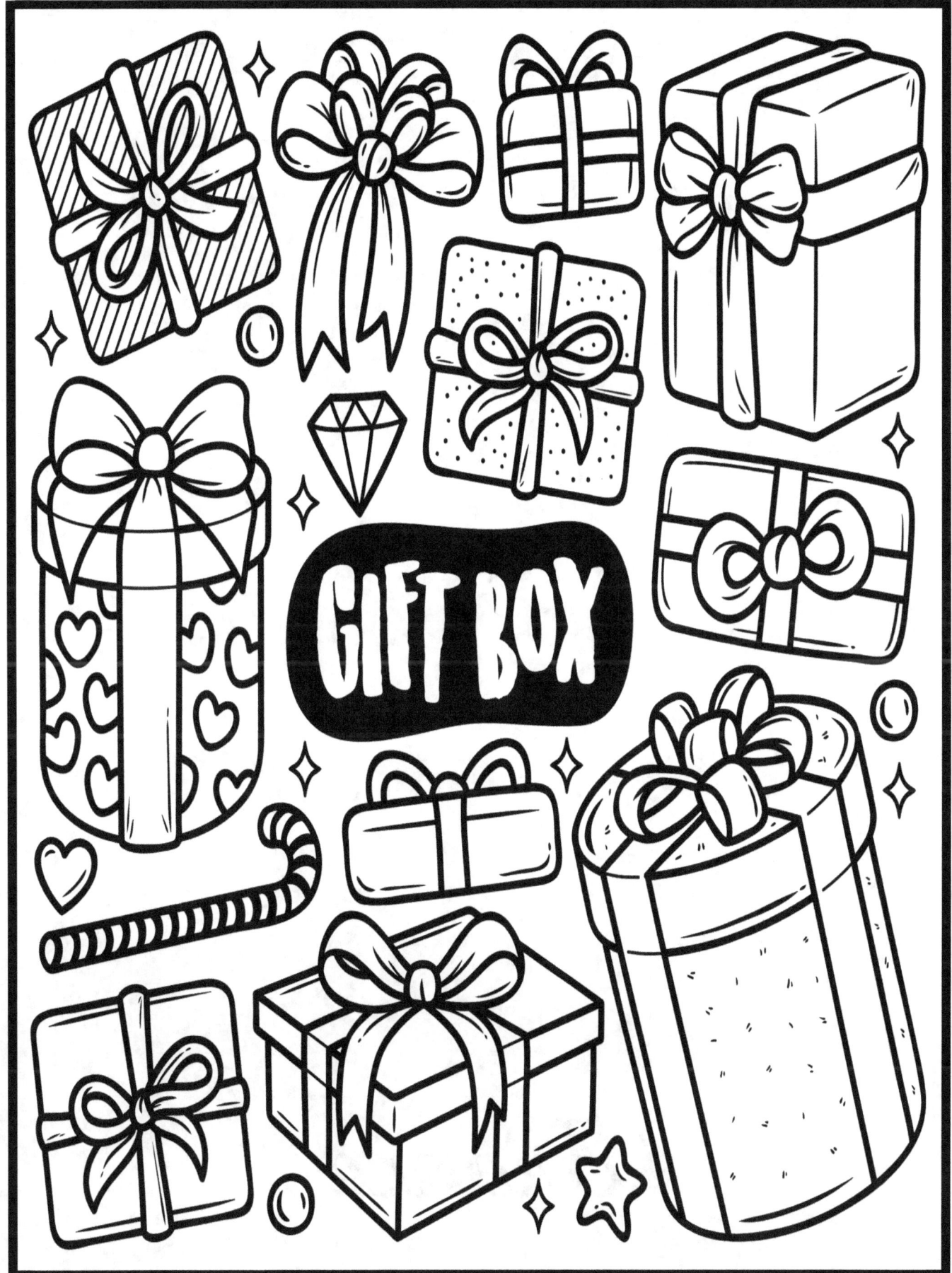

France

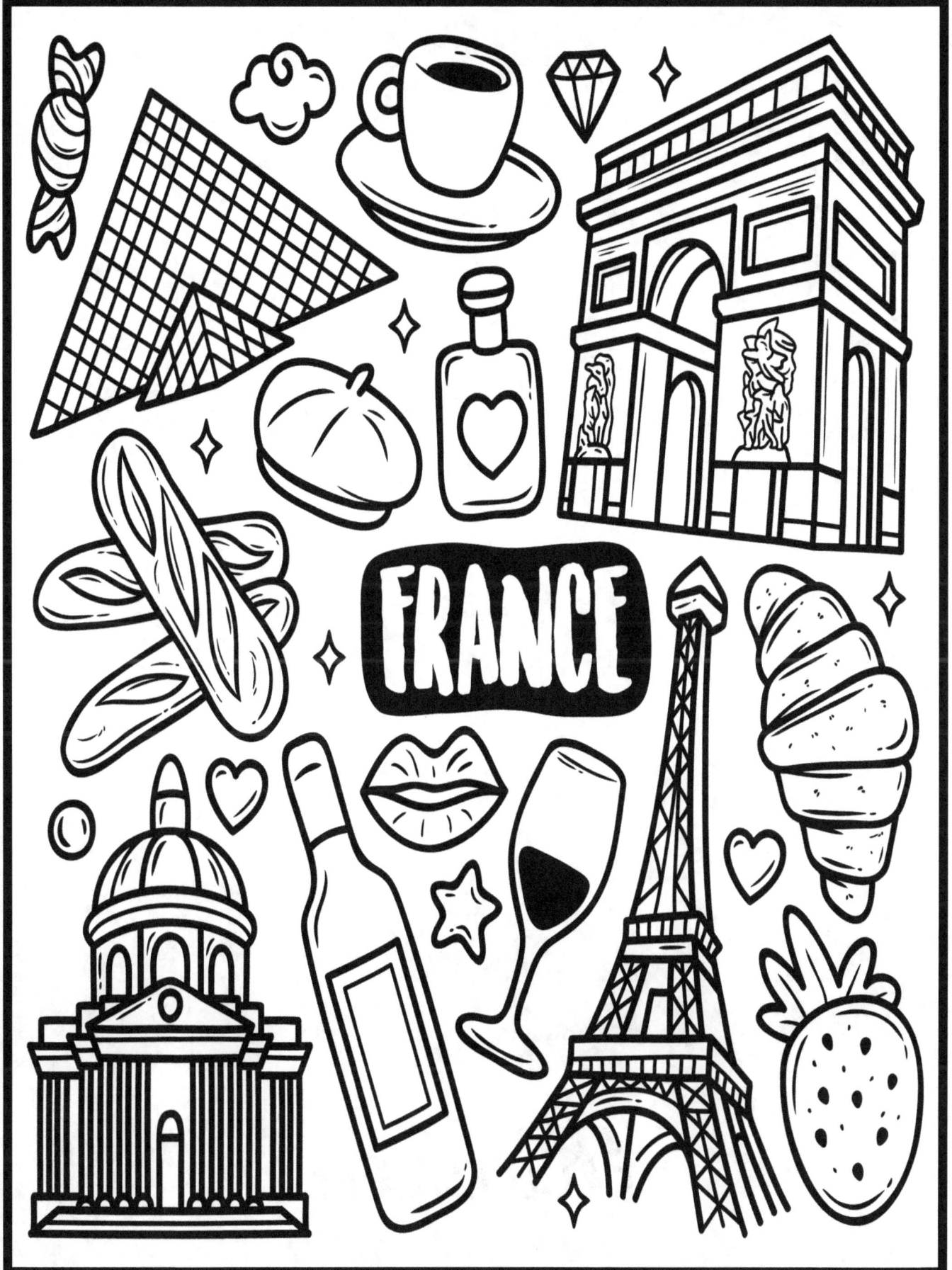

Kitchen

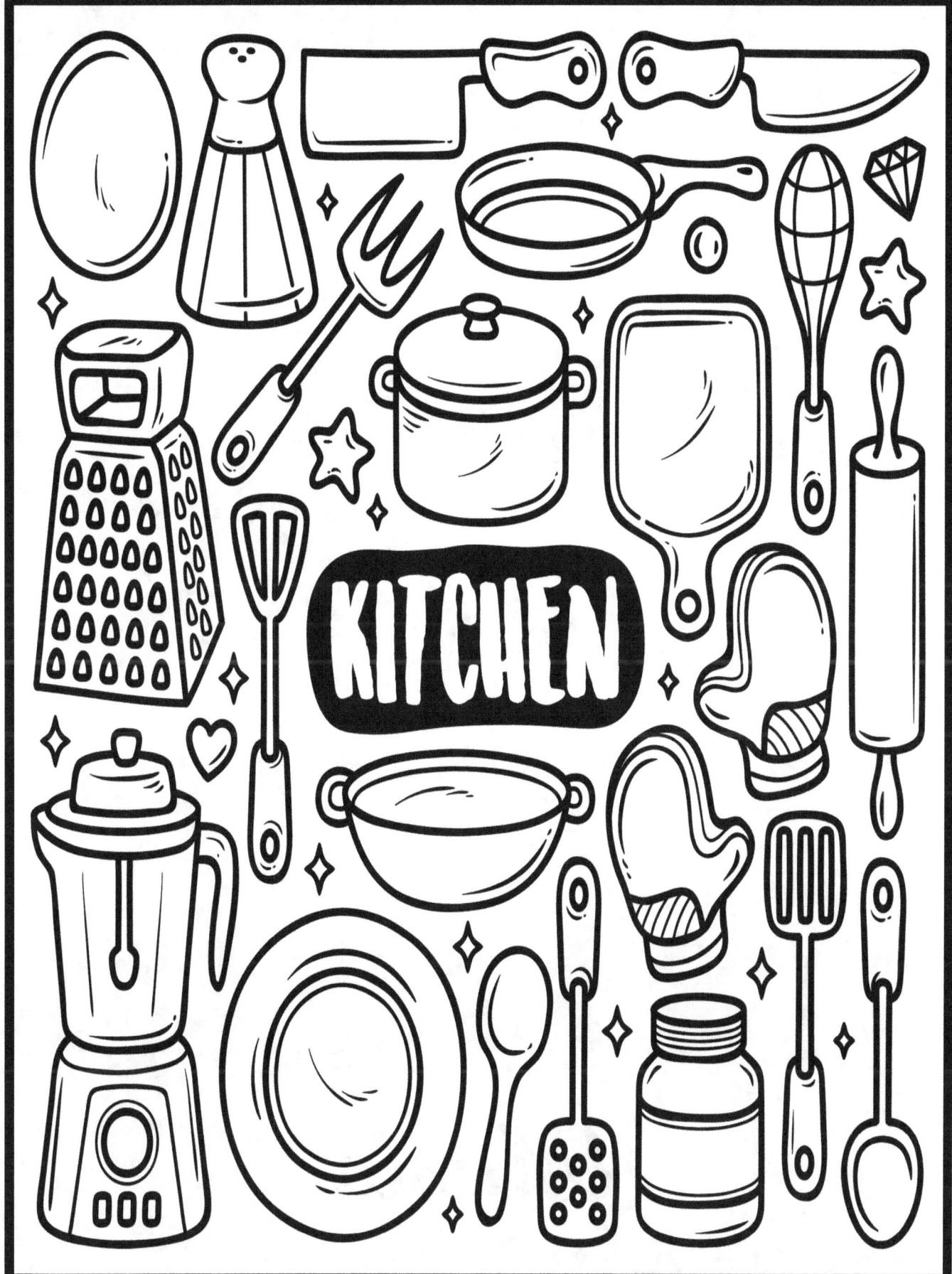

Music

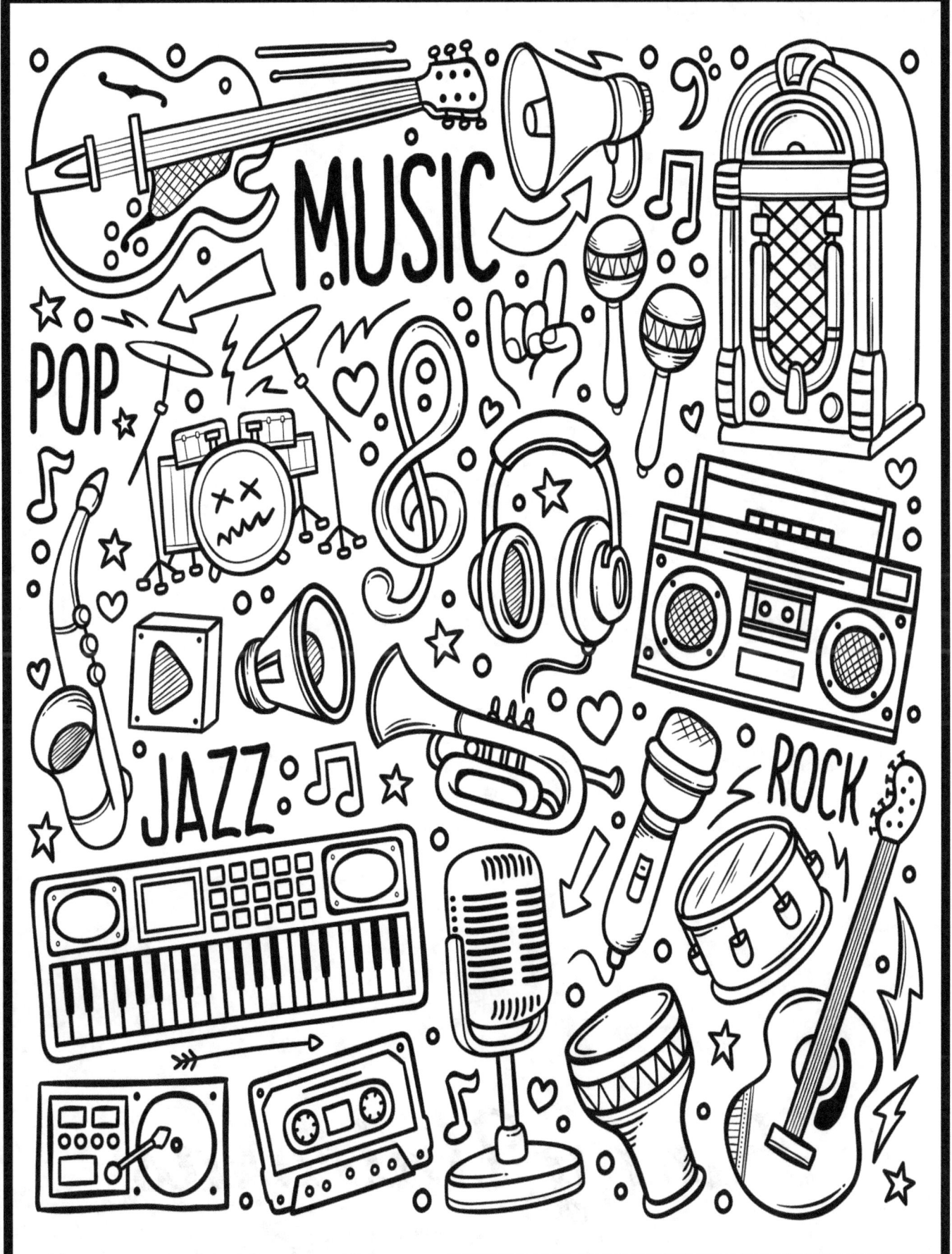

Funny Unicorns

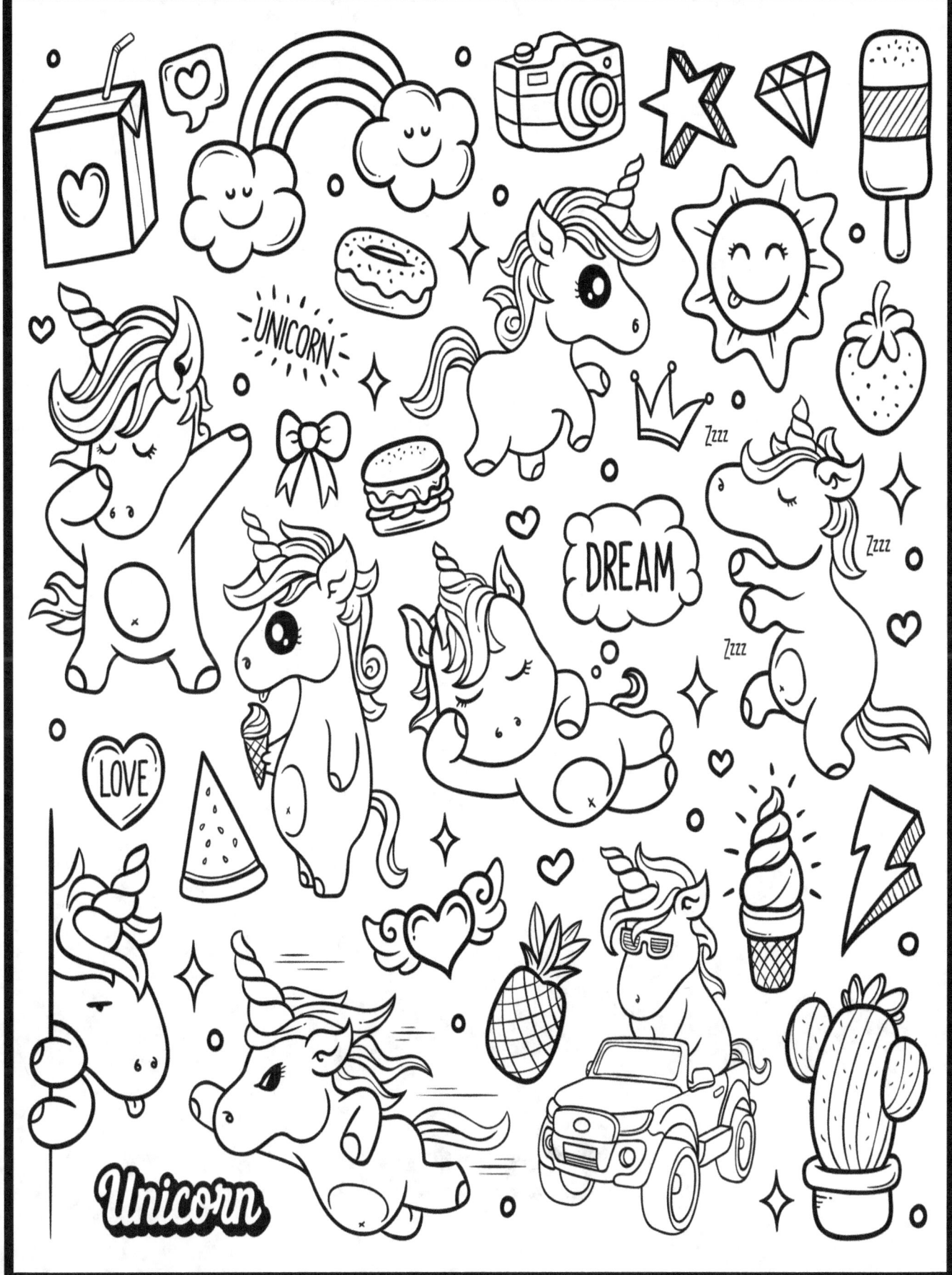

Cactus

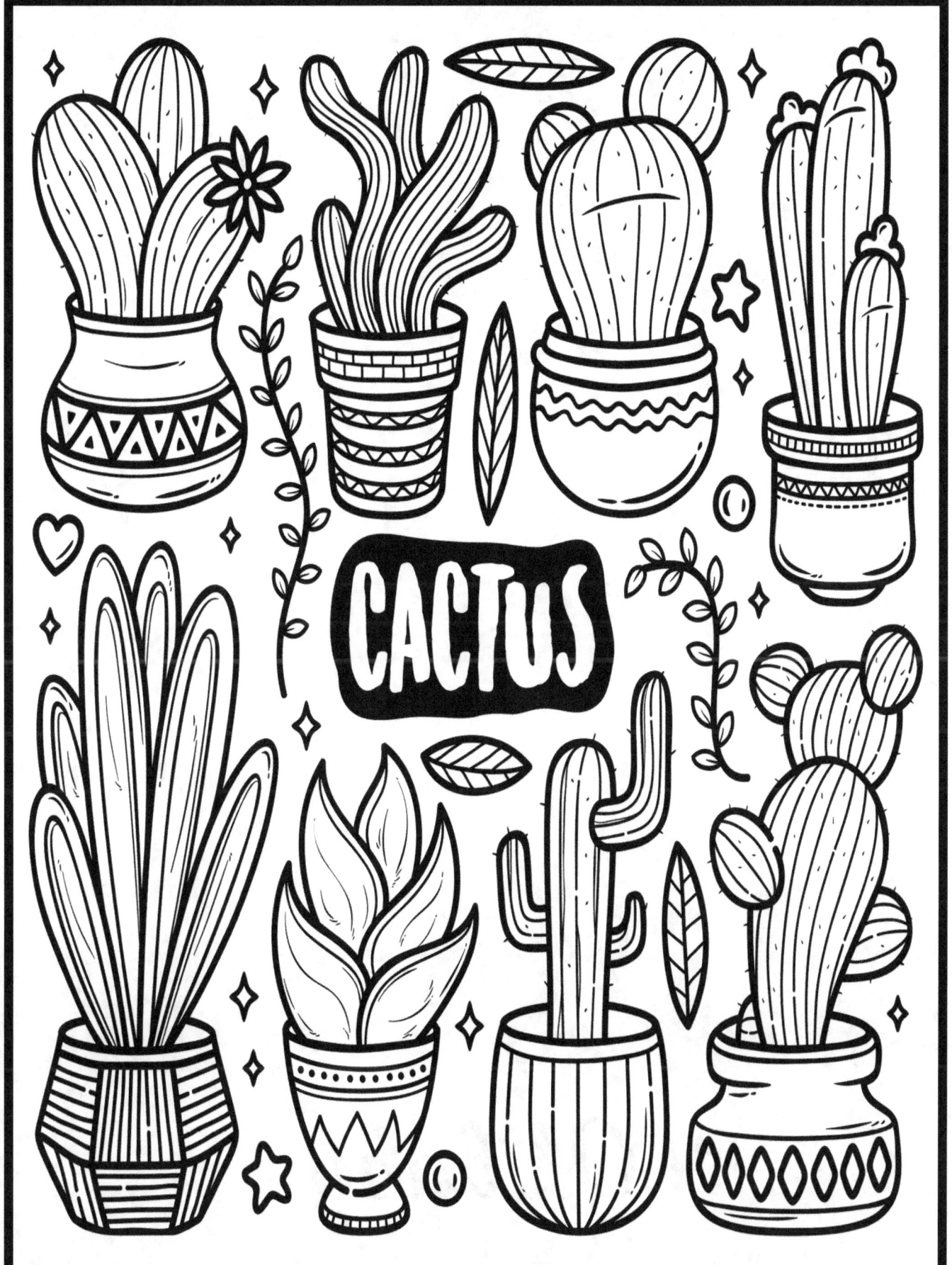

Oh baby

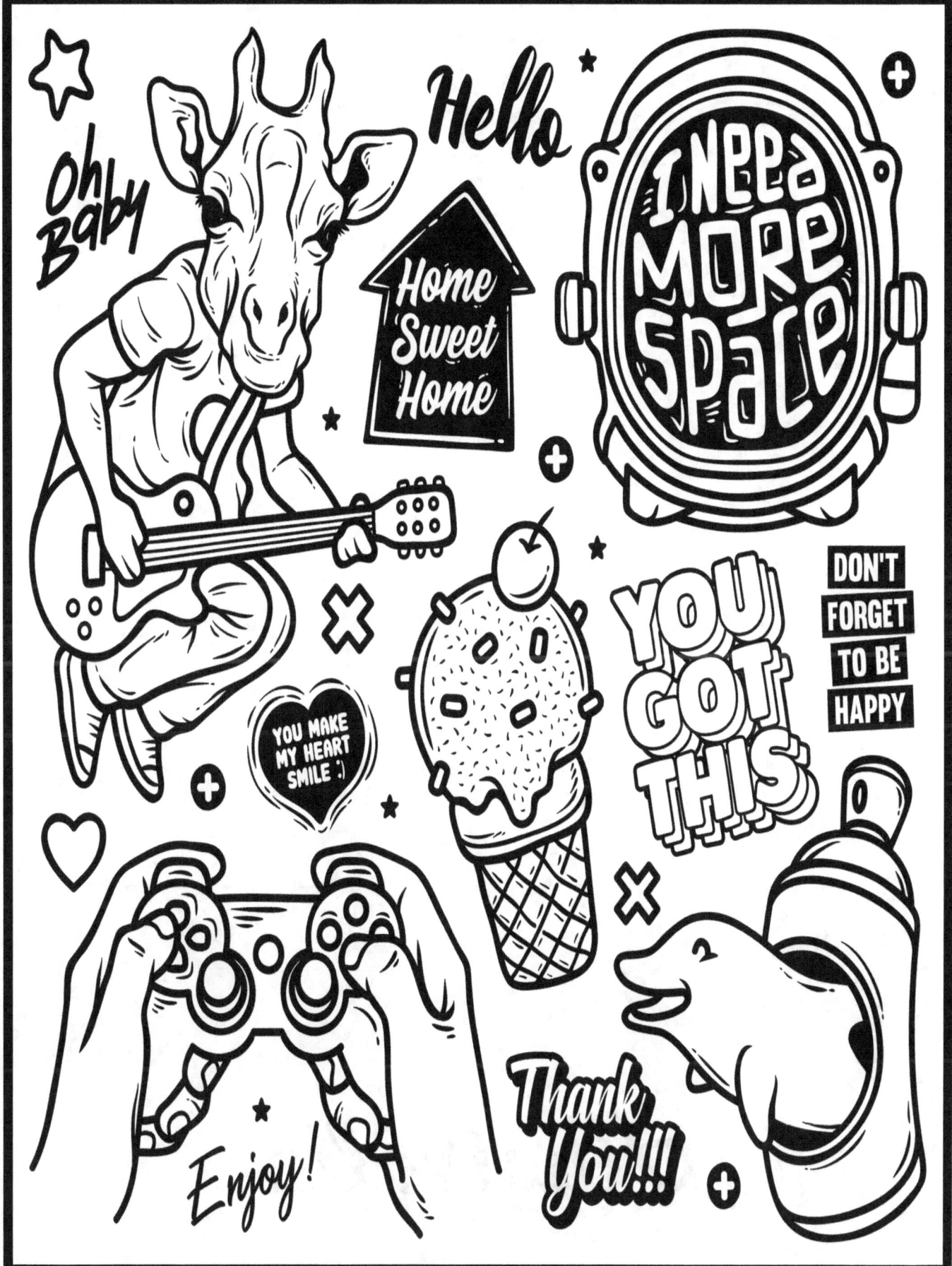

Australia

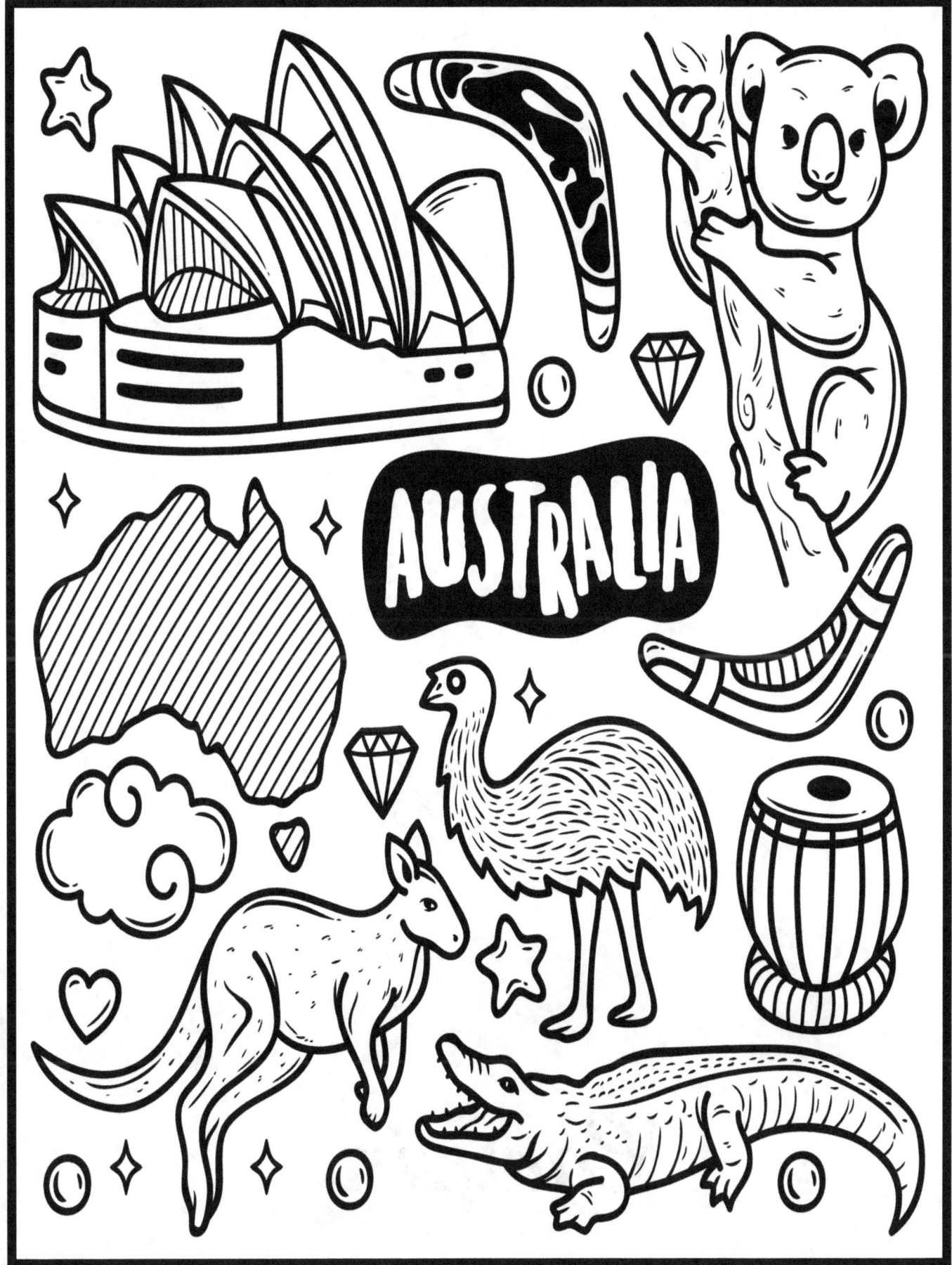

Camping

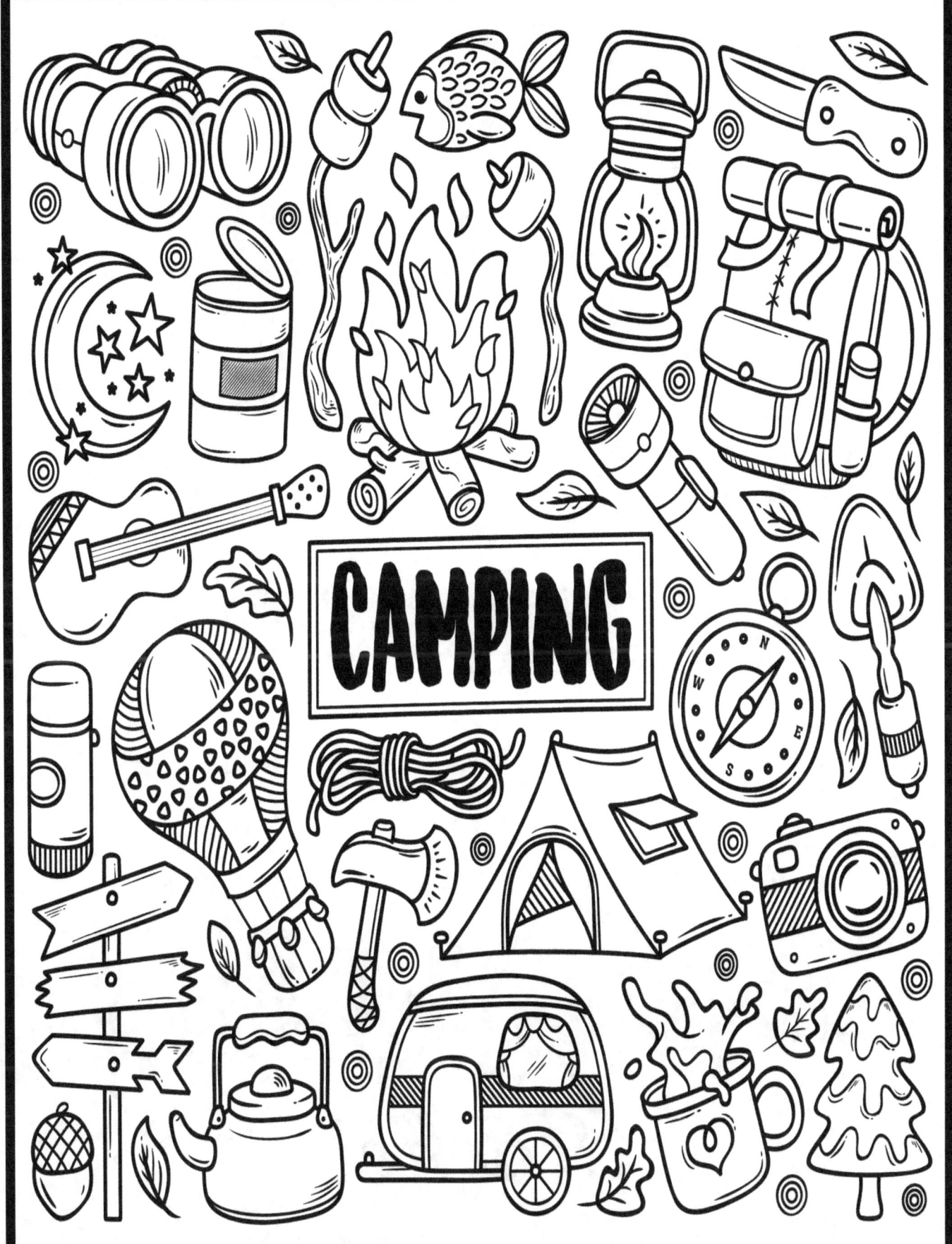

Rocket

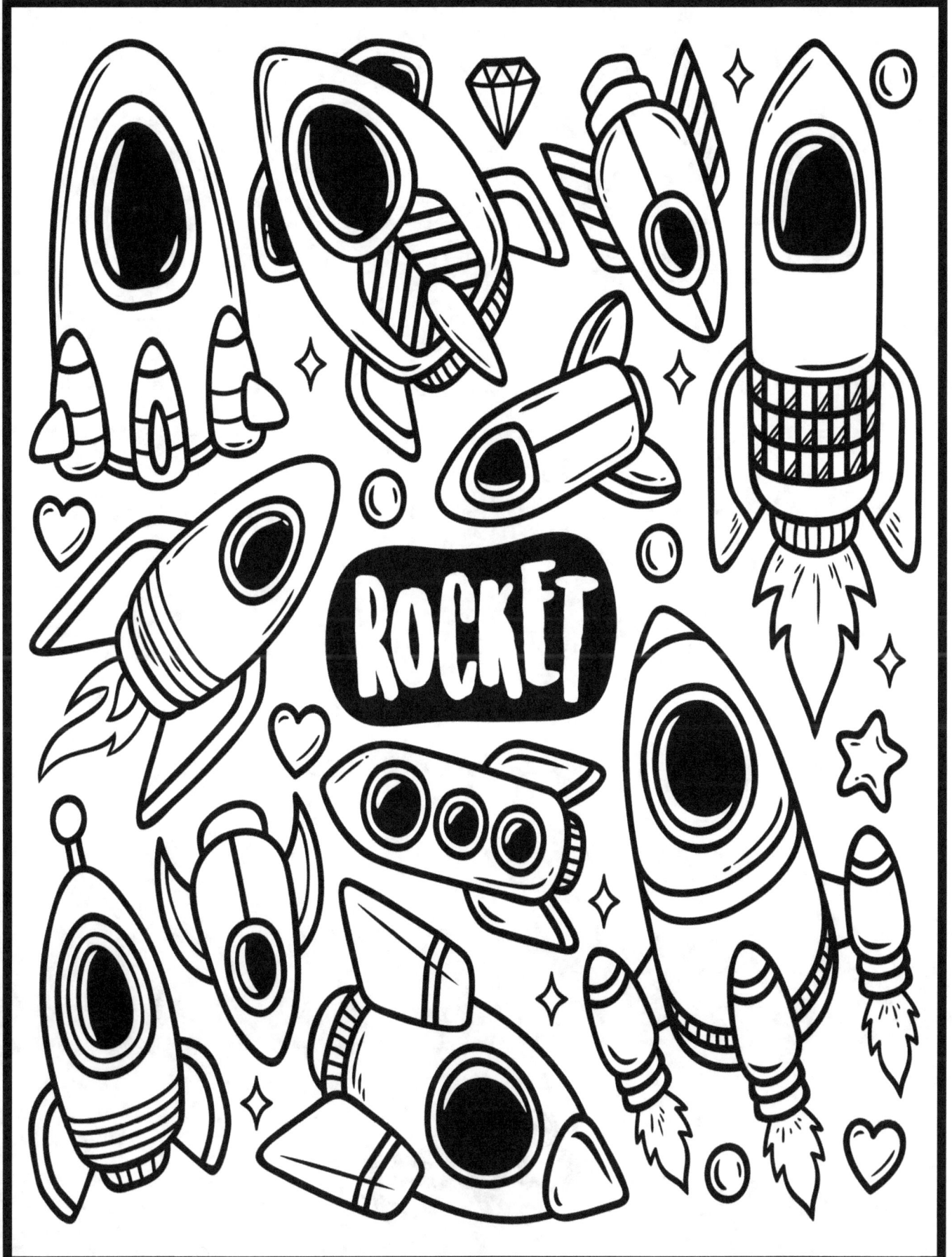

Enjoy

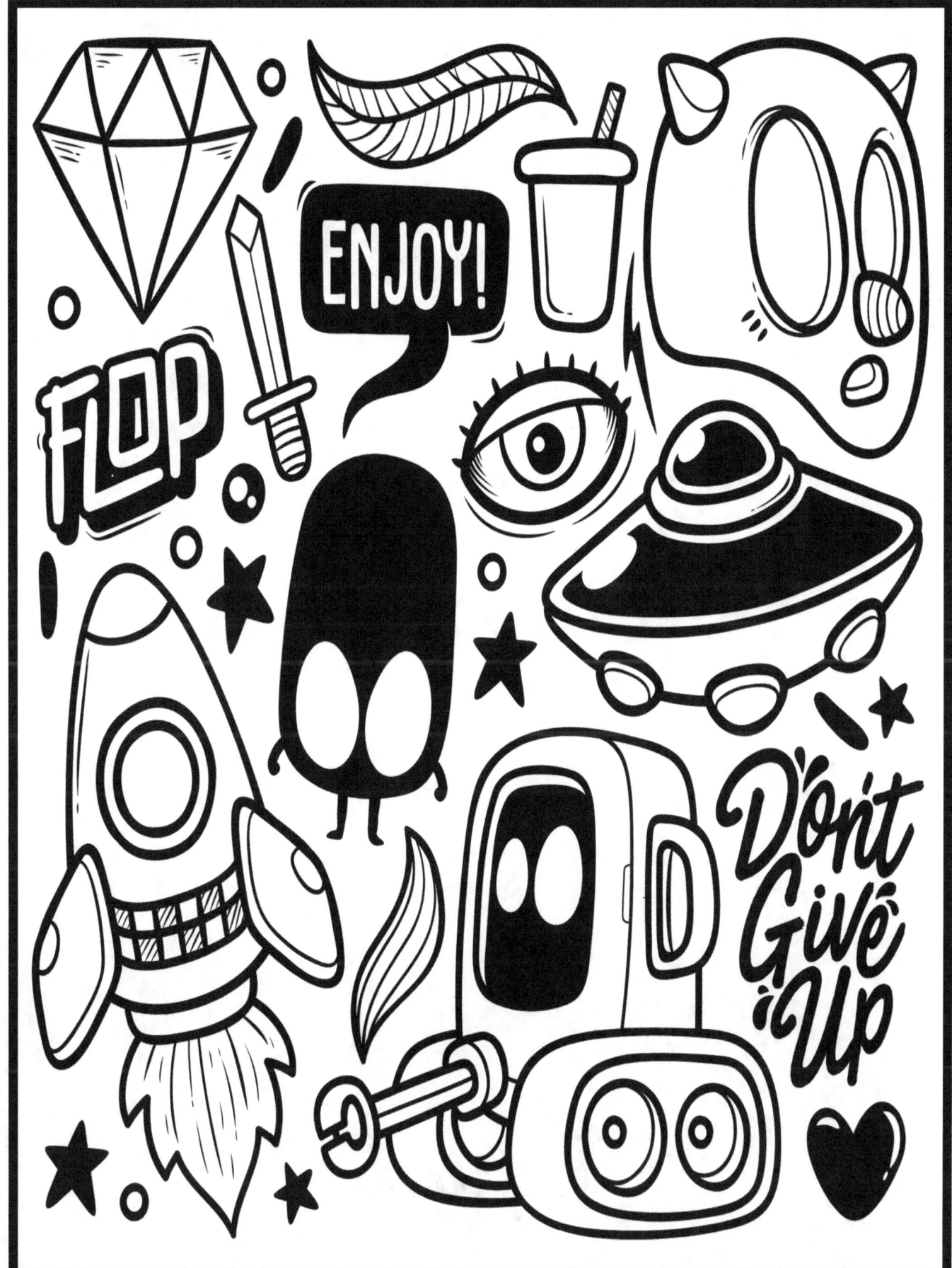

Egypt

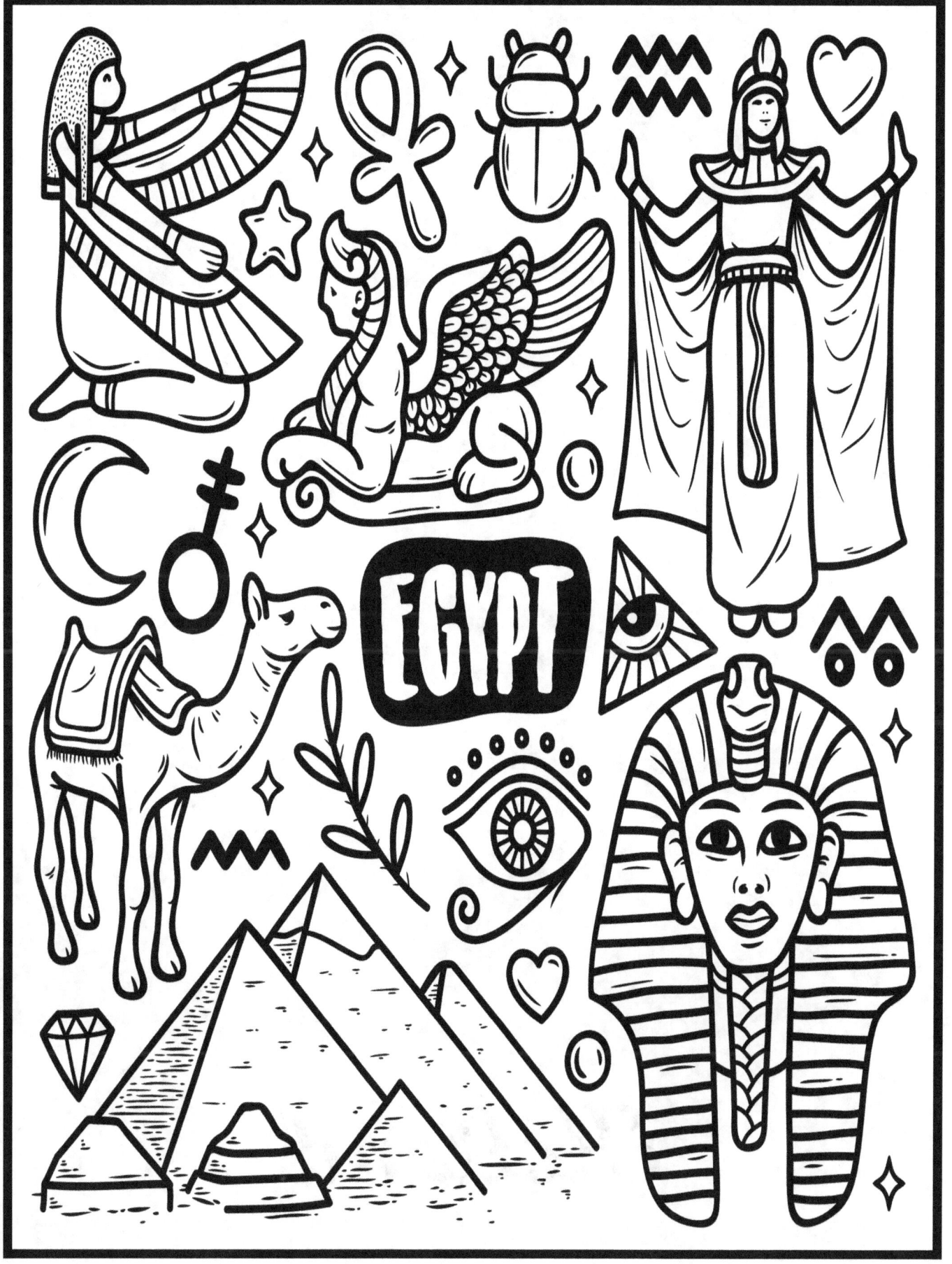

Holland

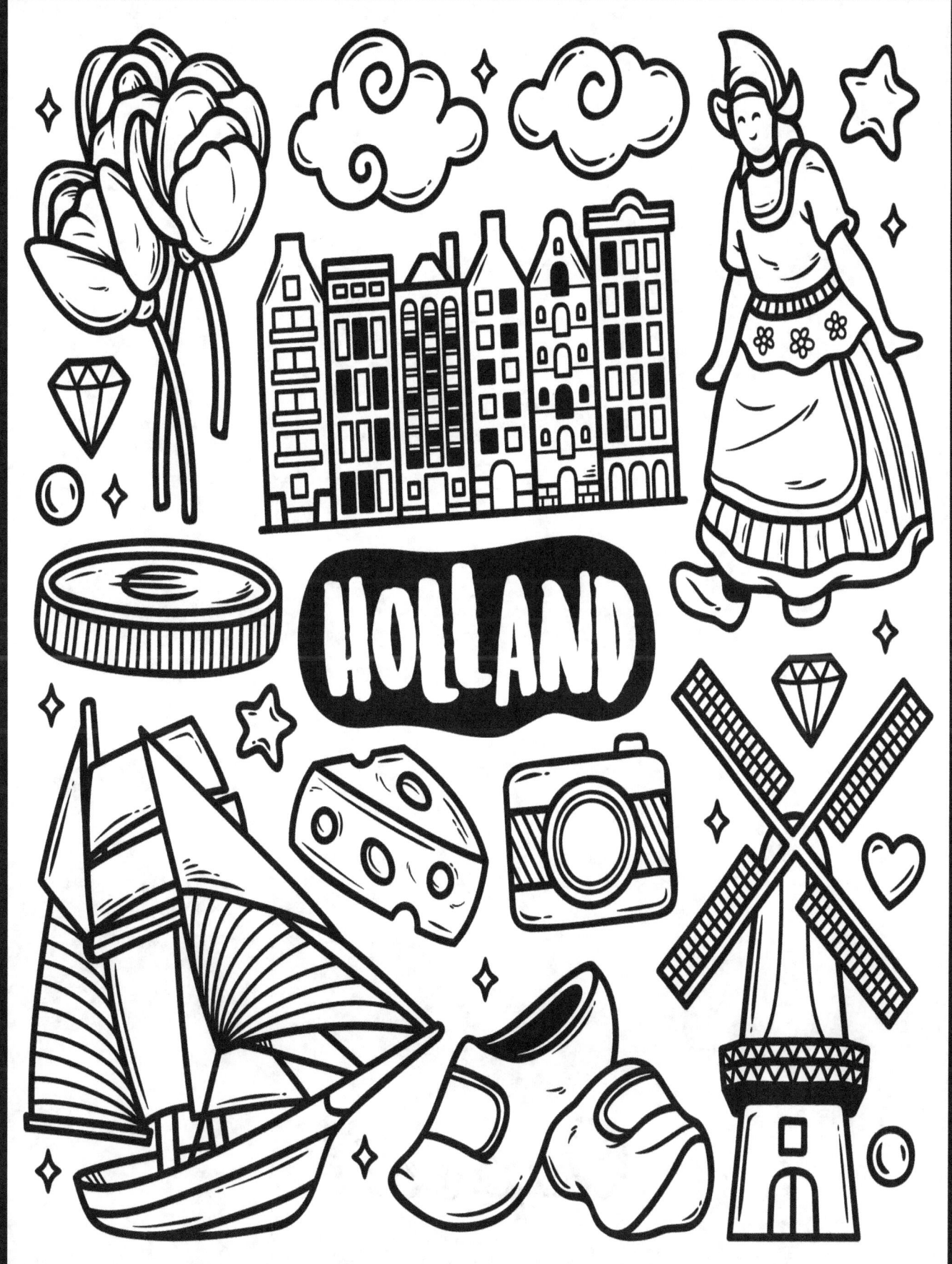

HOLLAND

Oopss!!

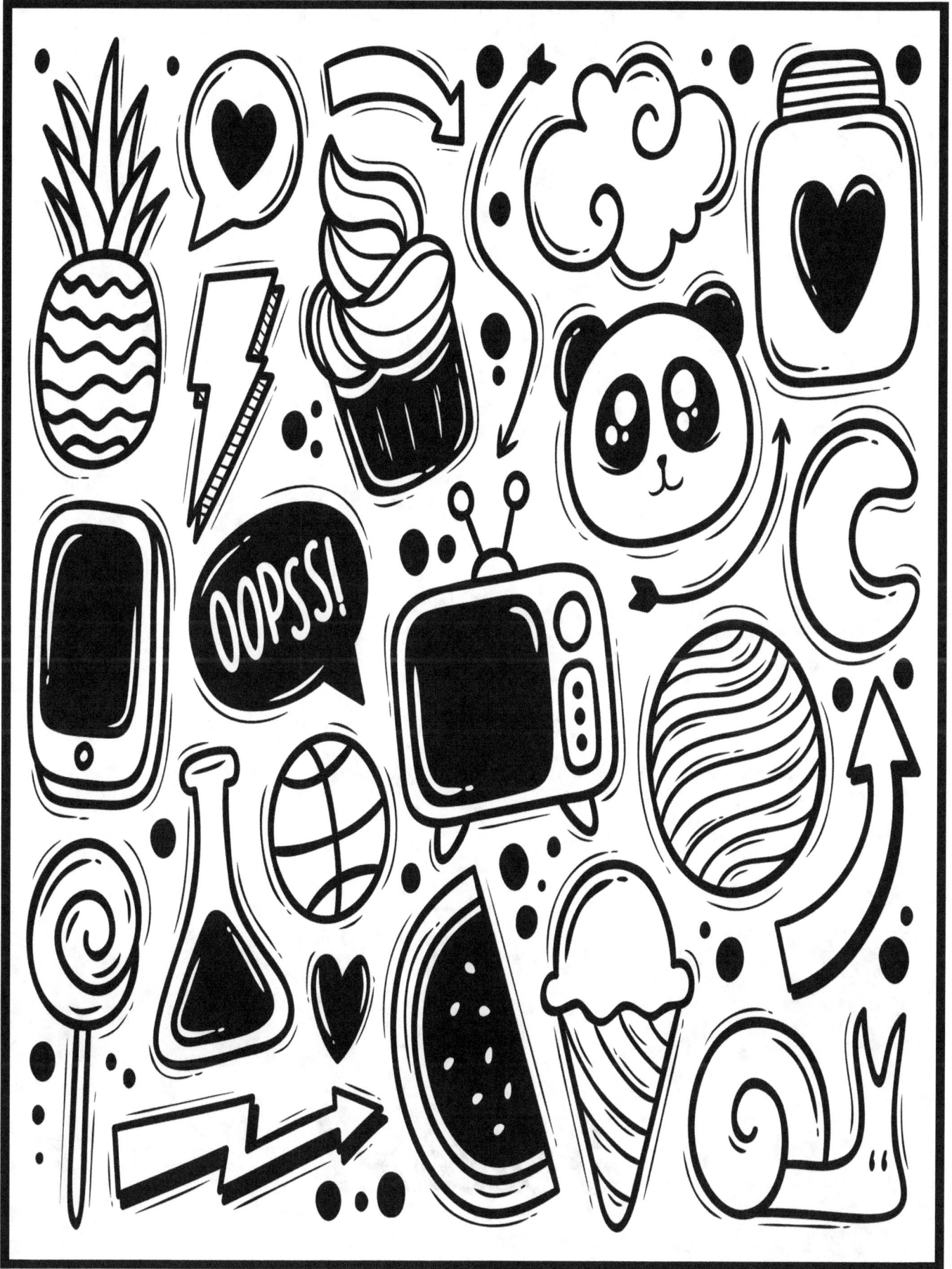

Relax!

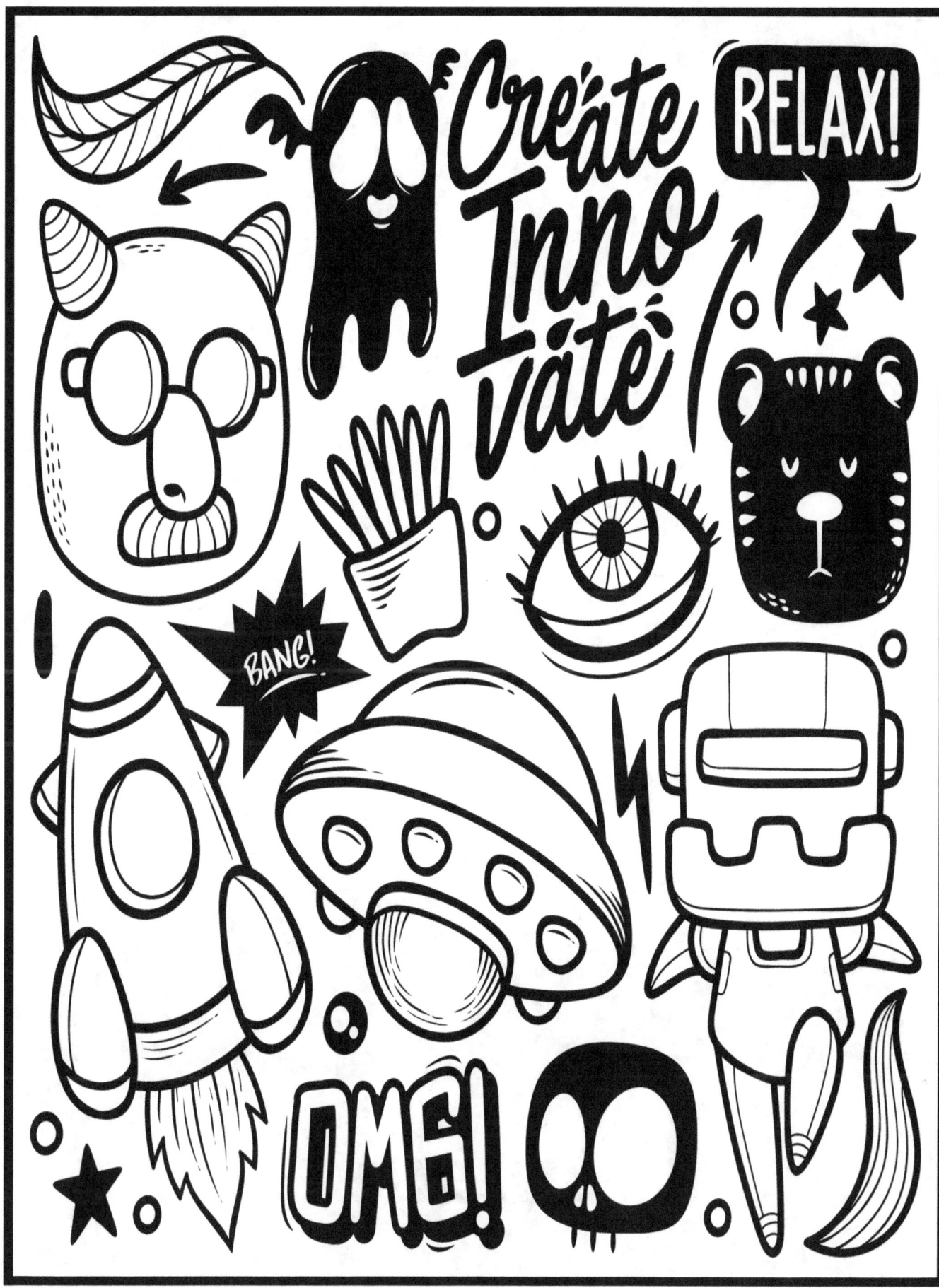

Spain

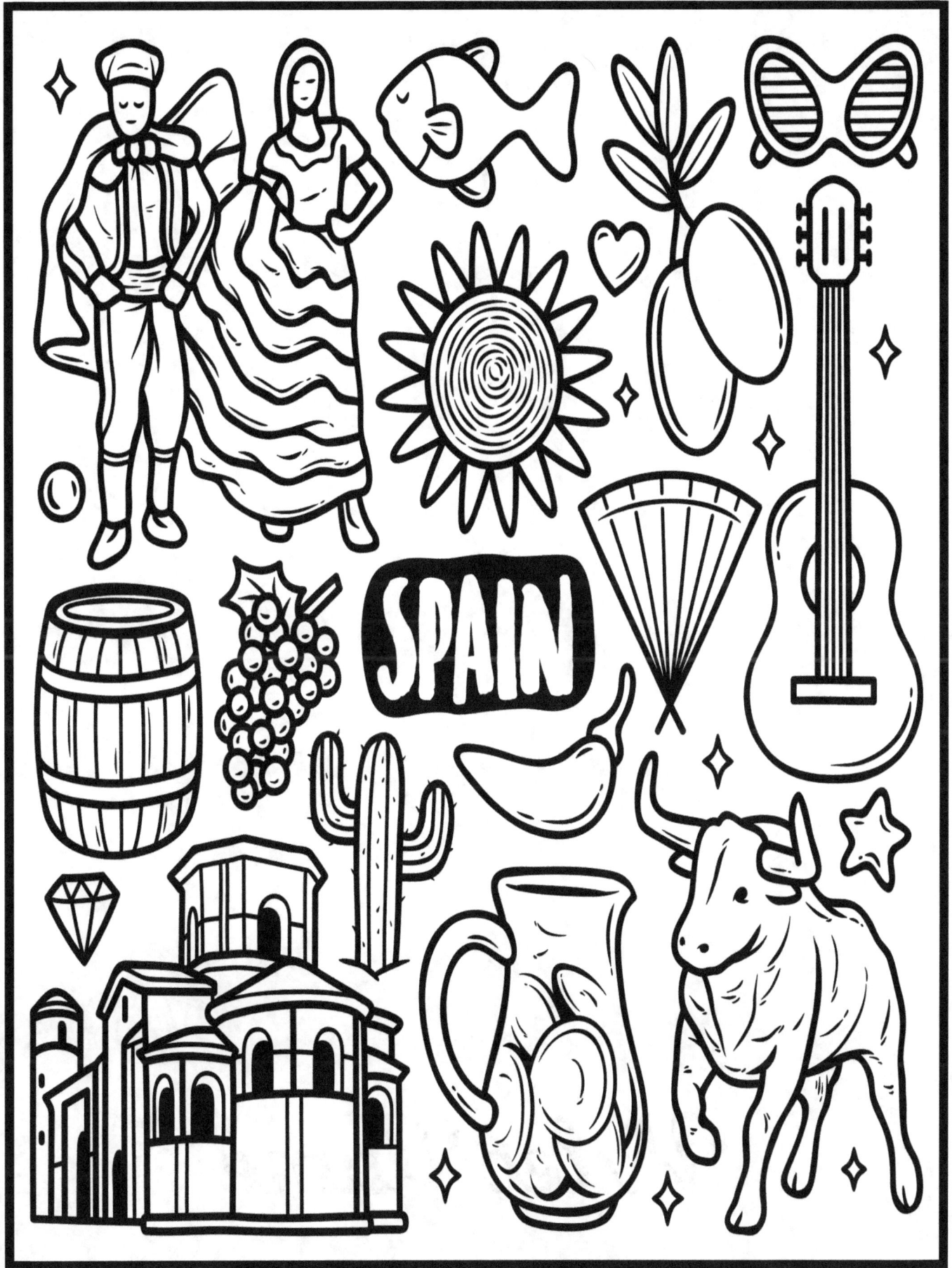

Video Game

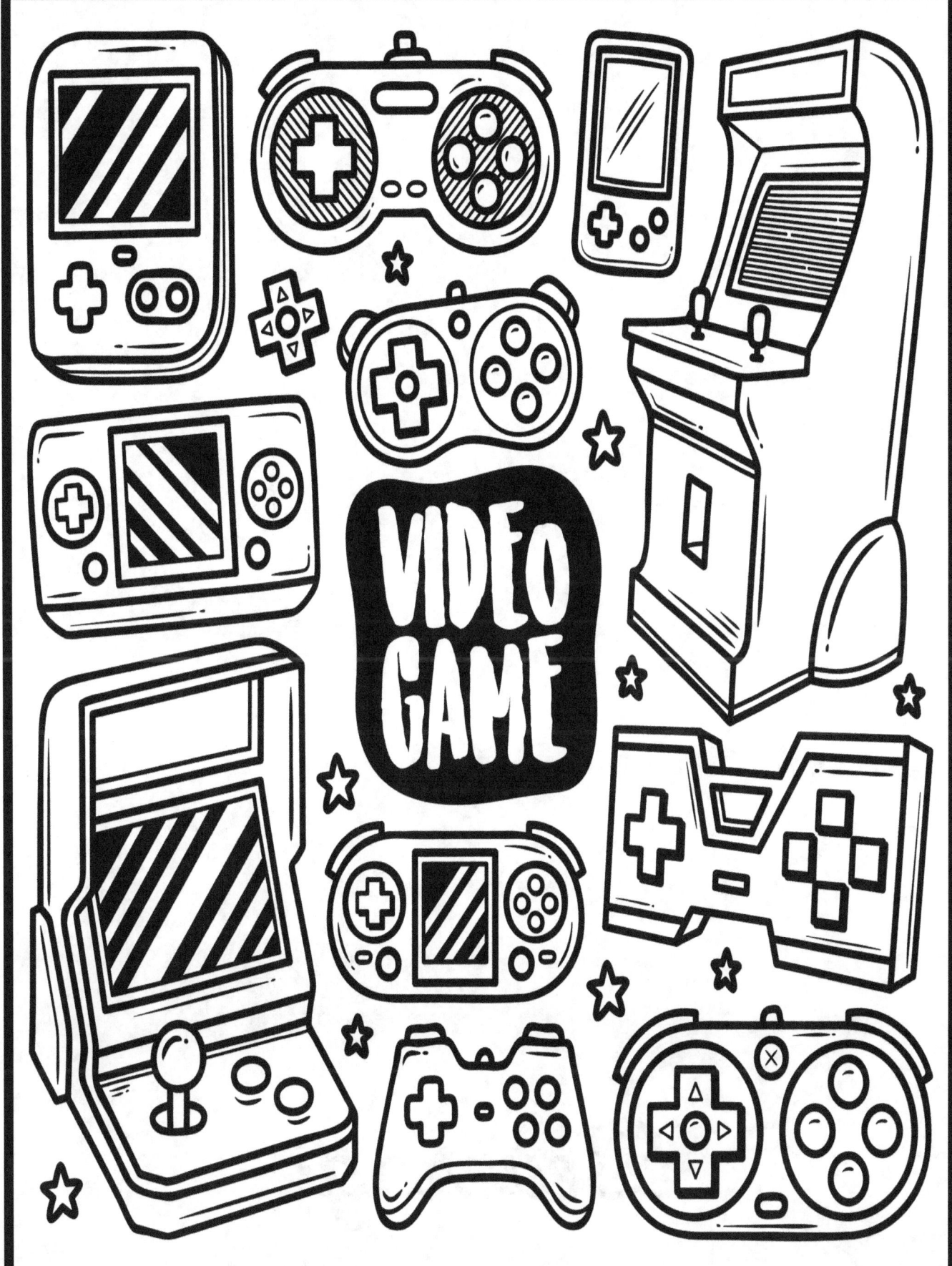

Beverage

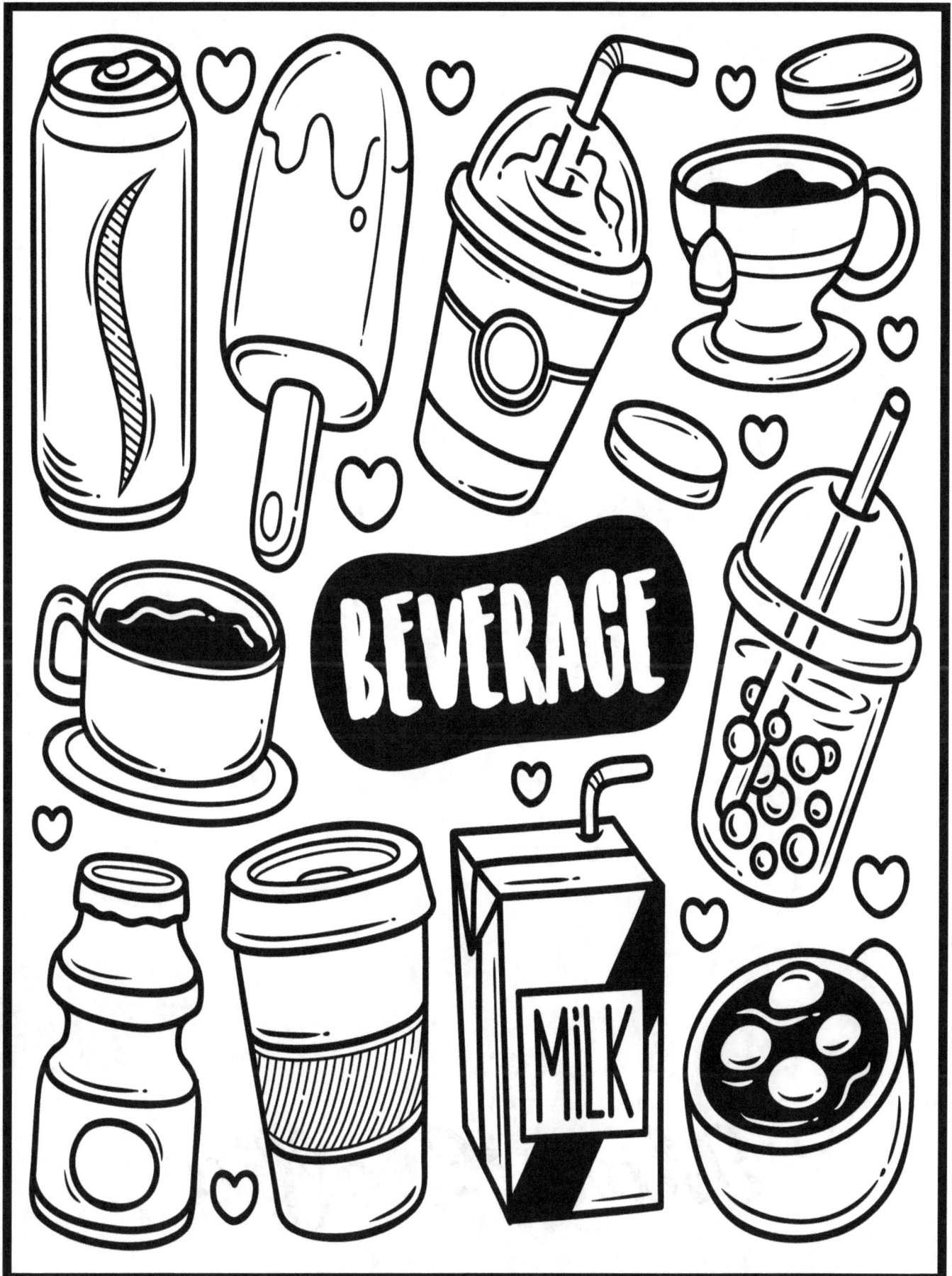

More Graffiti

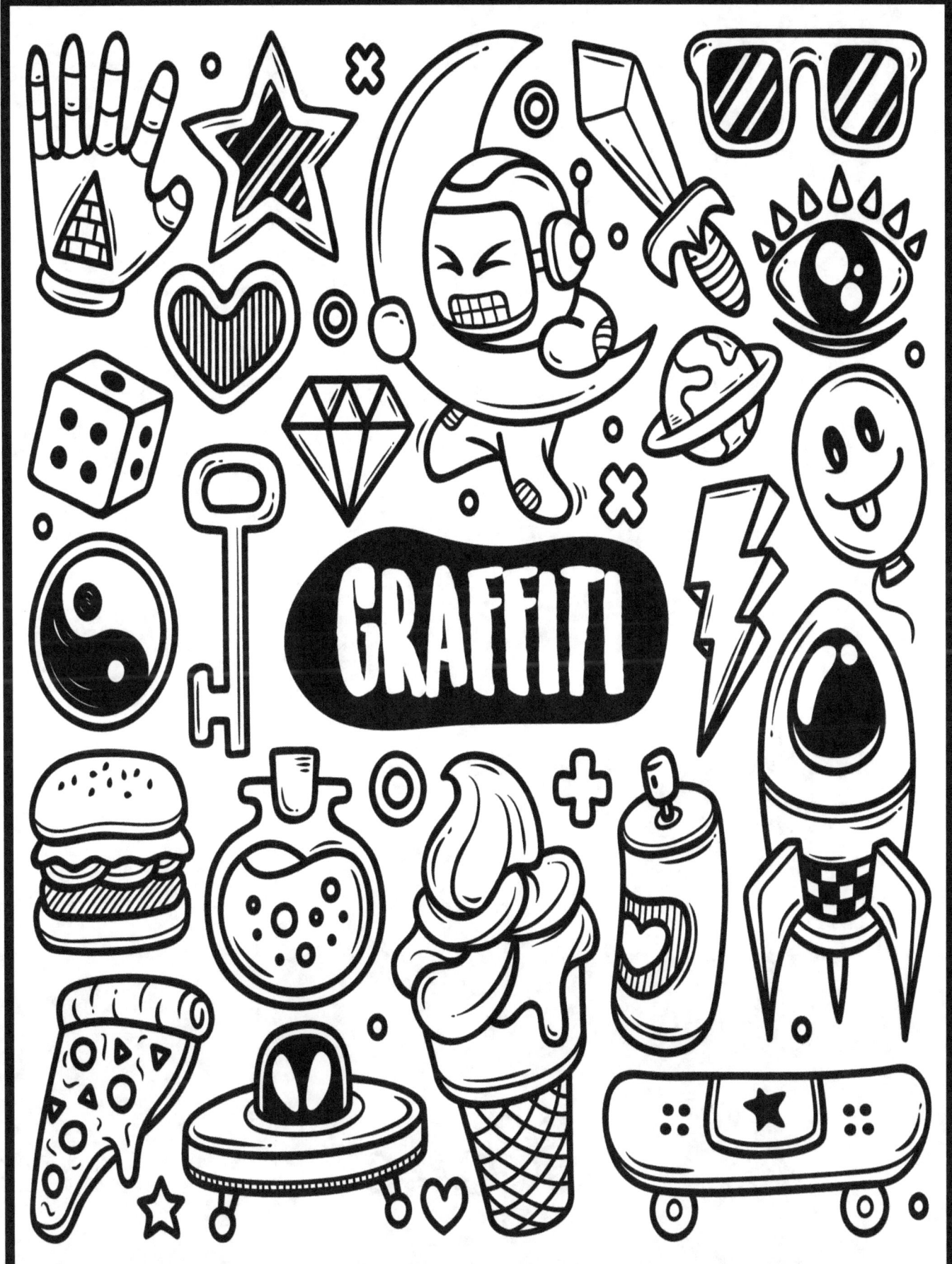

Love

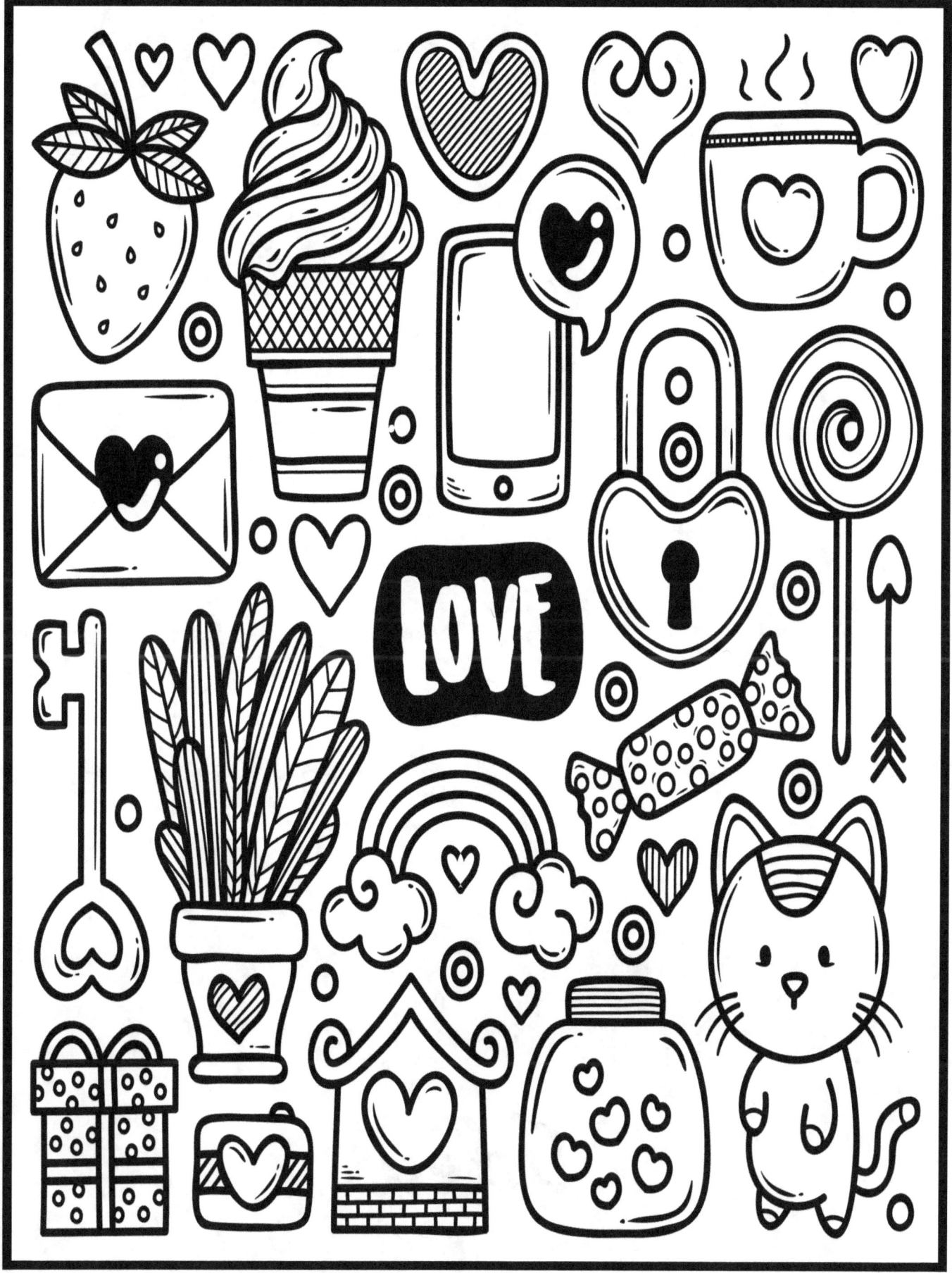

Idea

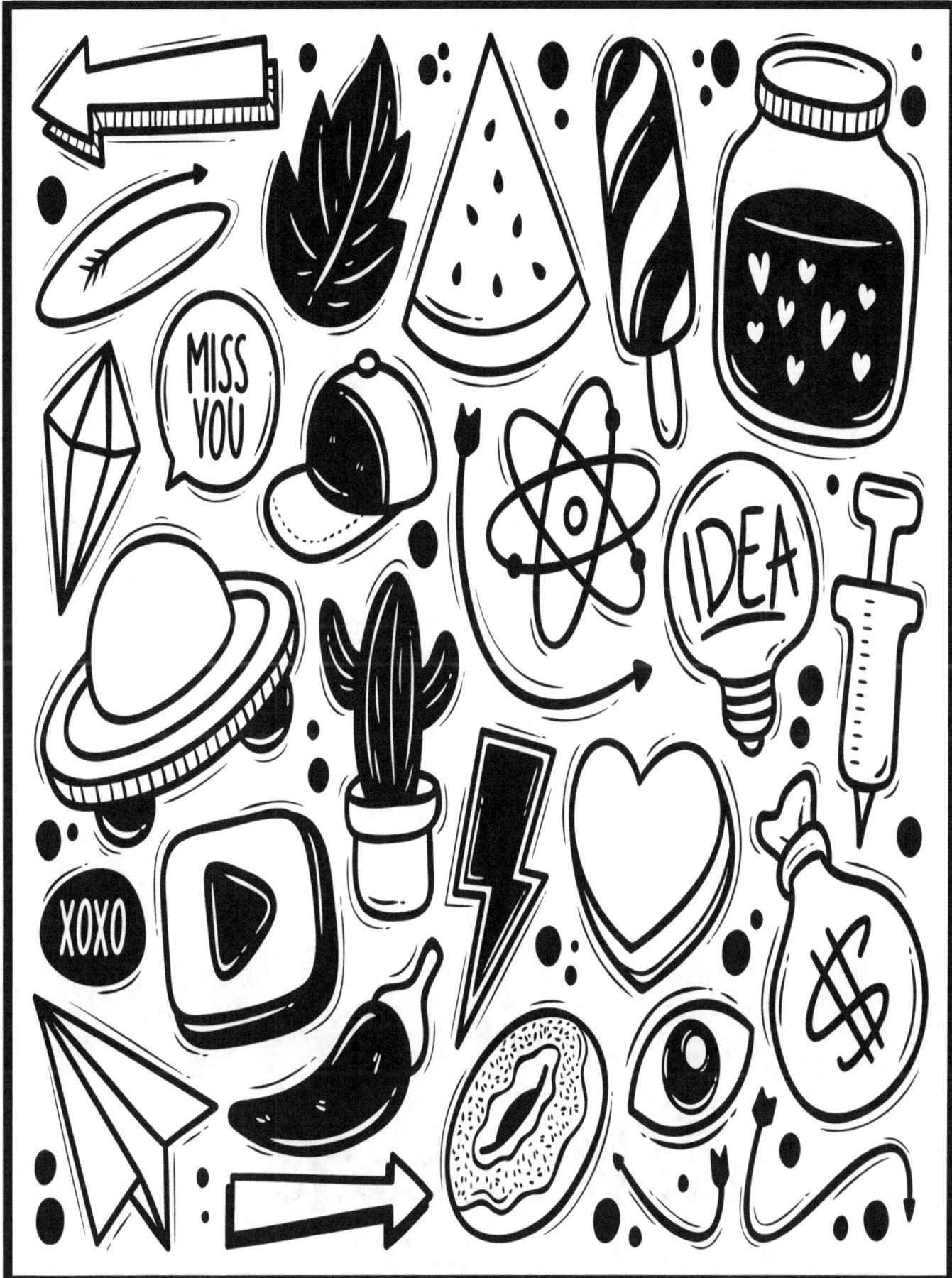

Mr Sloth

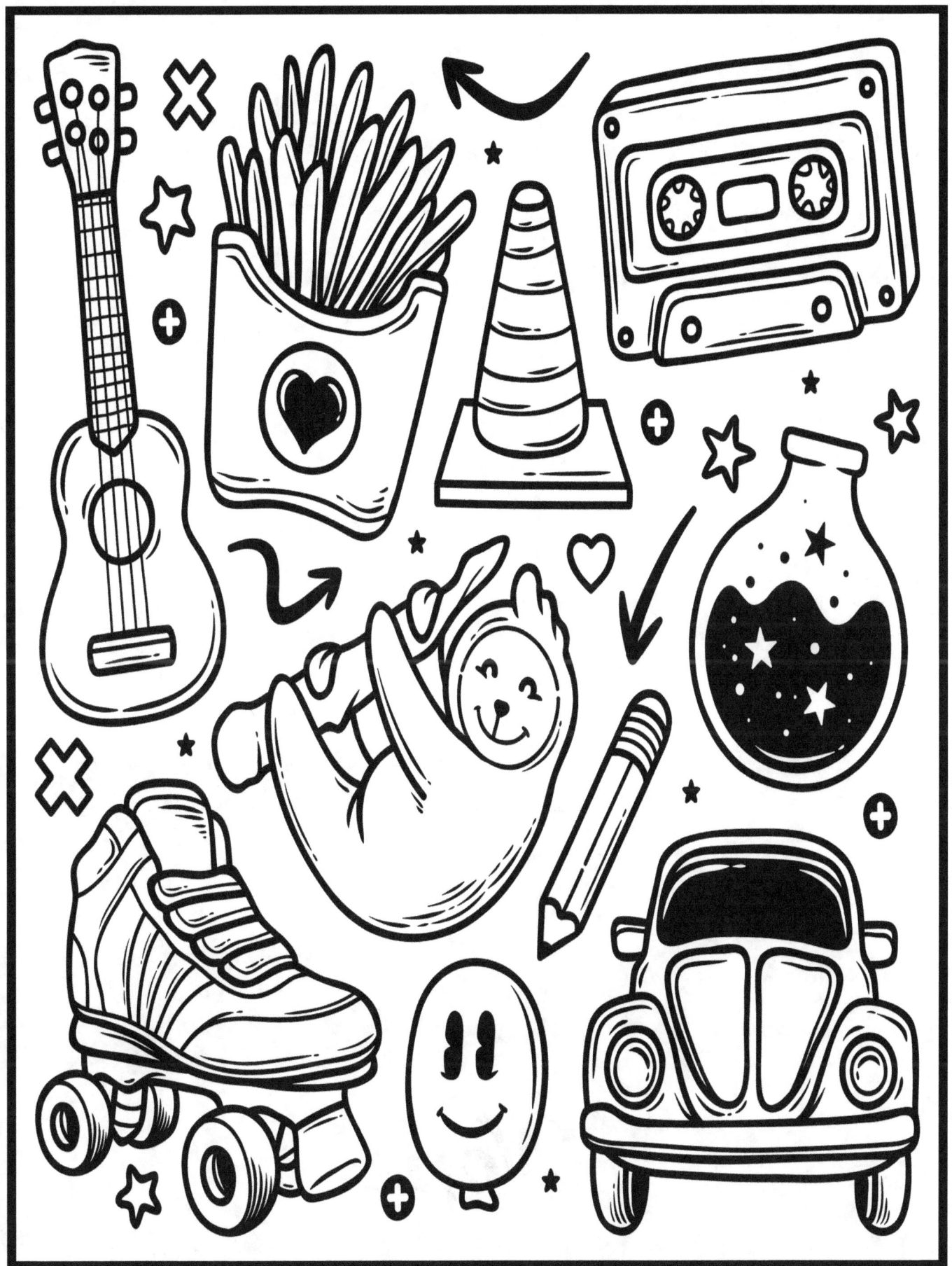

Nope

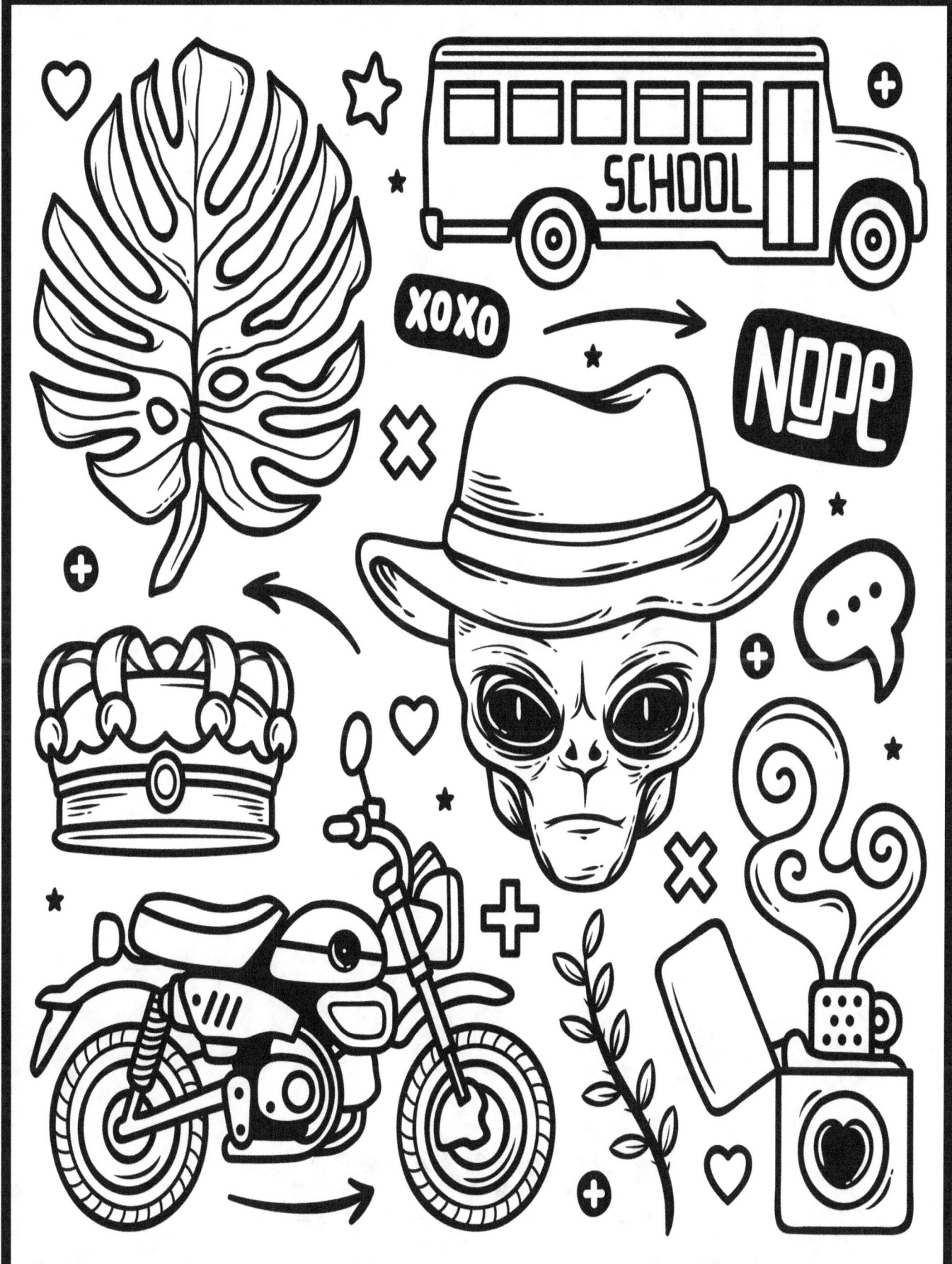

Germany

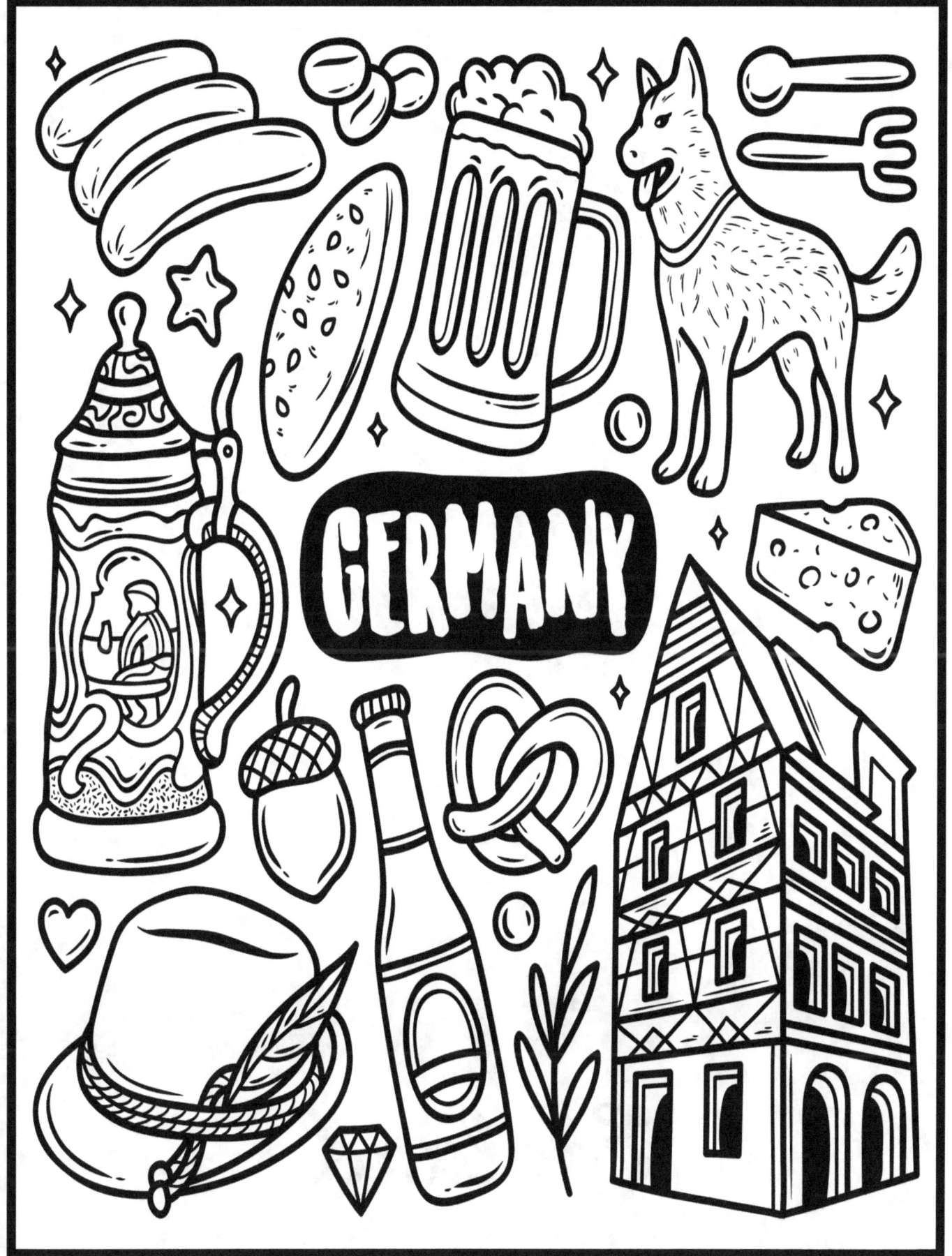

England

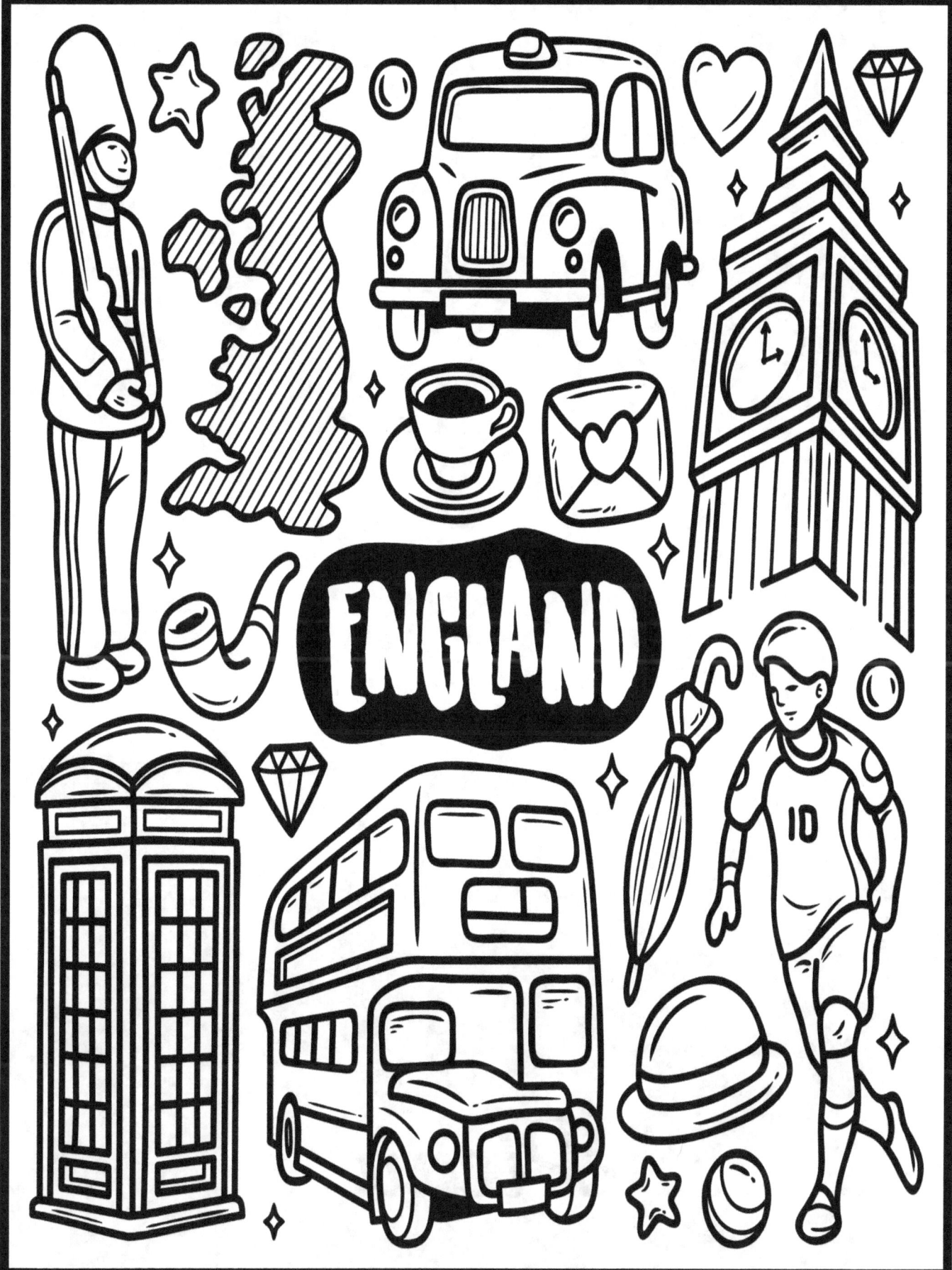

Picnic

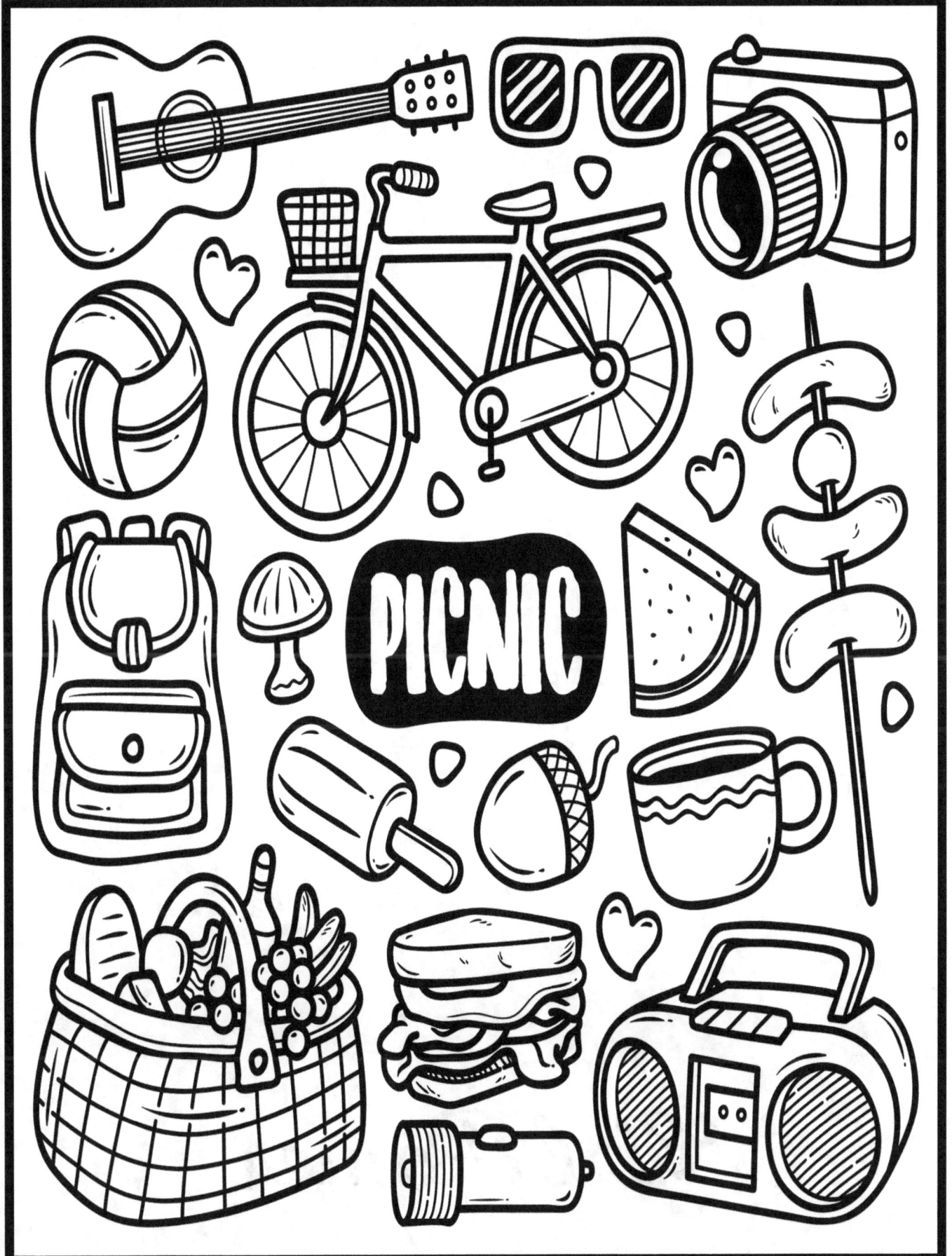

Girl Power

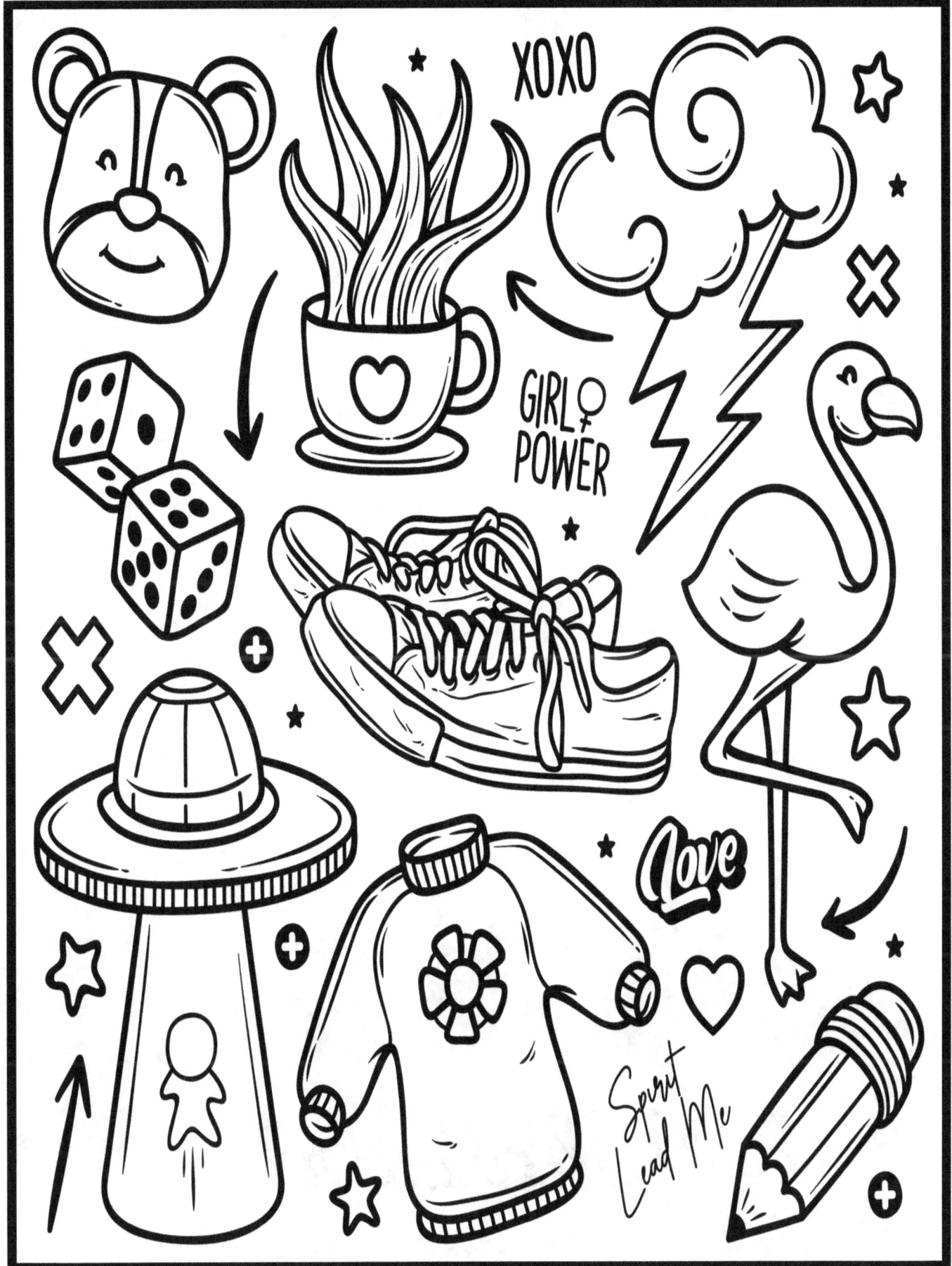

Whatever!

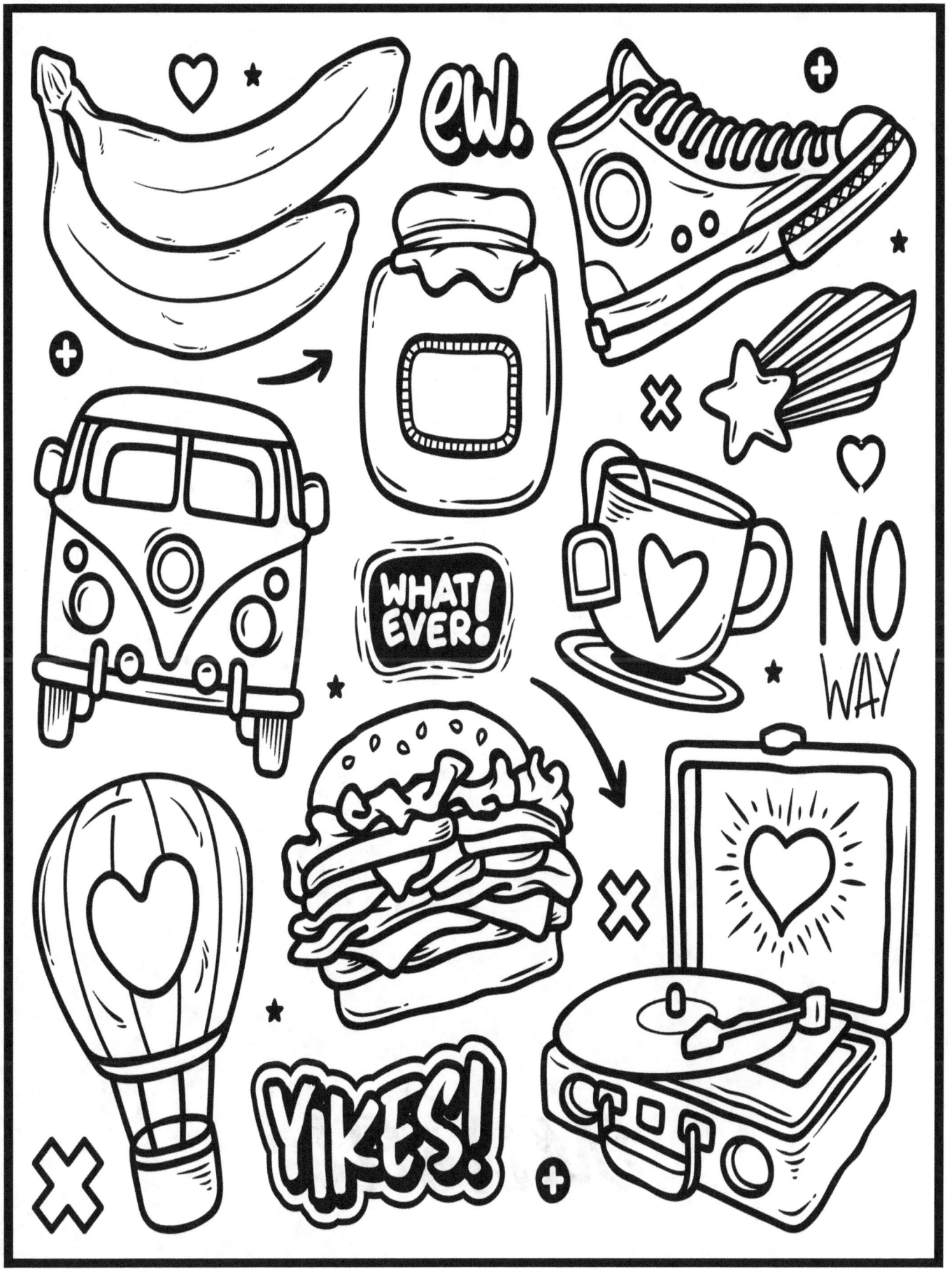

Miss U

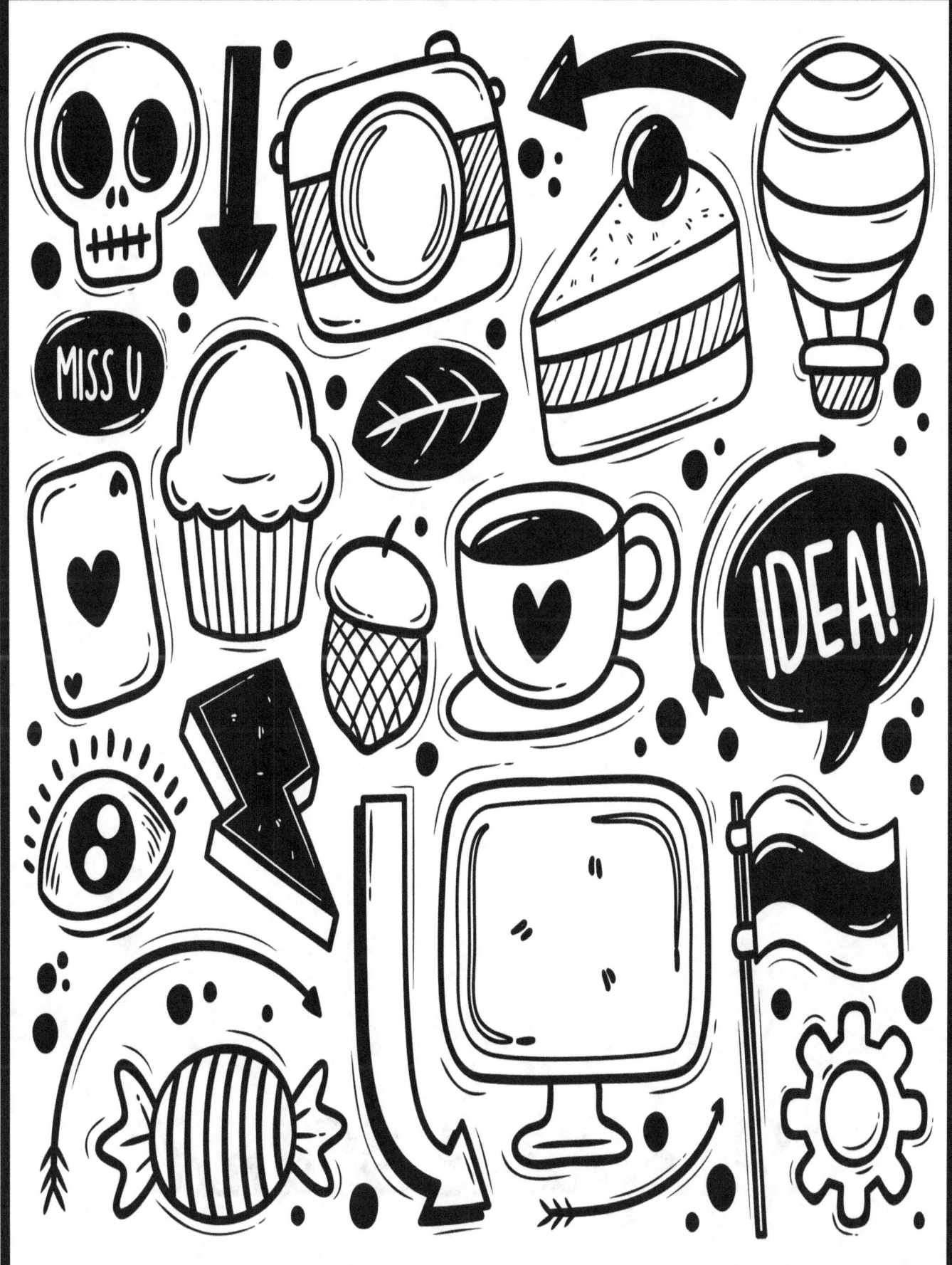

Magical Land

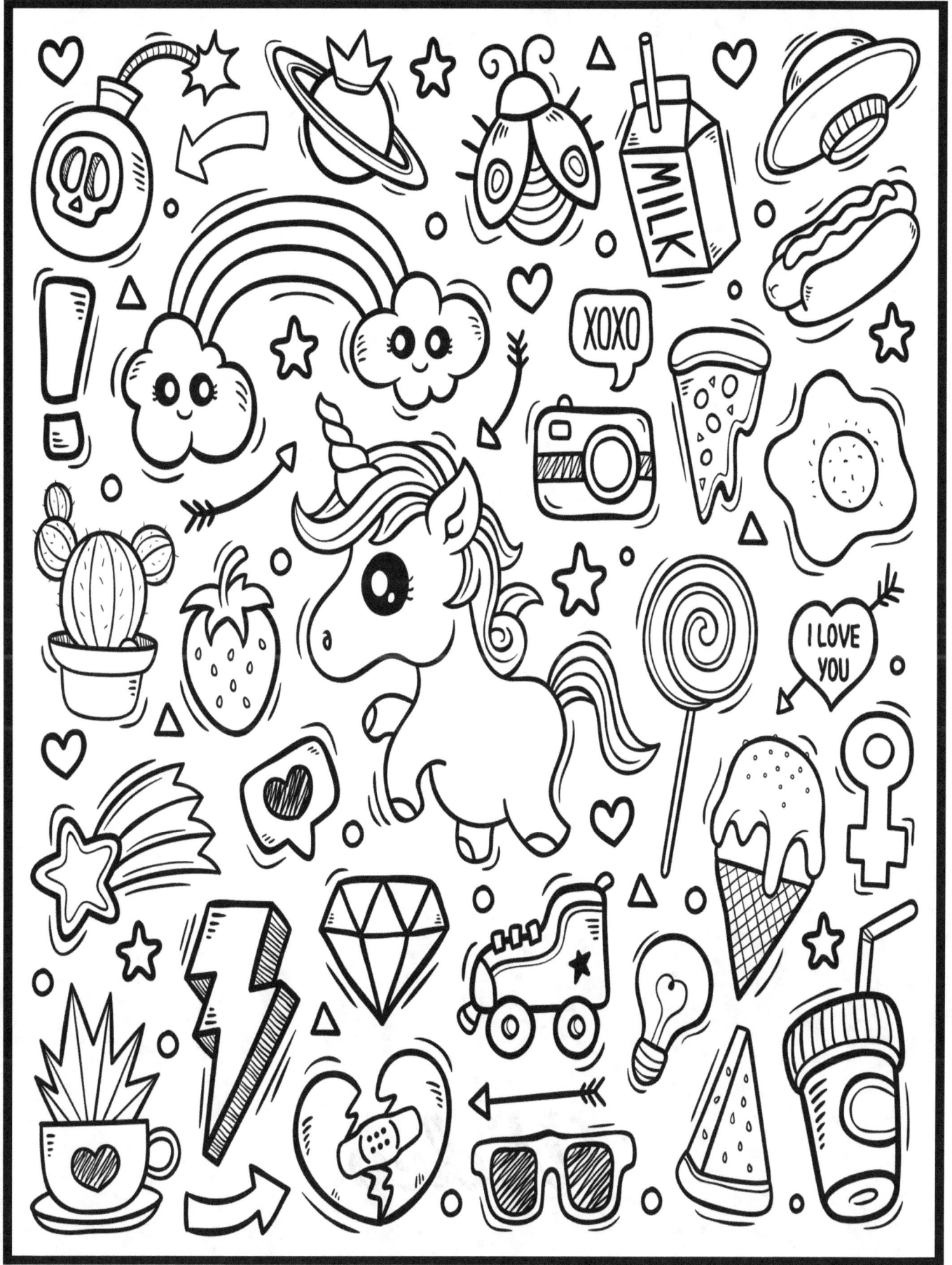

Video

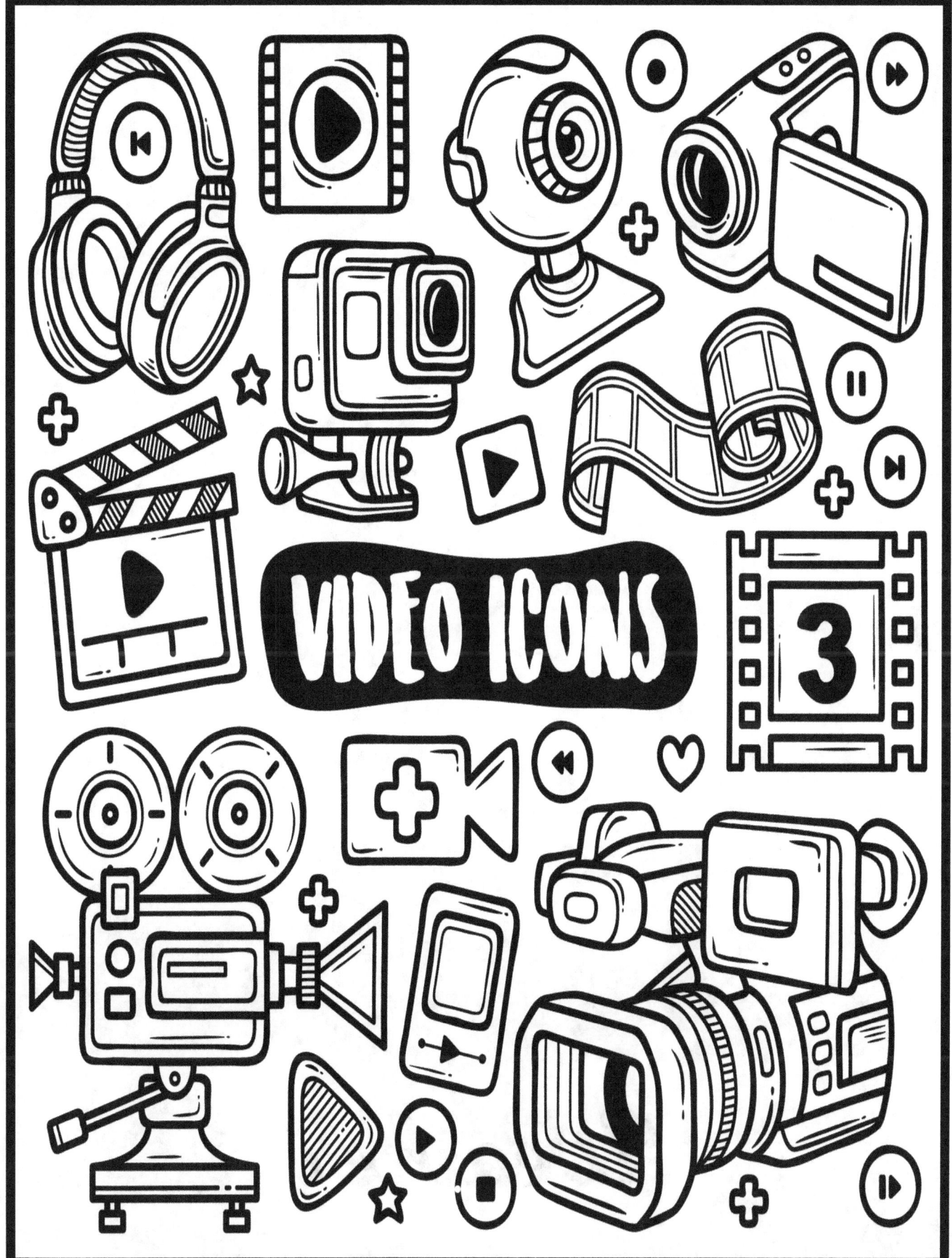

Weather

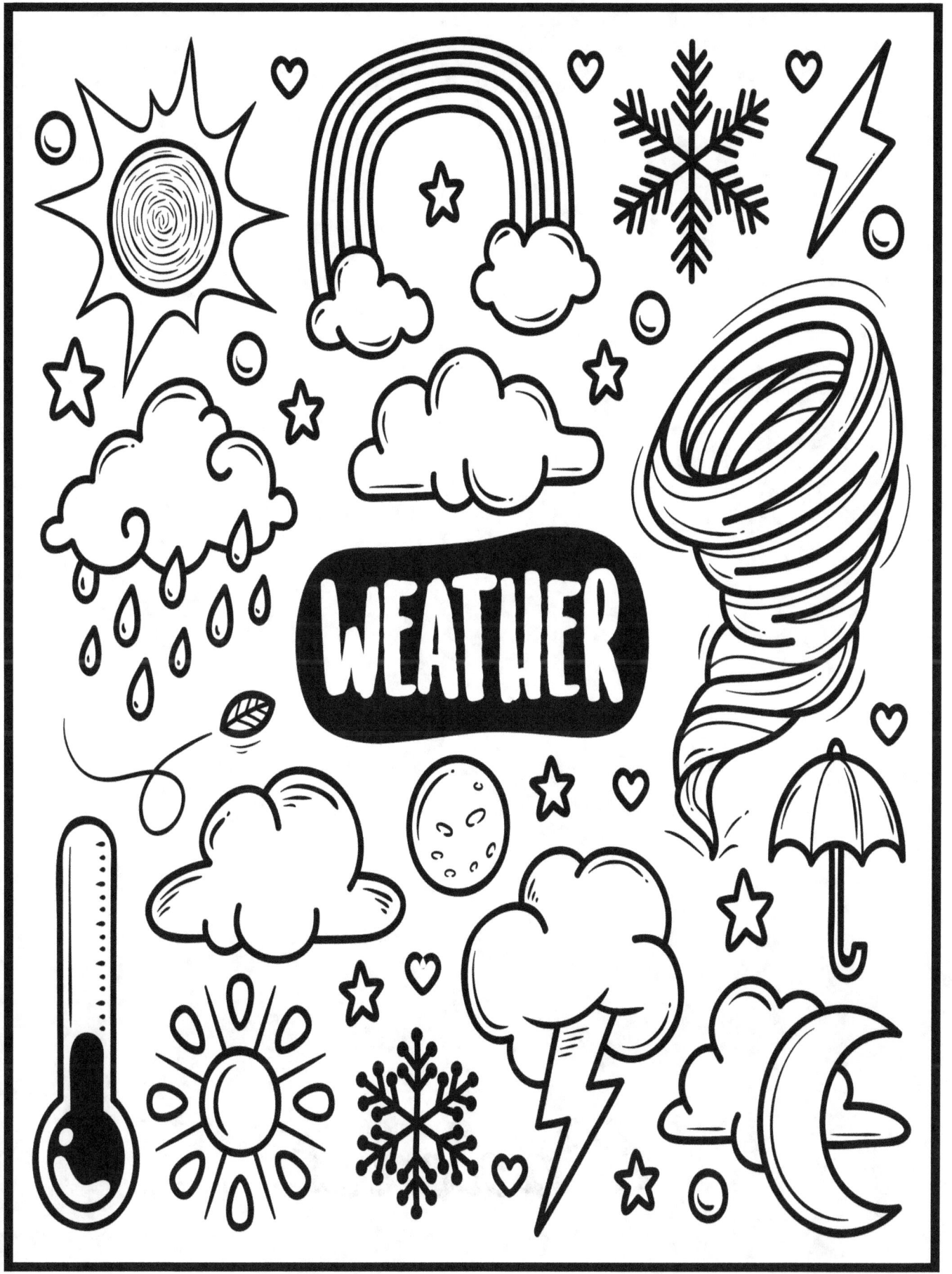

Podcast

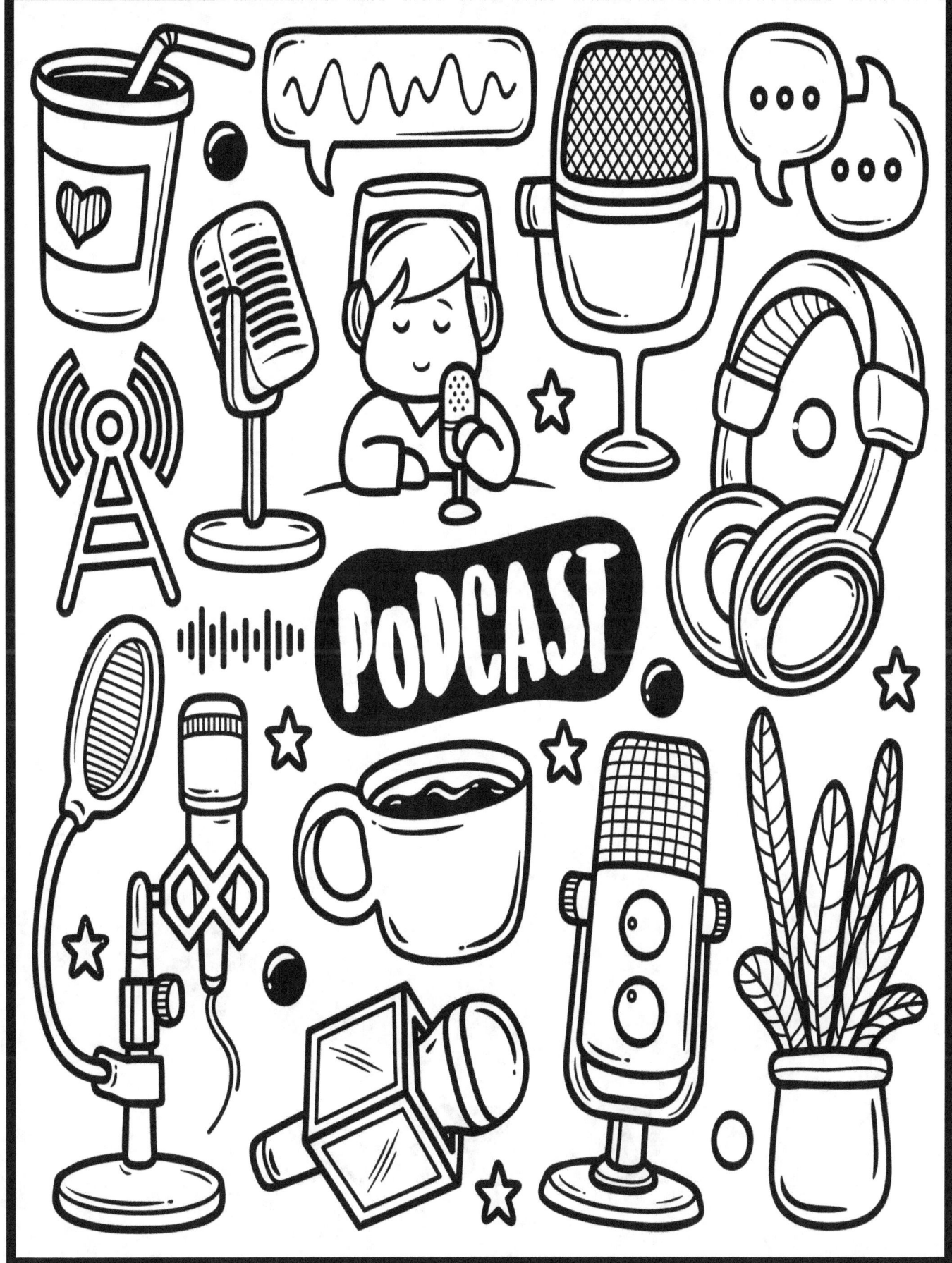

Be Lind

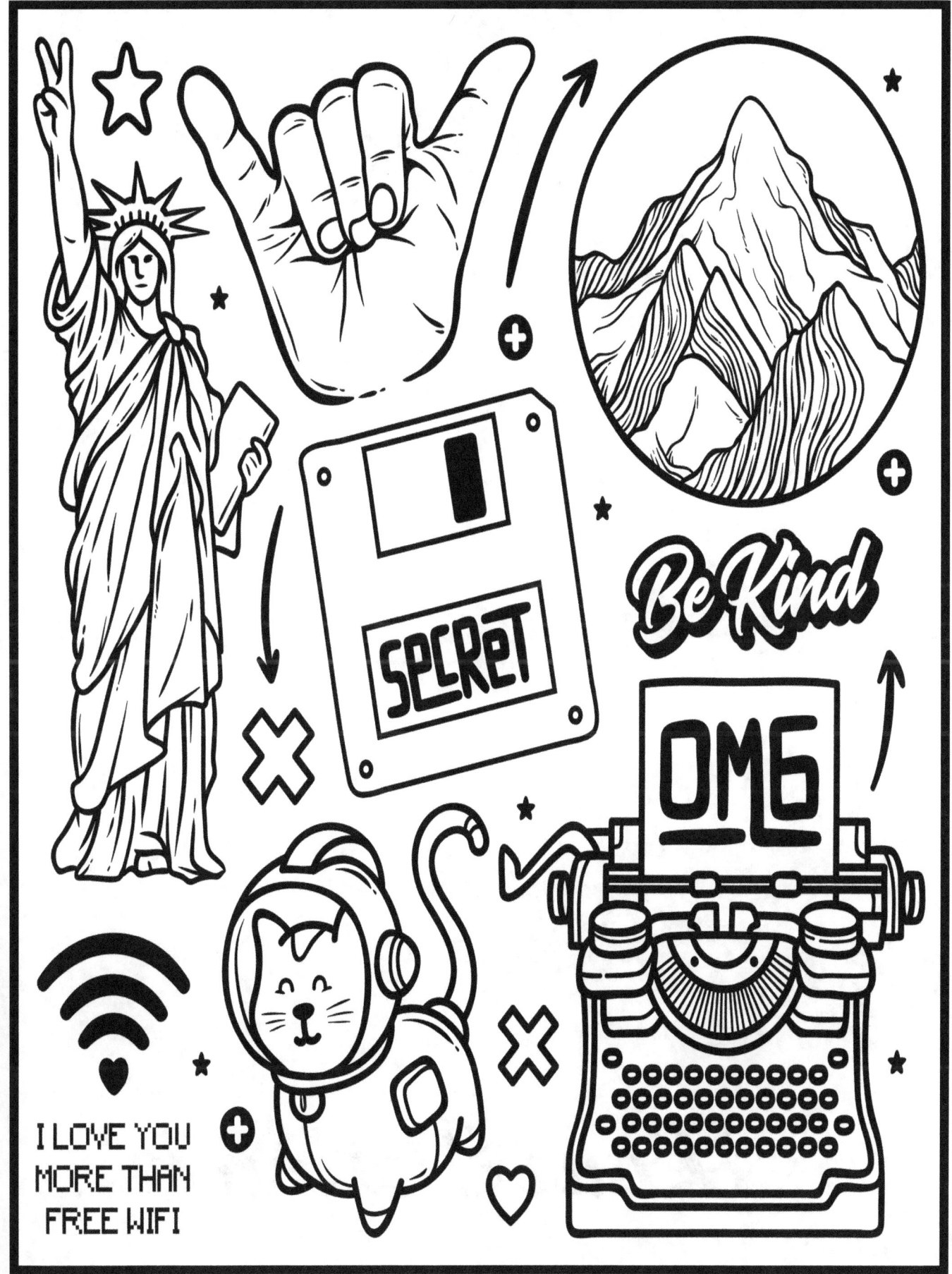

Love Potion

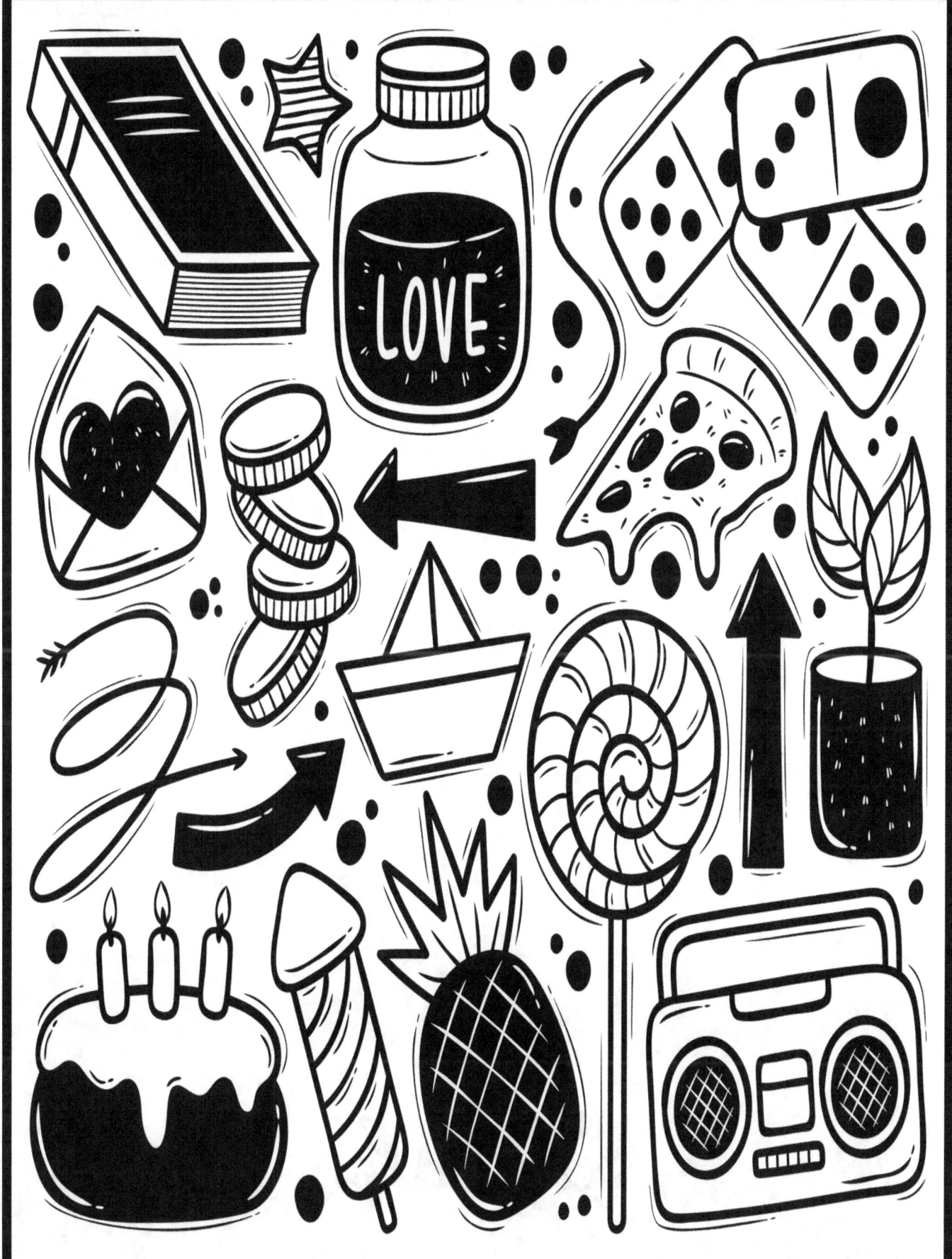

Fresh

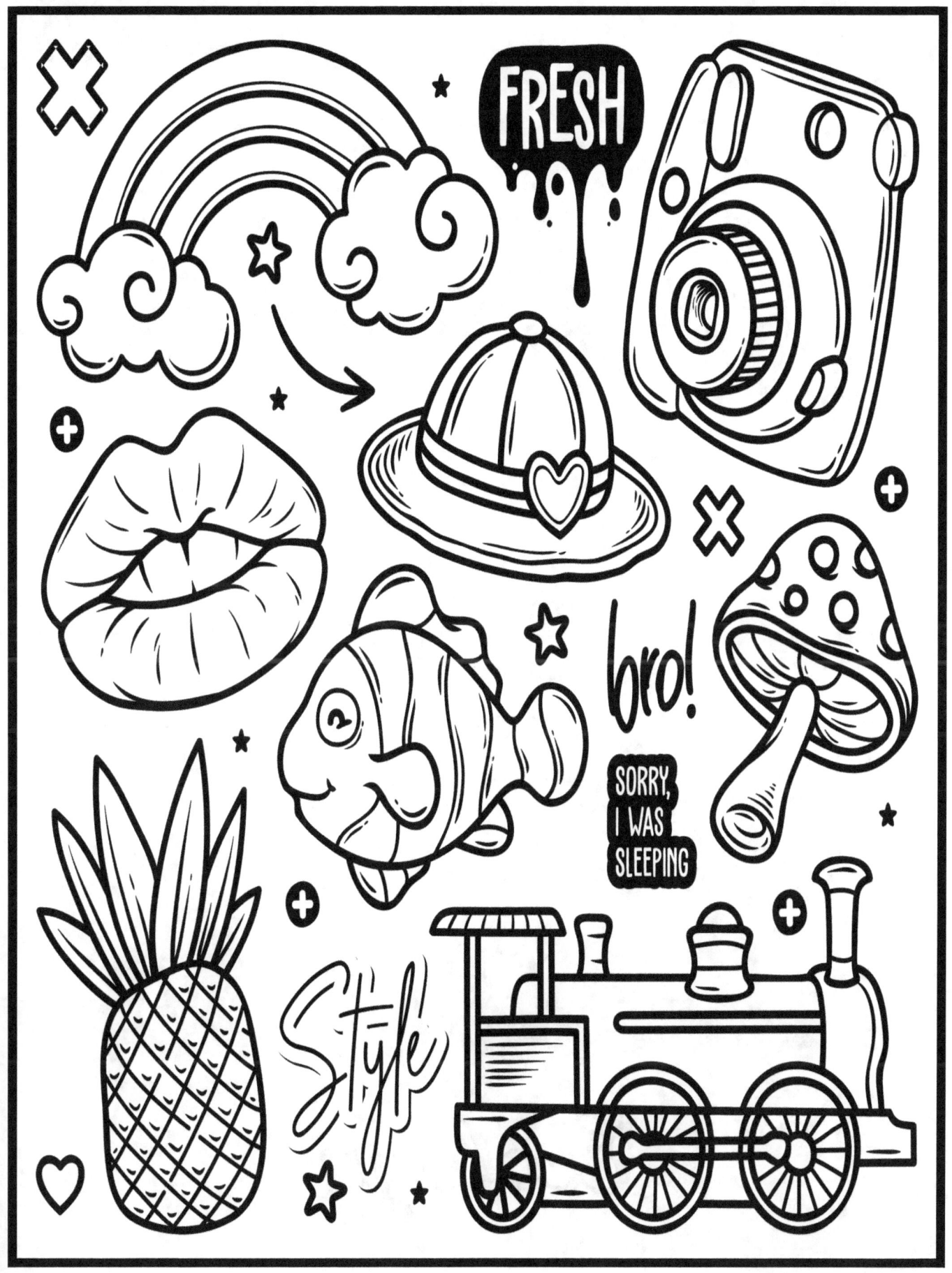

Ecology

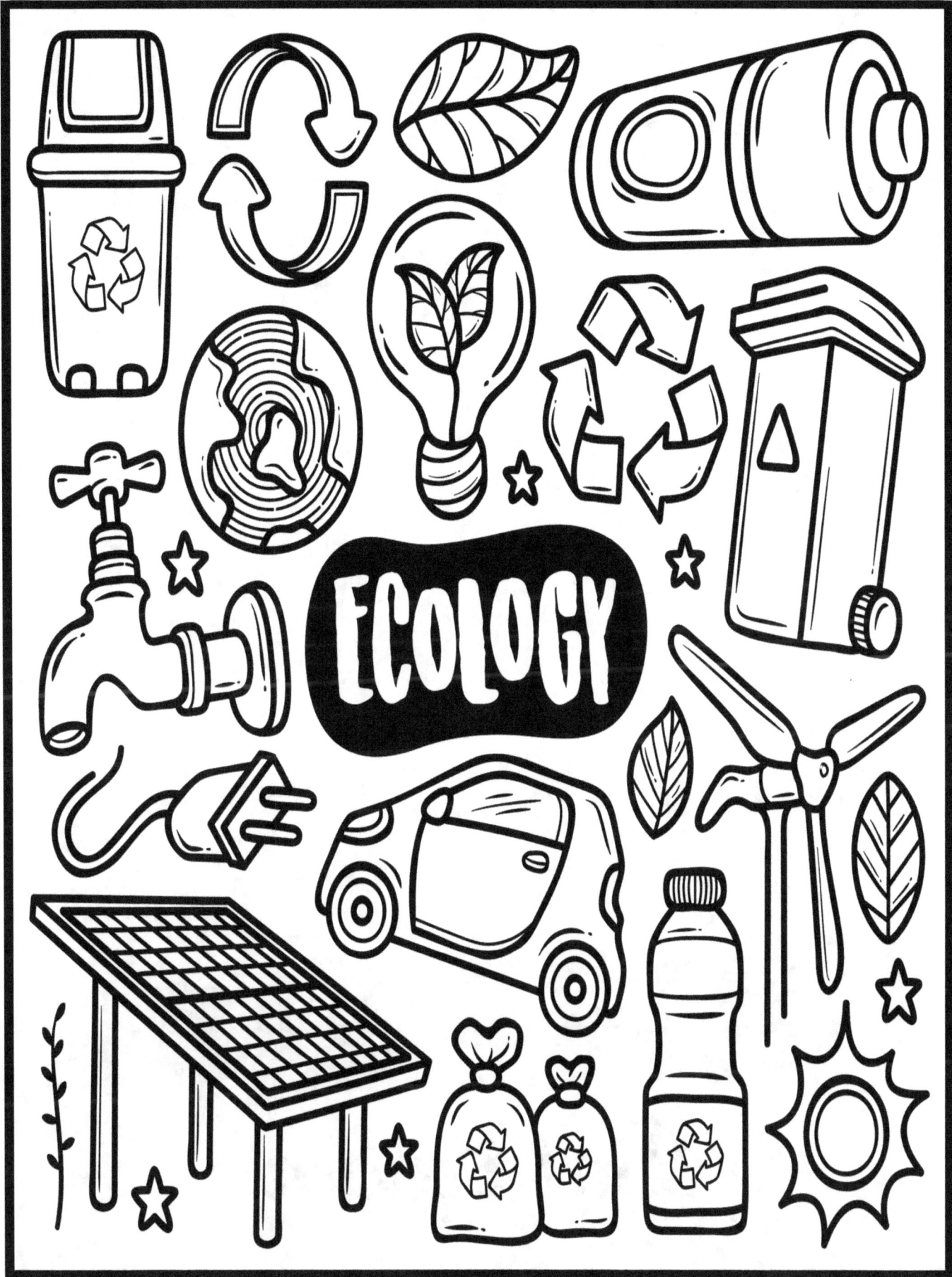

Bathroom

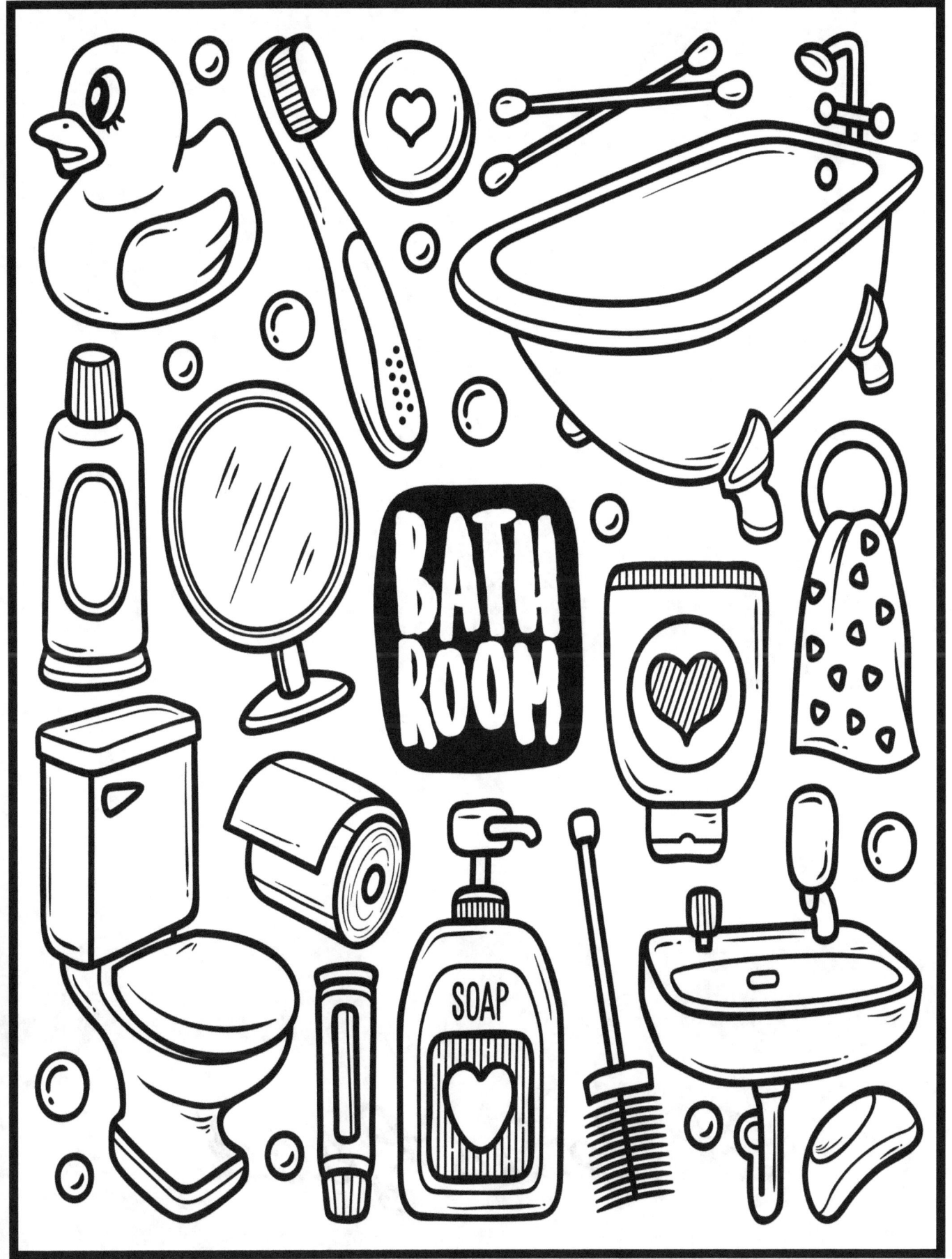

Life Is Good

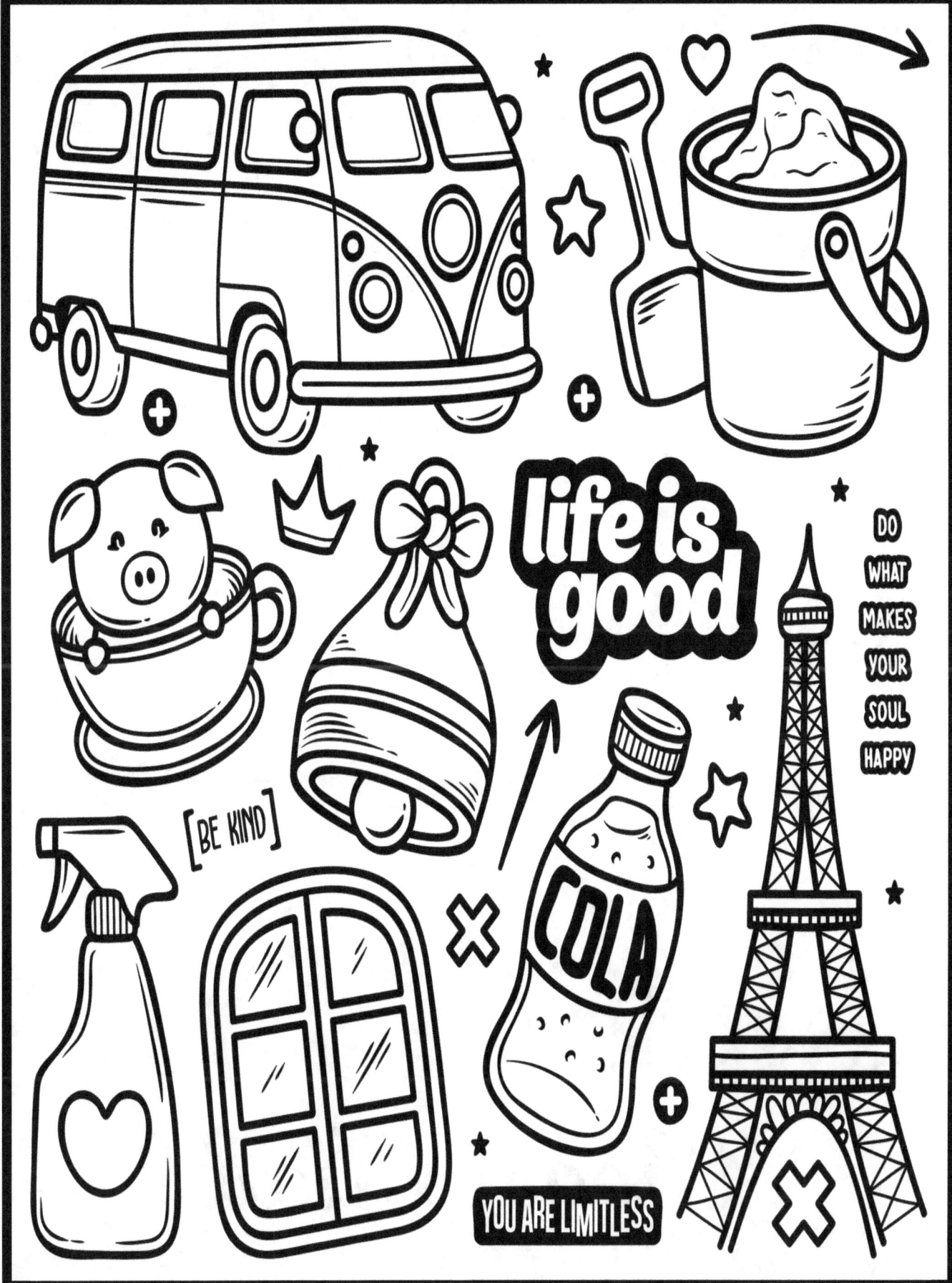

Choose Kind

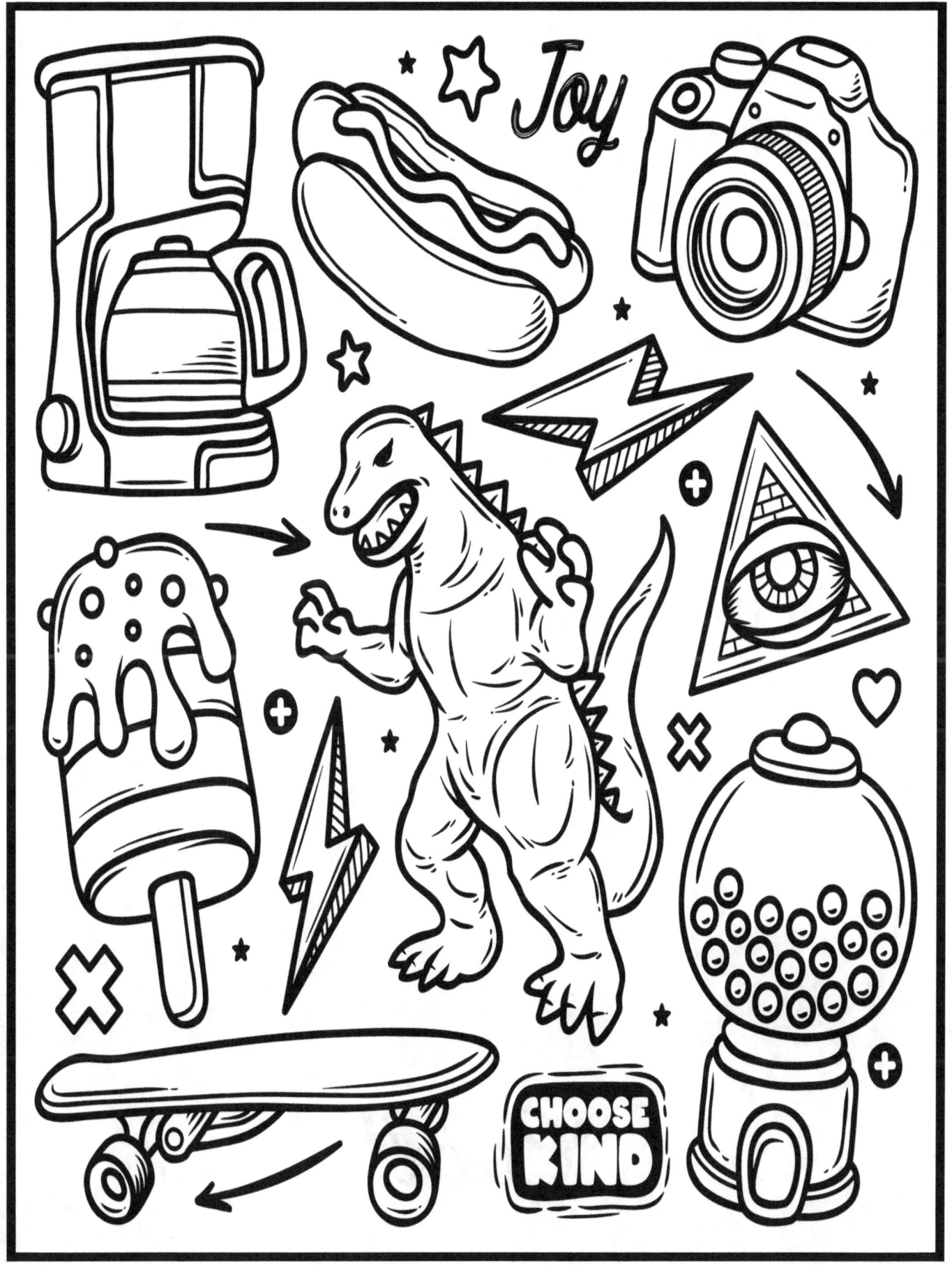

Cool!

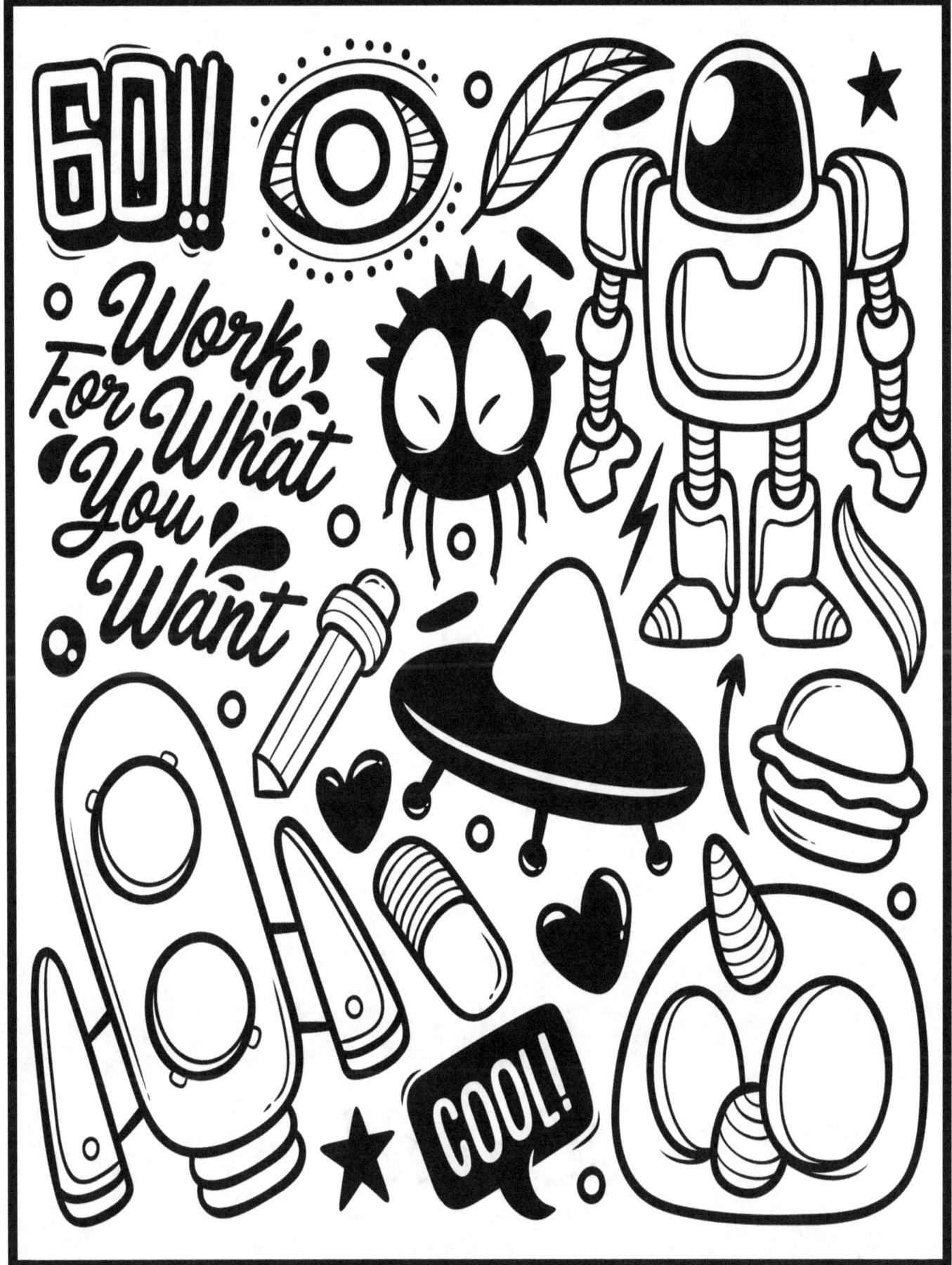

Booh!

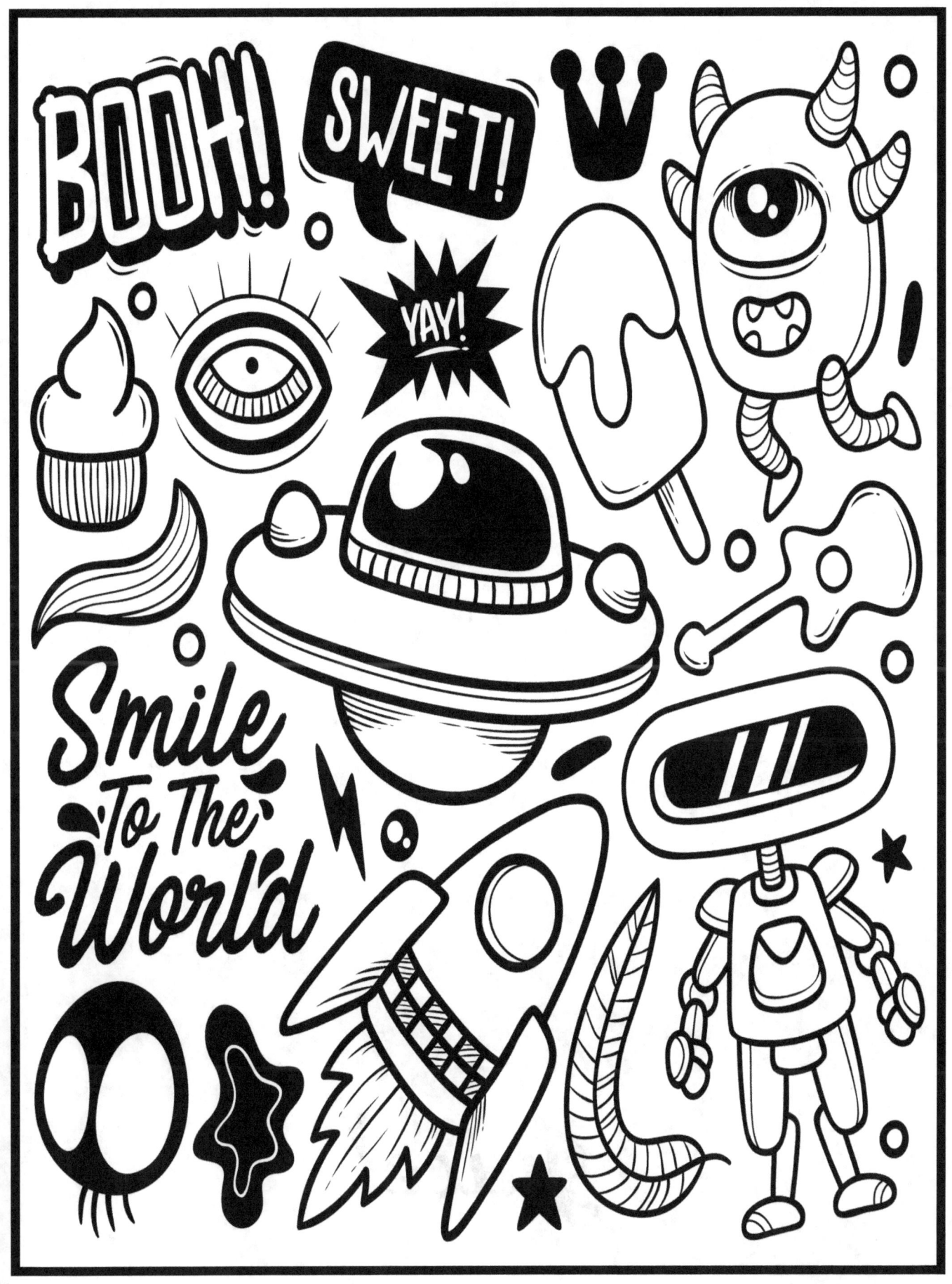

Juice!

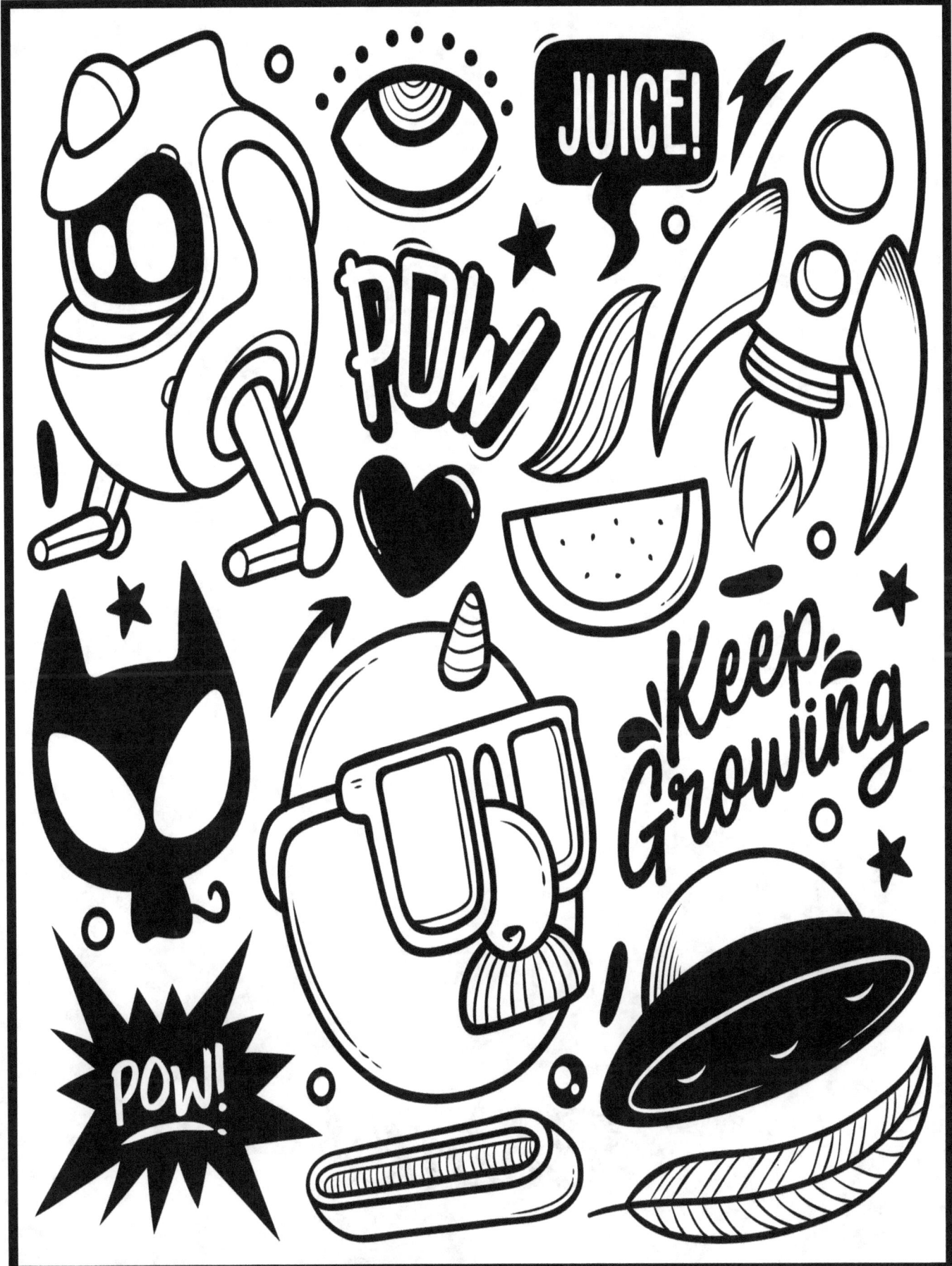

Boink!

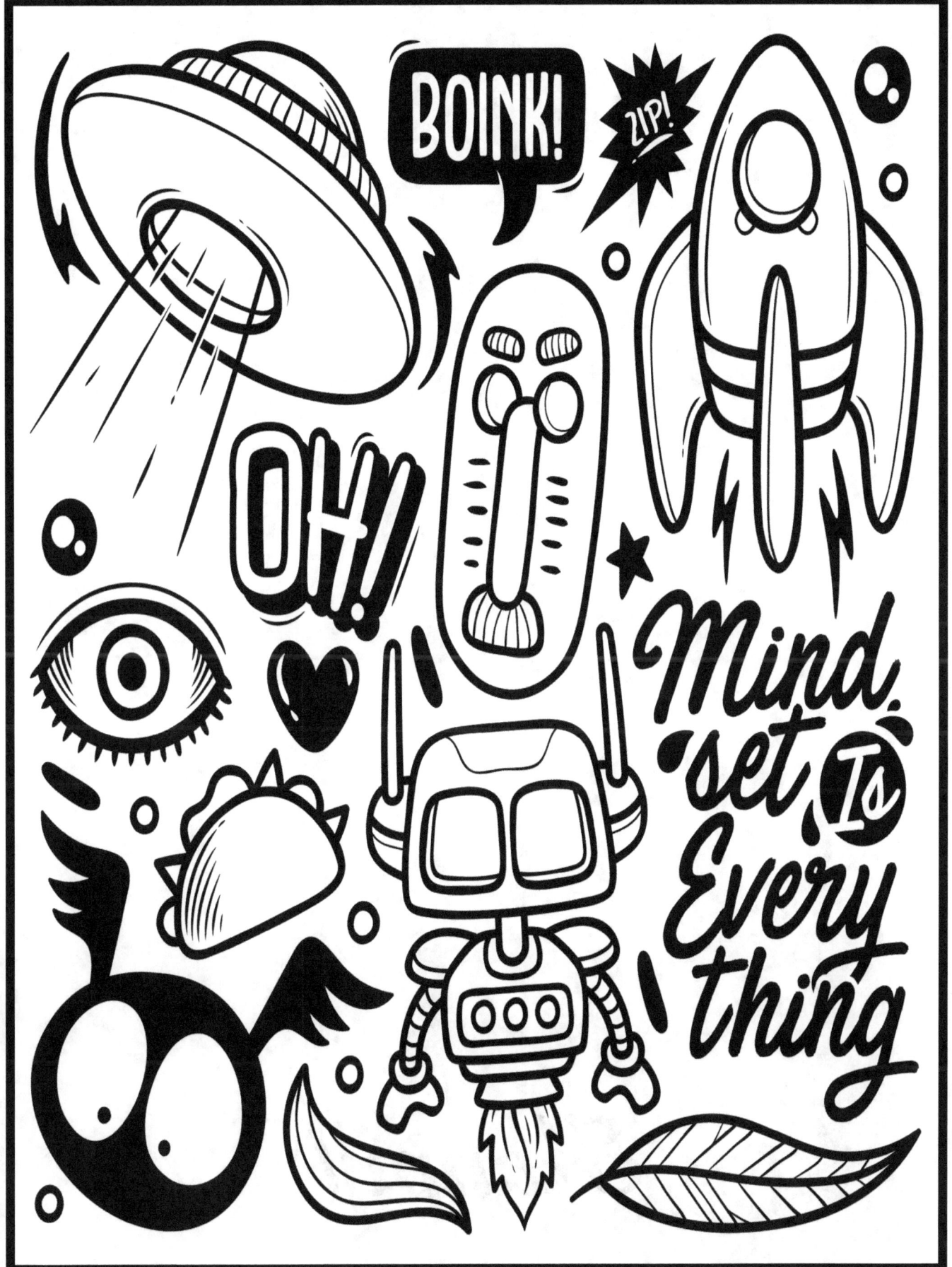

Happy!

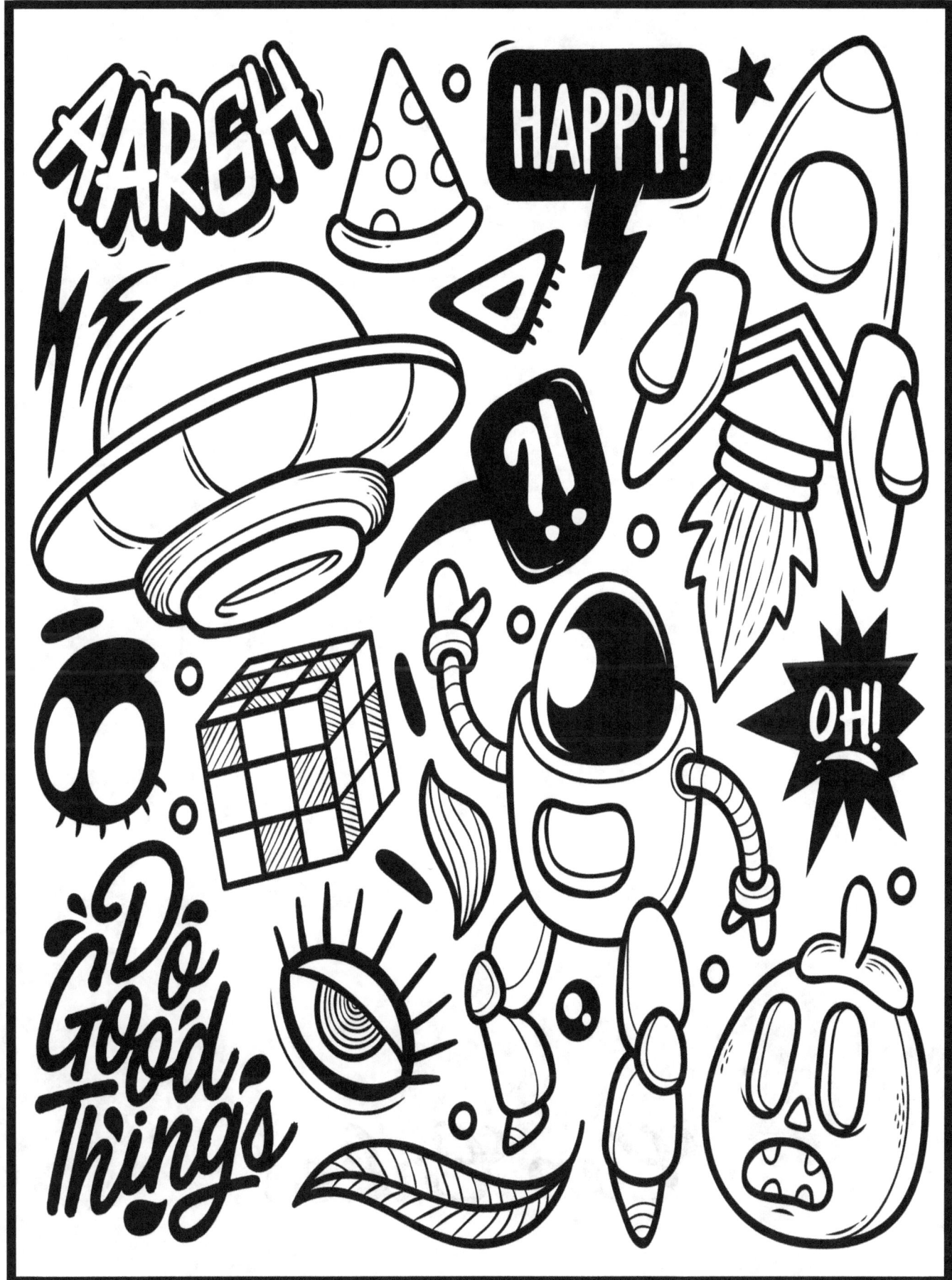

Cup Cakes

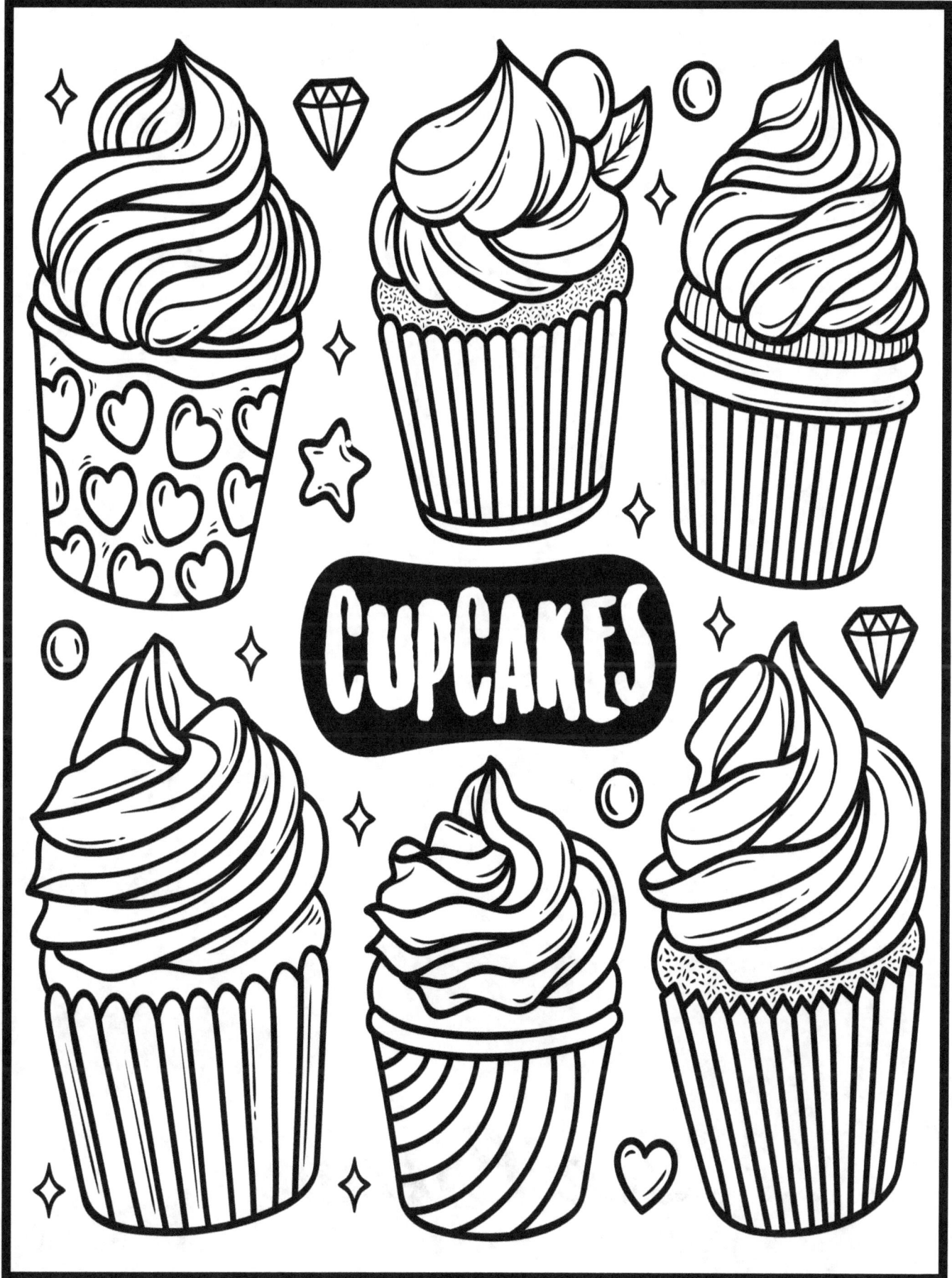

Ice Cream

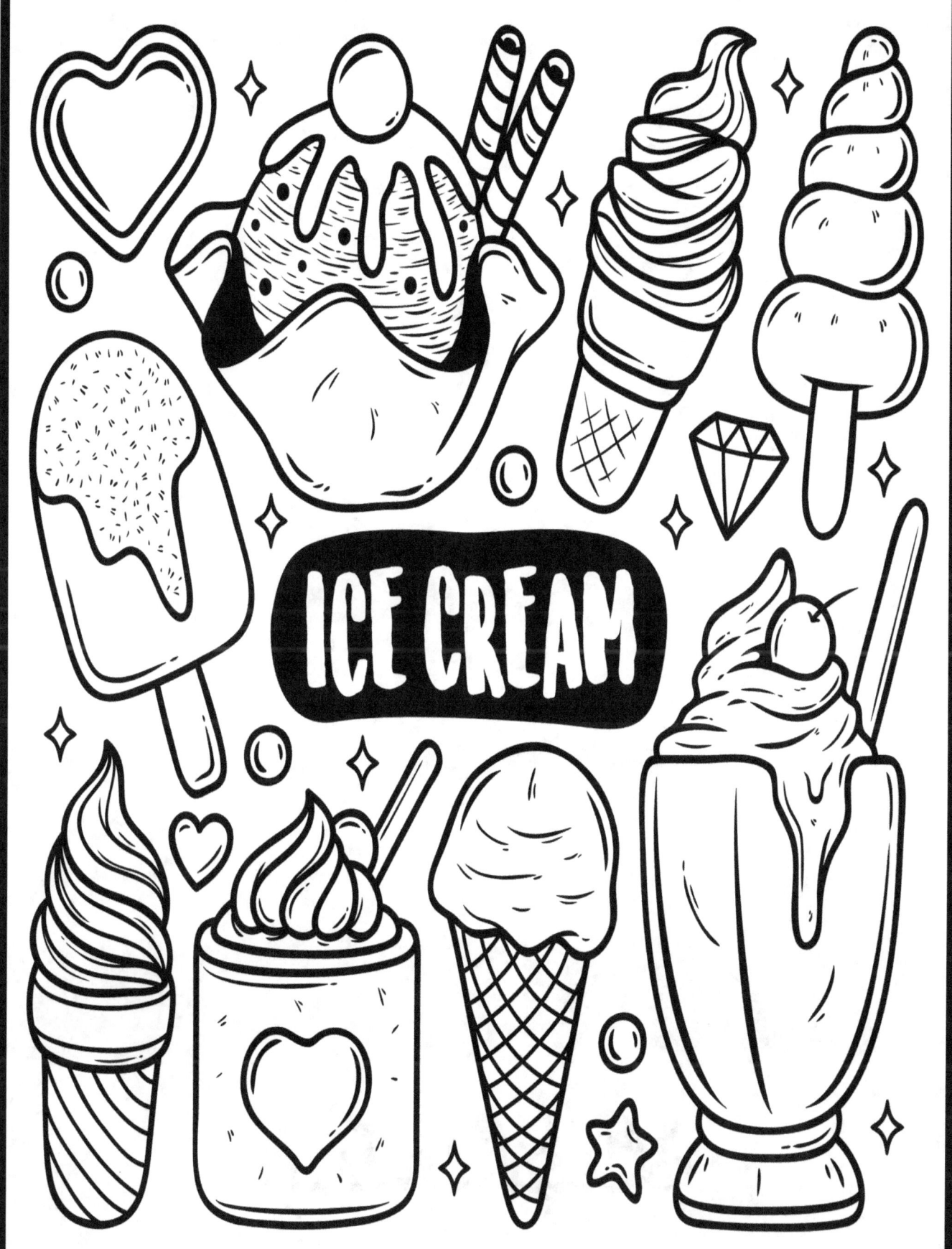

Lightning

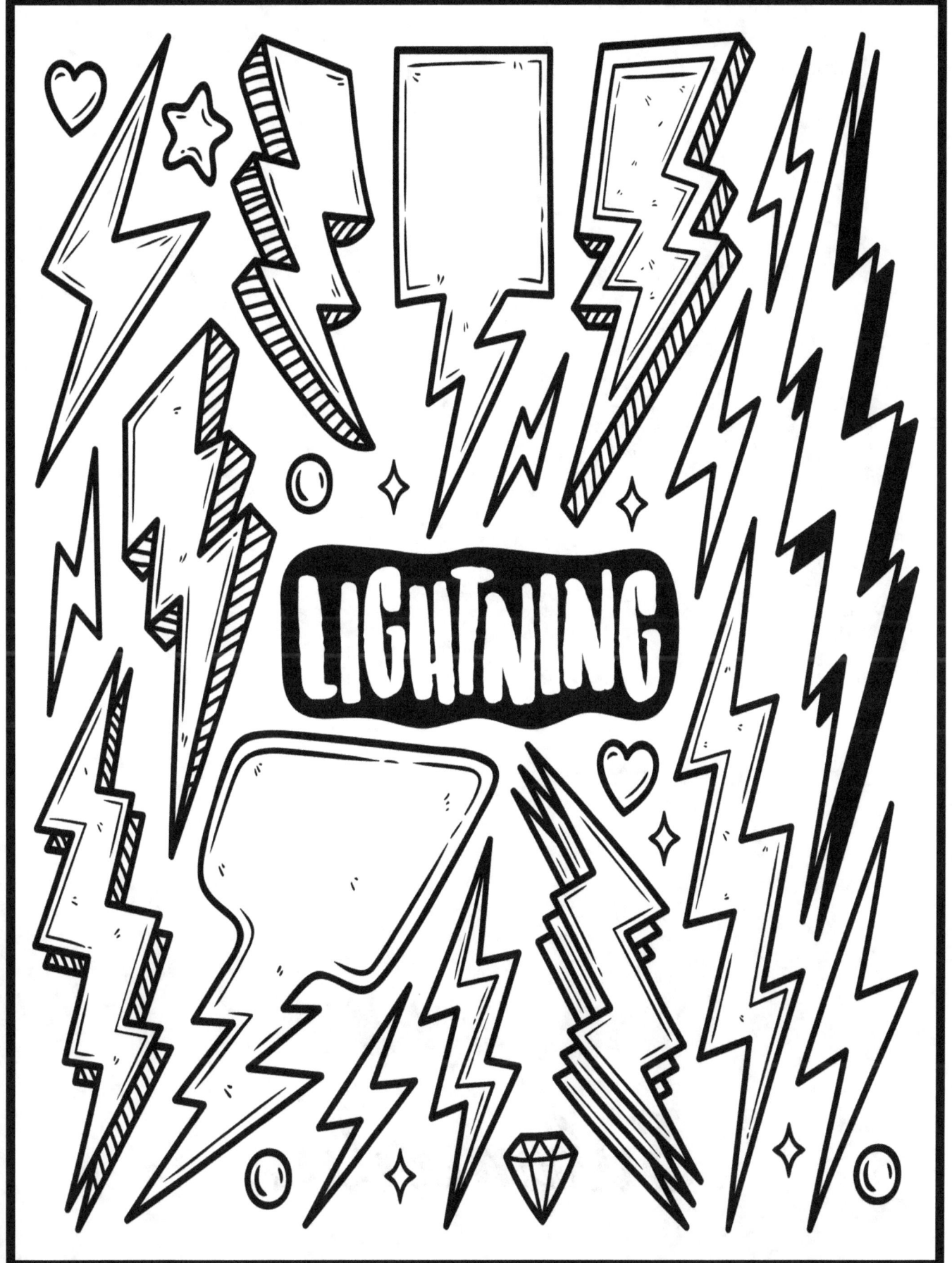

Submarine

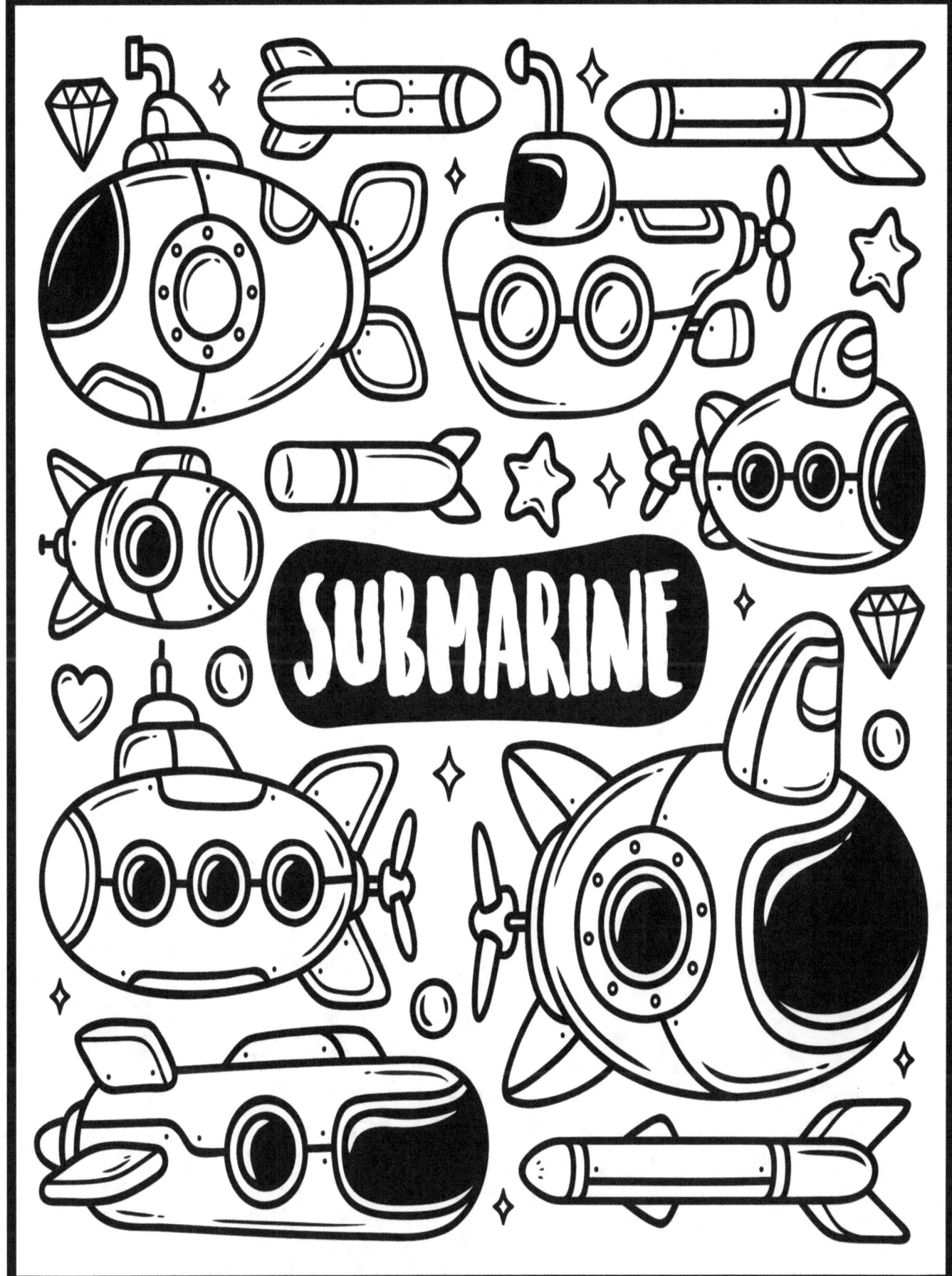

Roar!

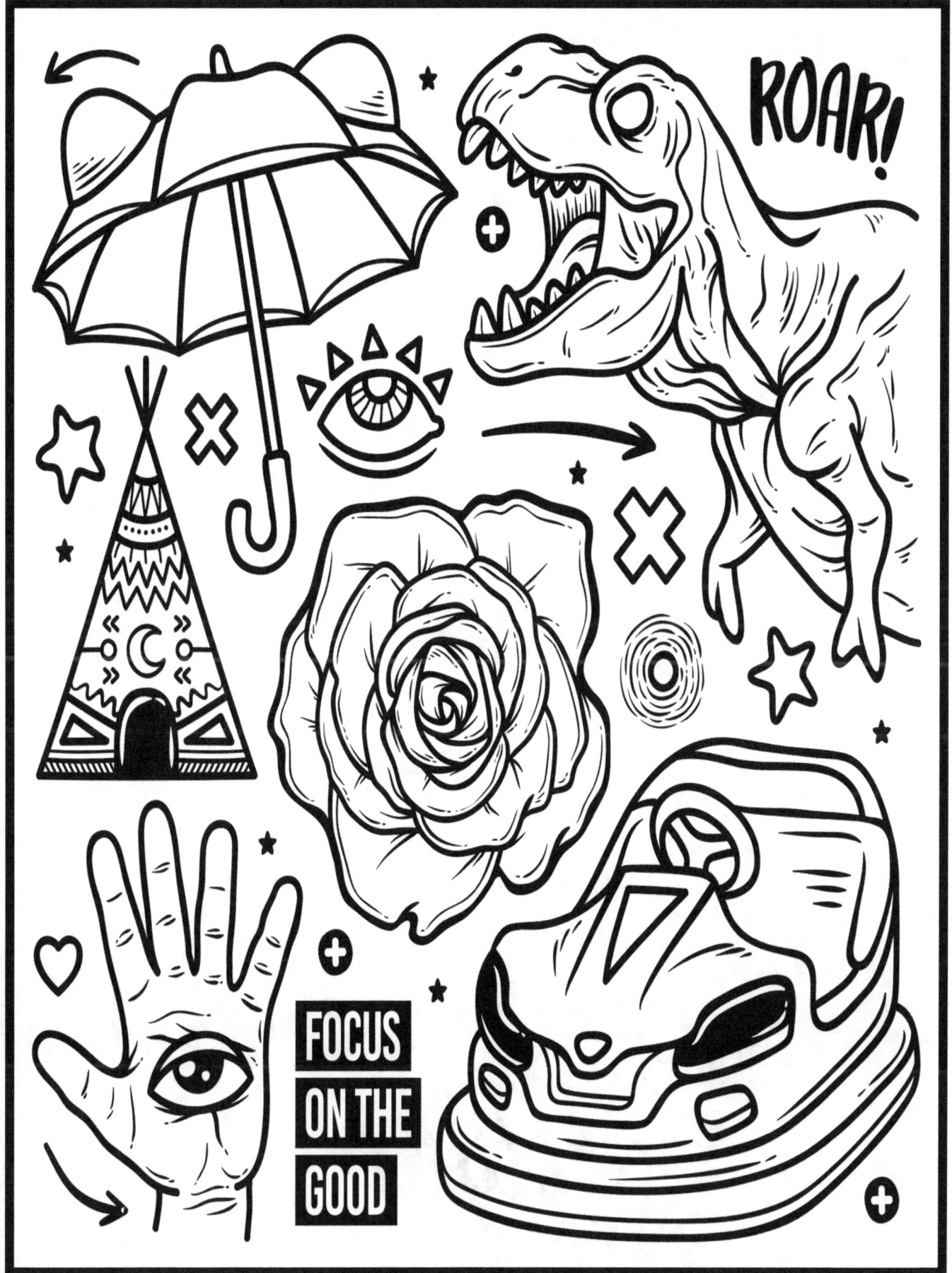

Ugh!

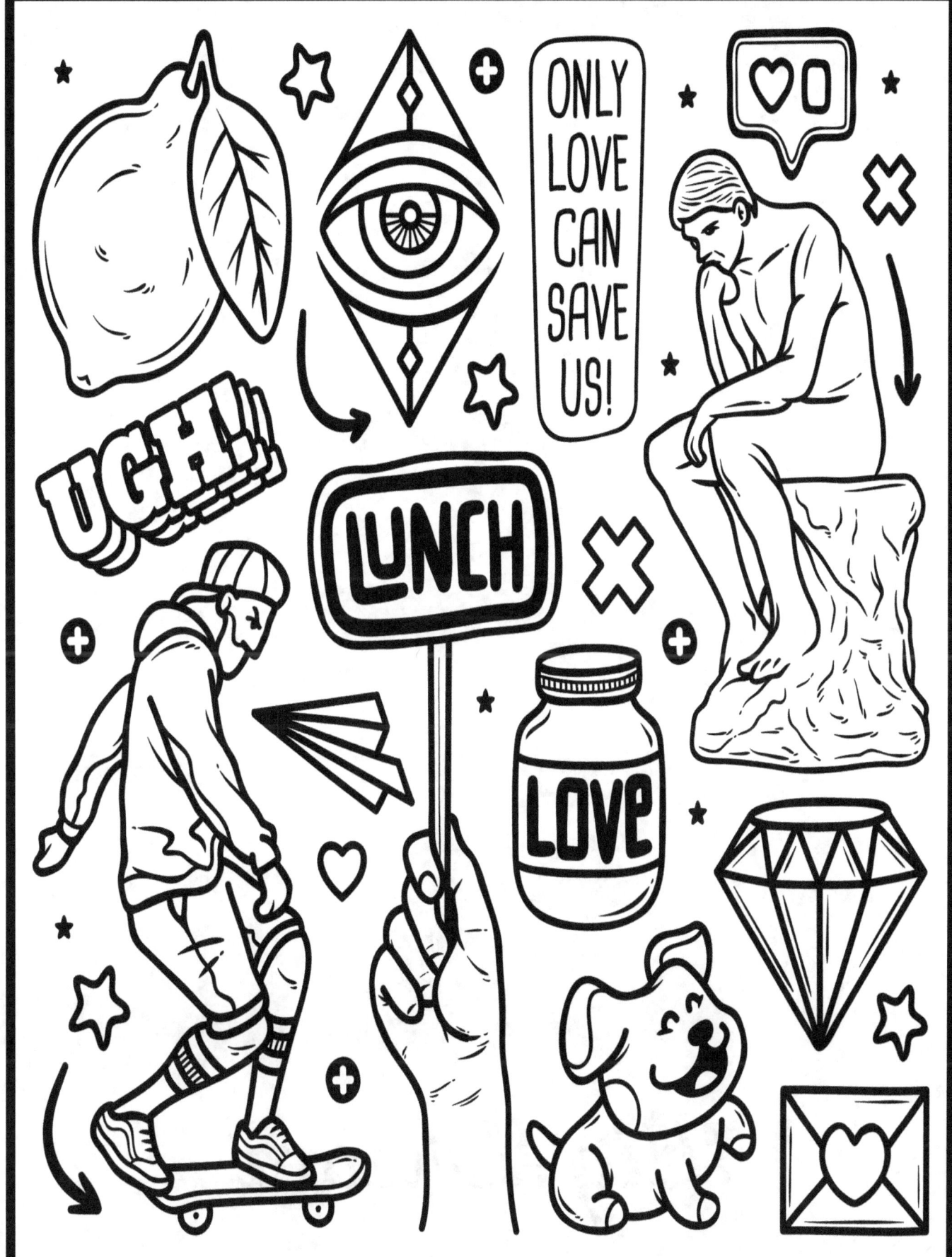

Big Dream

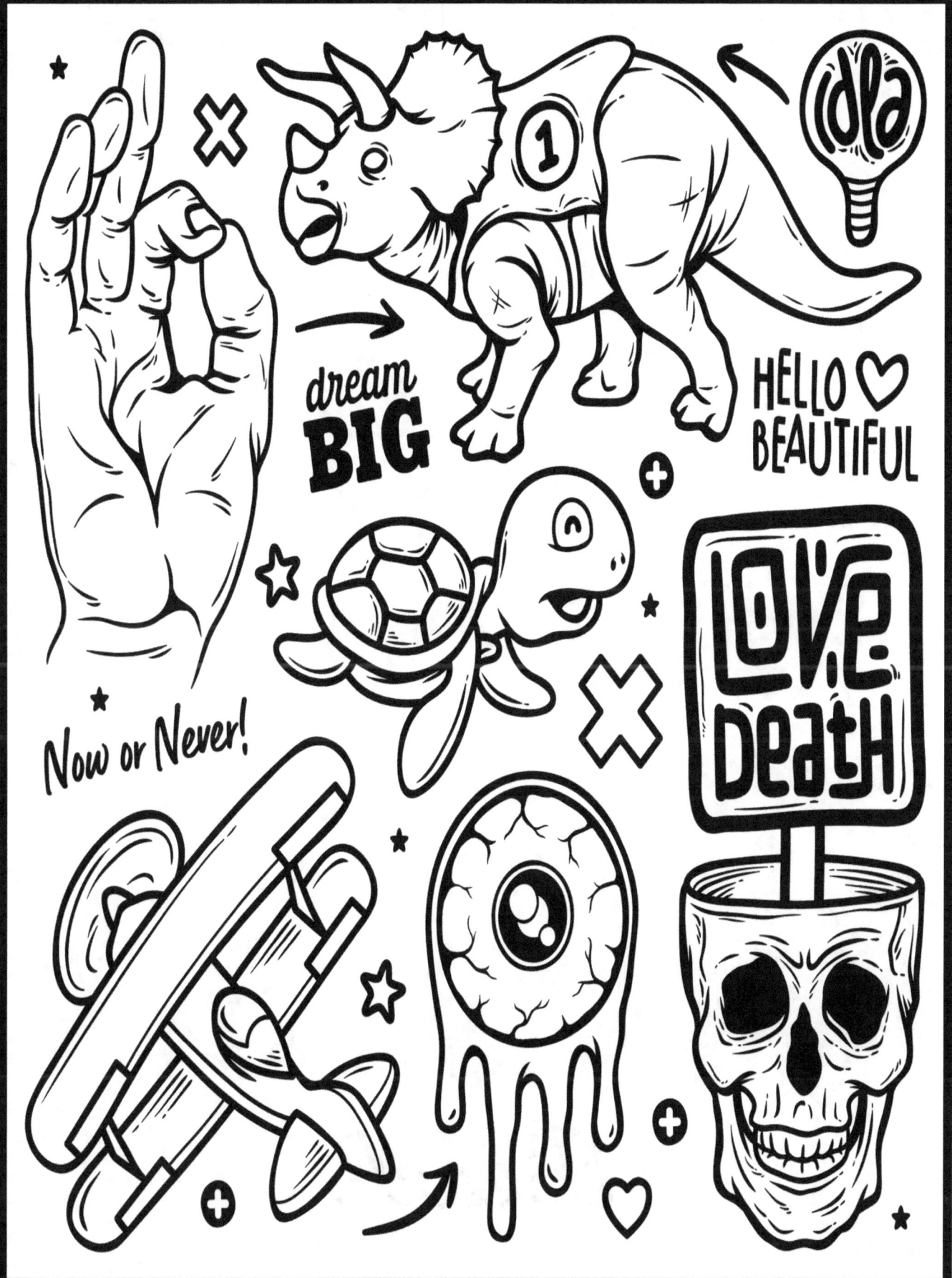

Beach

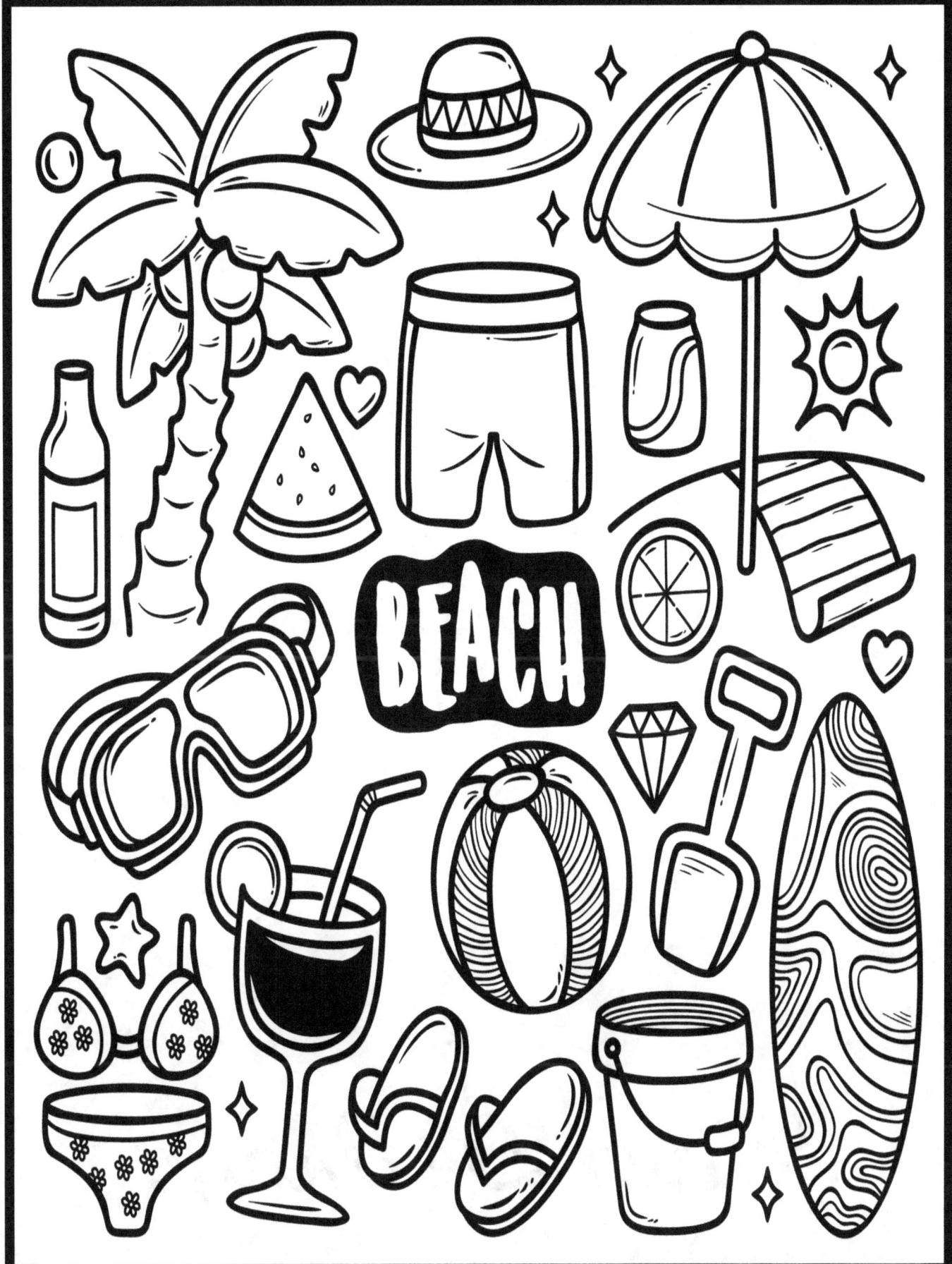

Cinco De Mayo

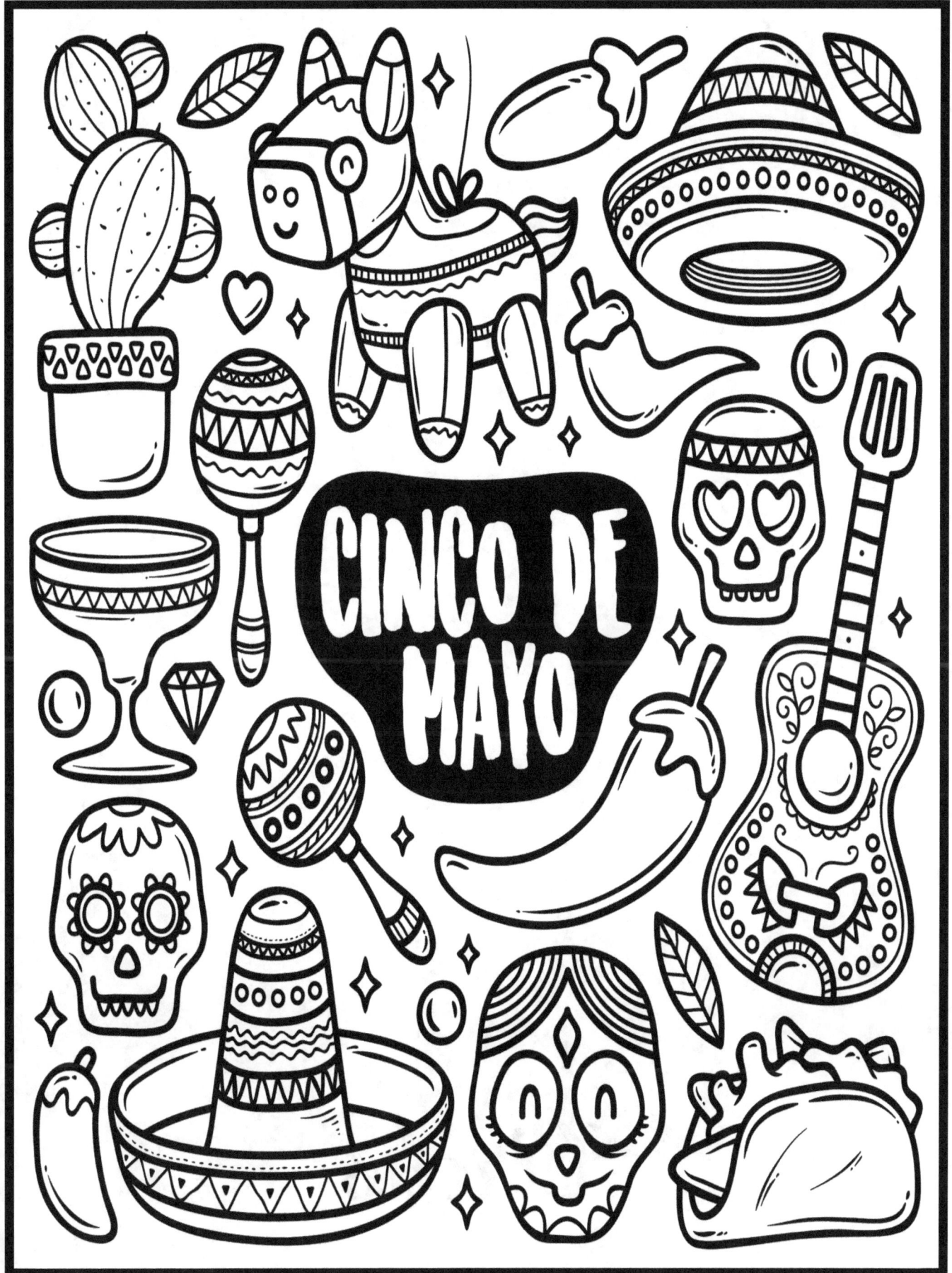

Circus

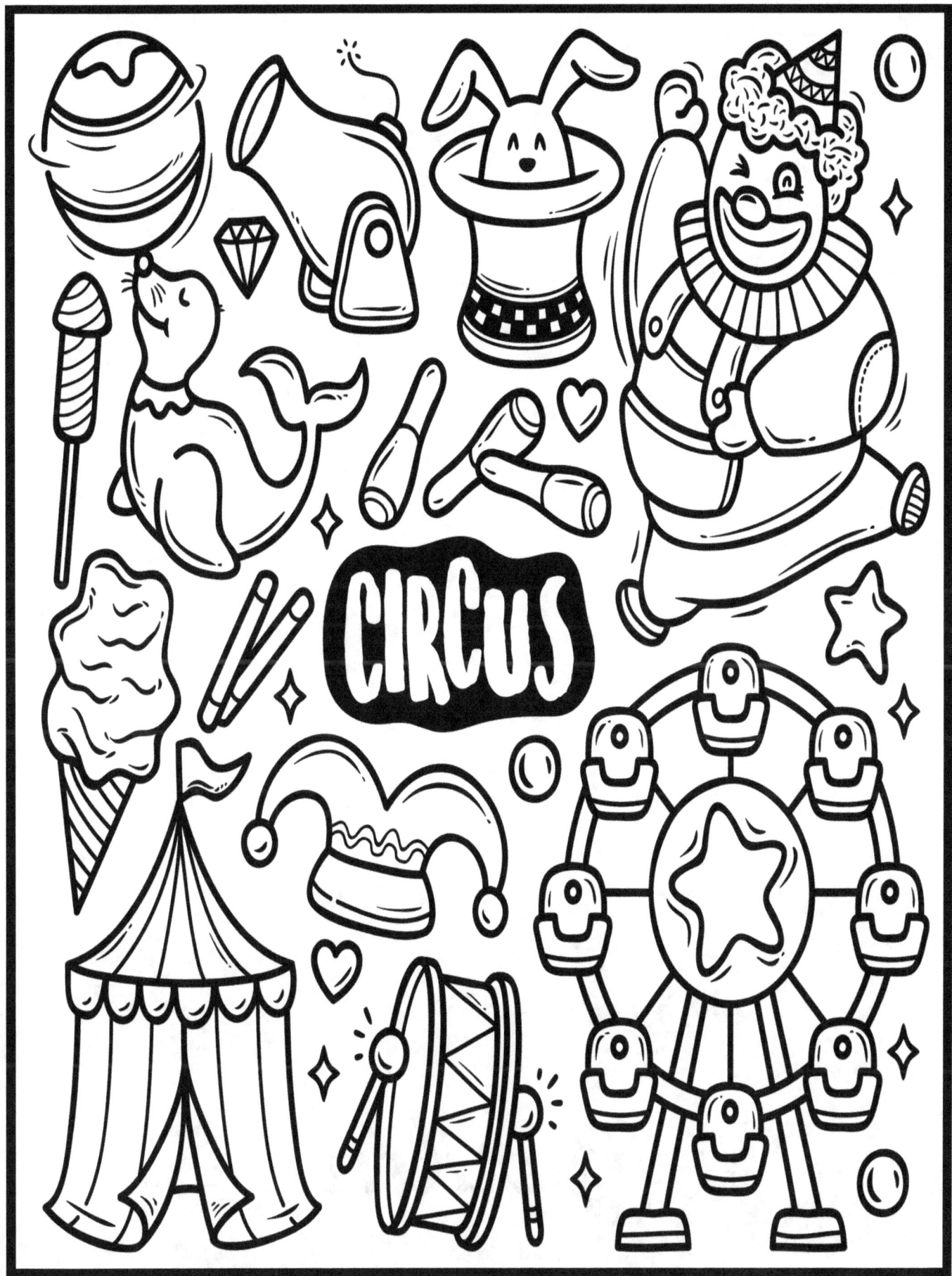

CIRCUS

Garden

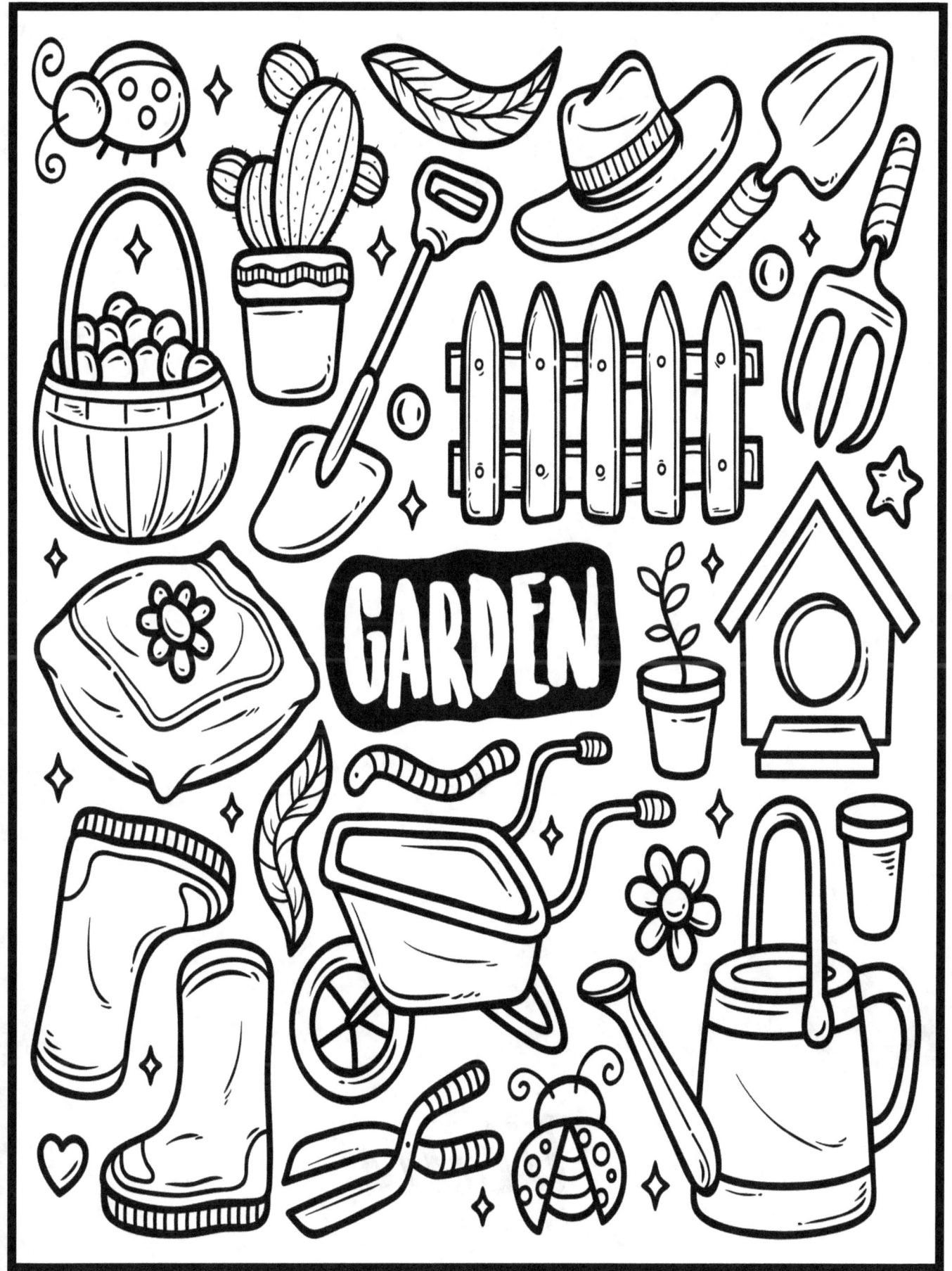

Virus

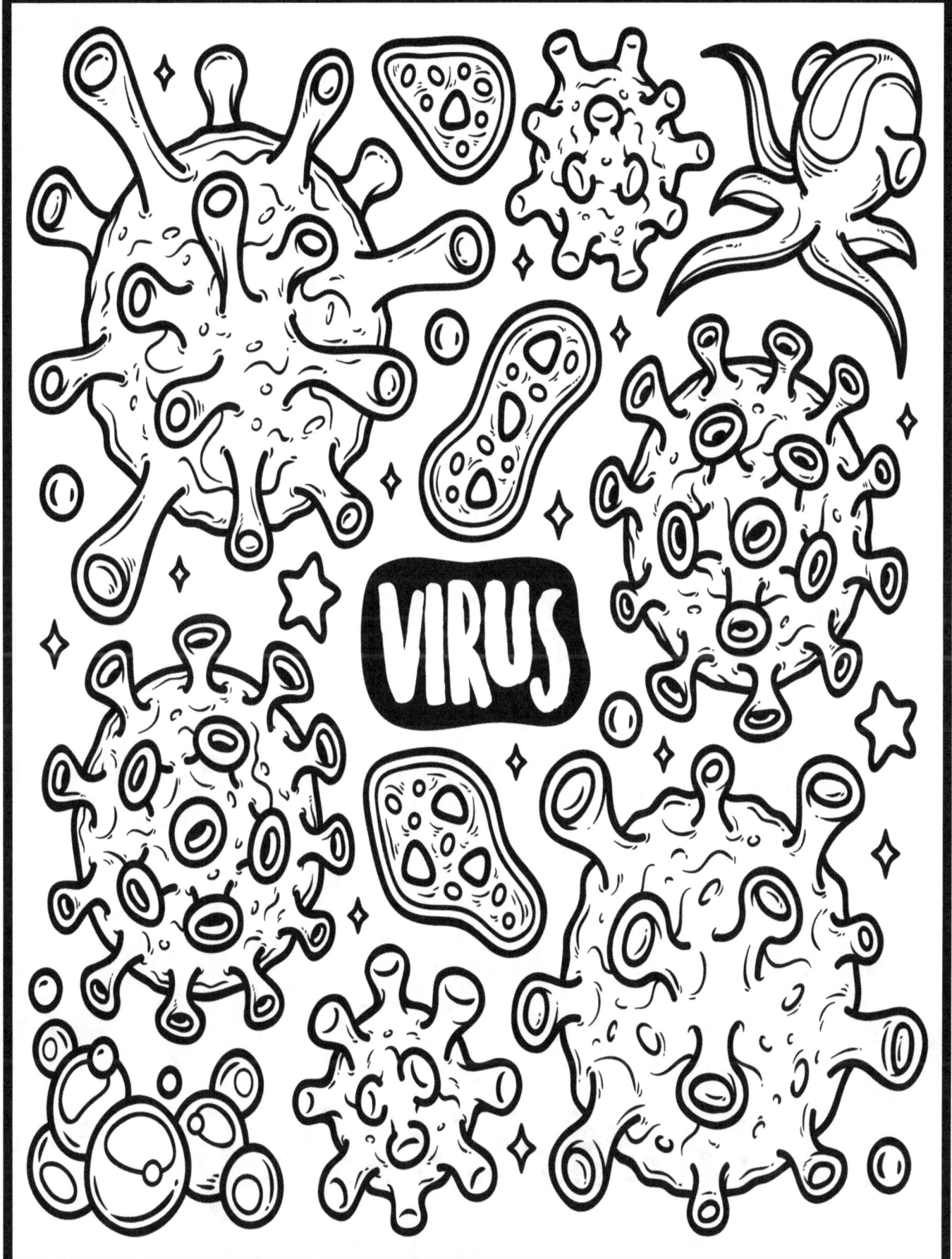

Father's Day

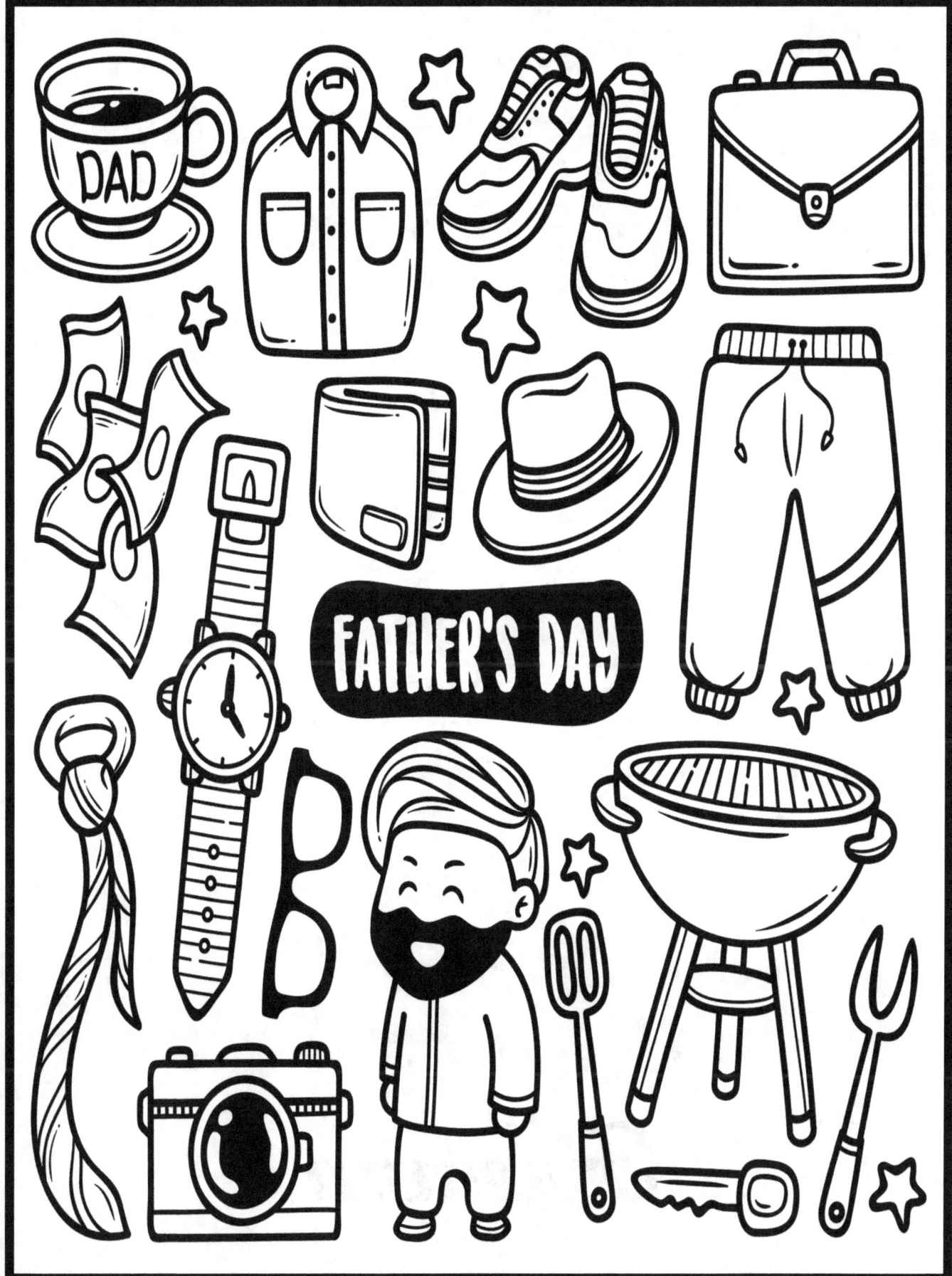

Fireman

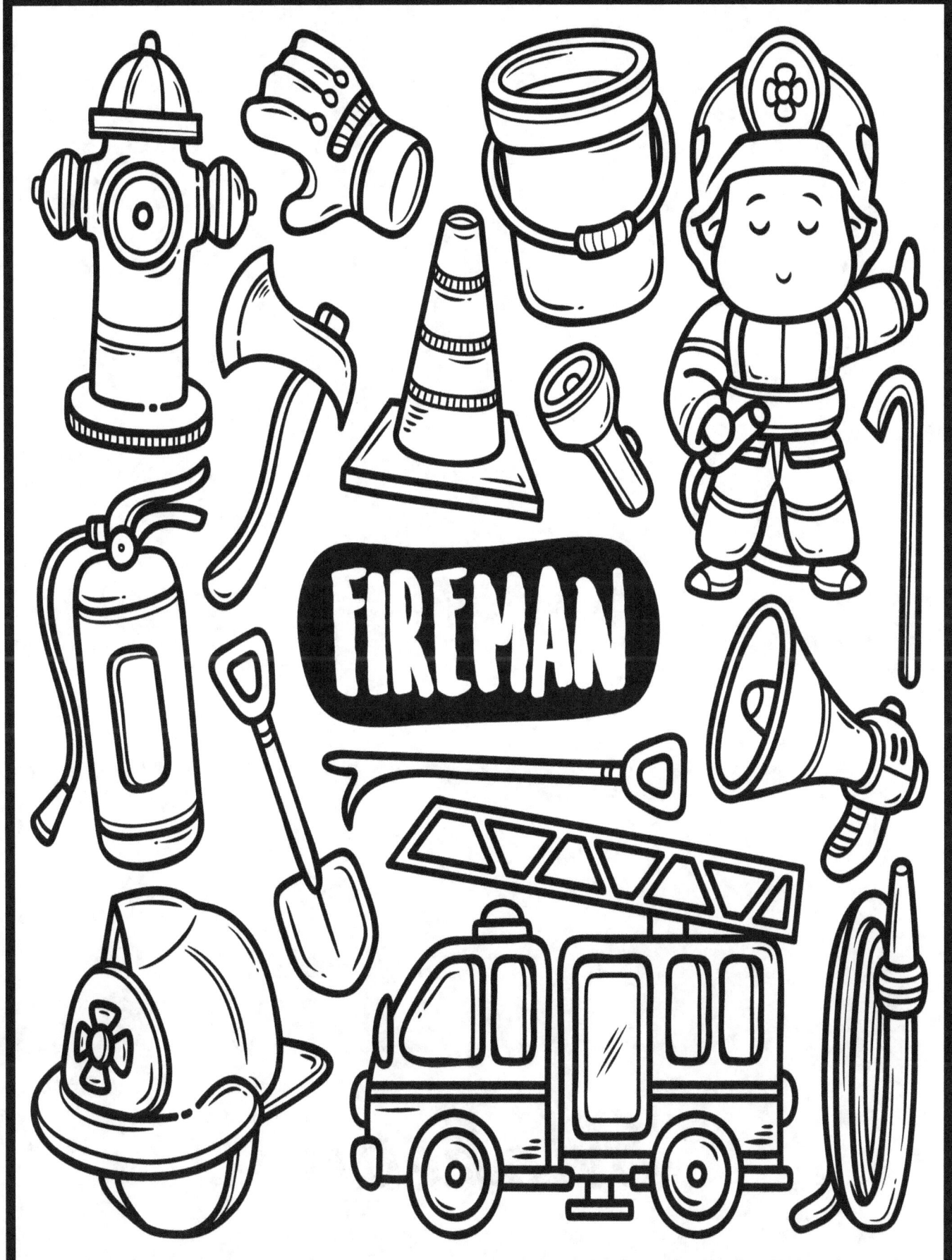

FIREMAN

Makeup

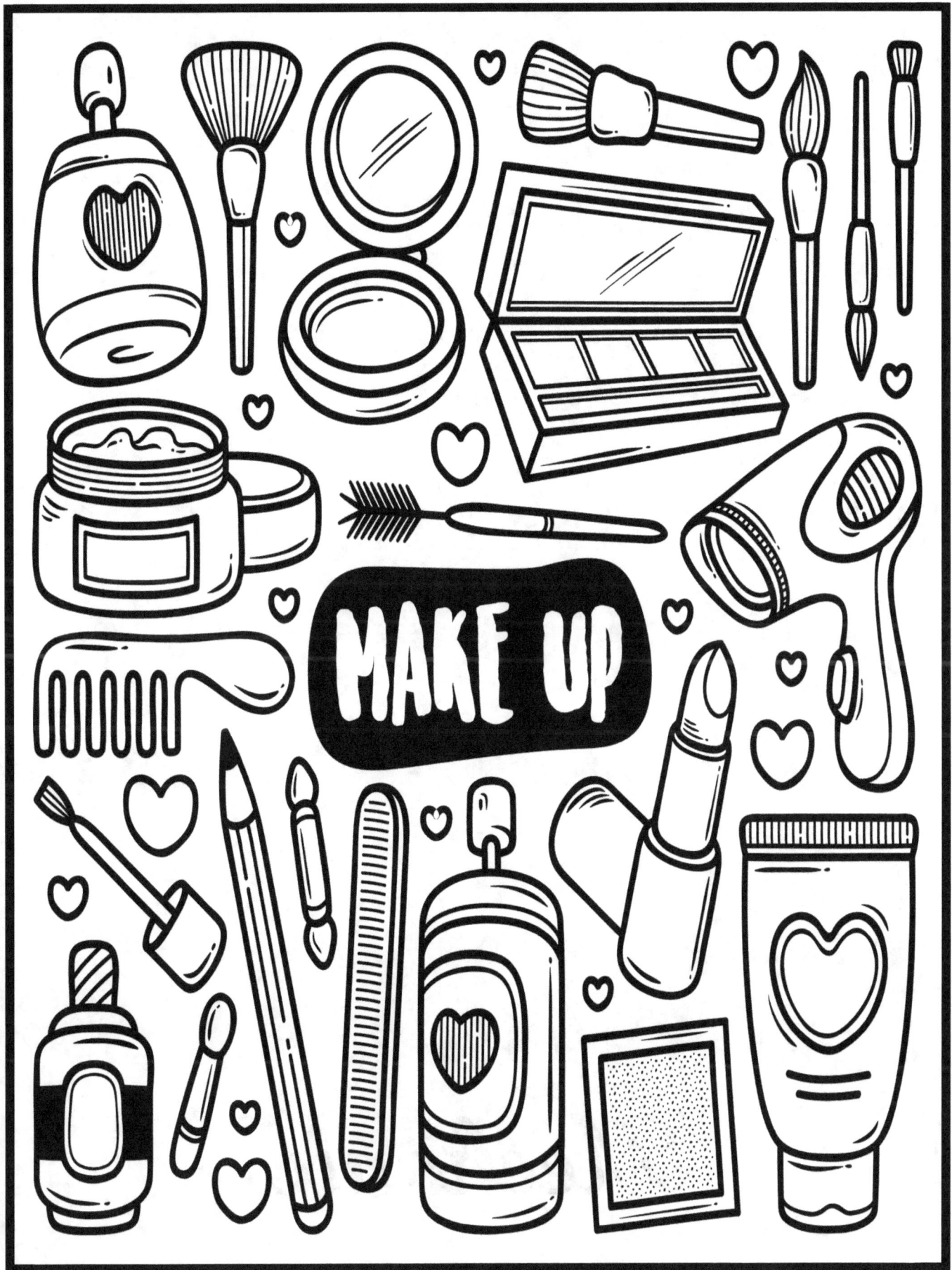

Mechanic

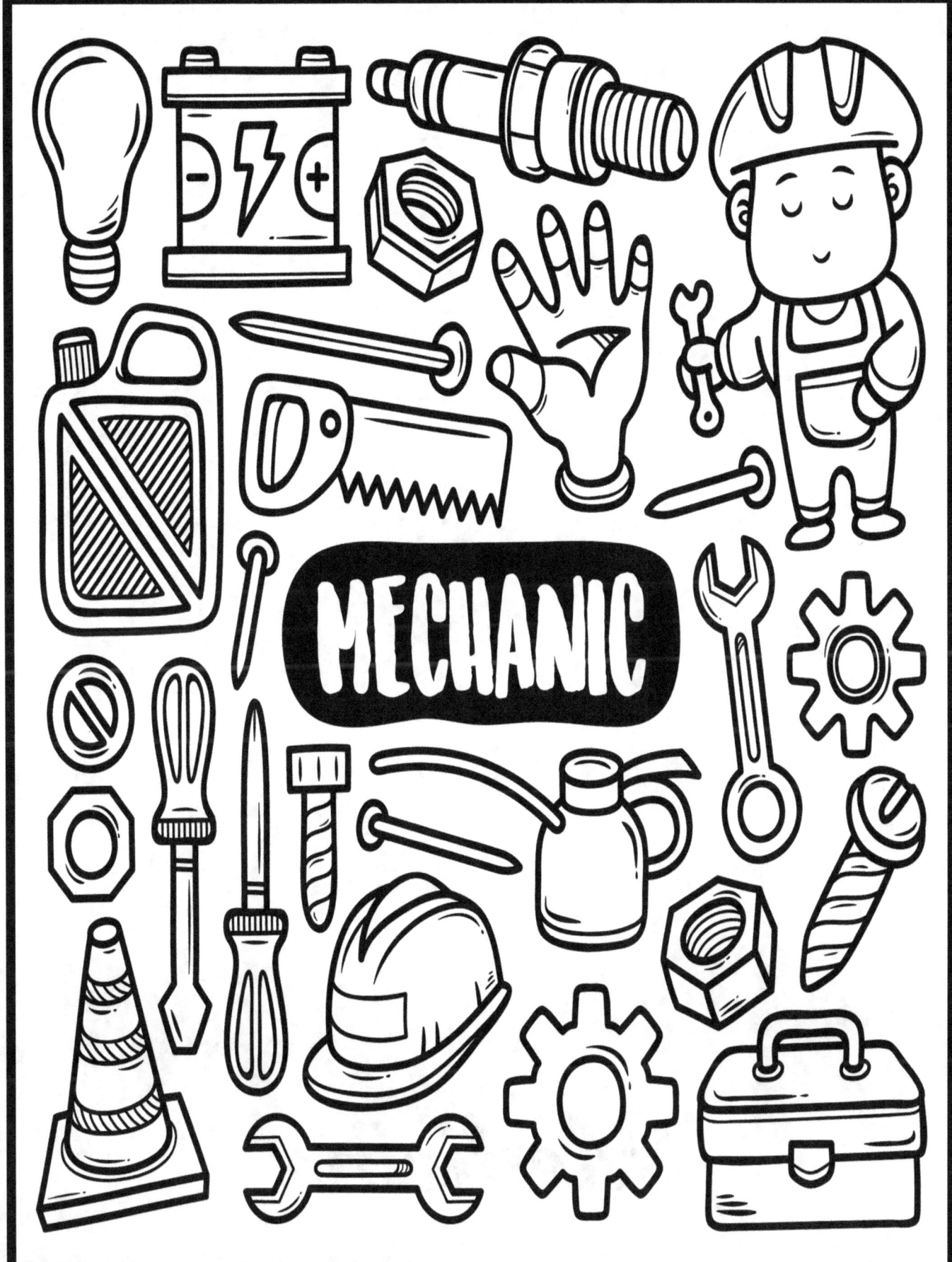

Medicine

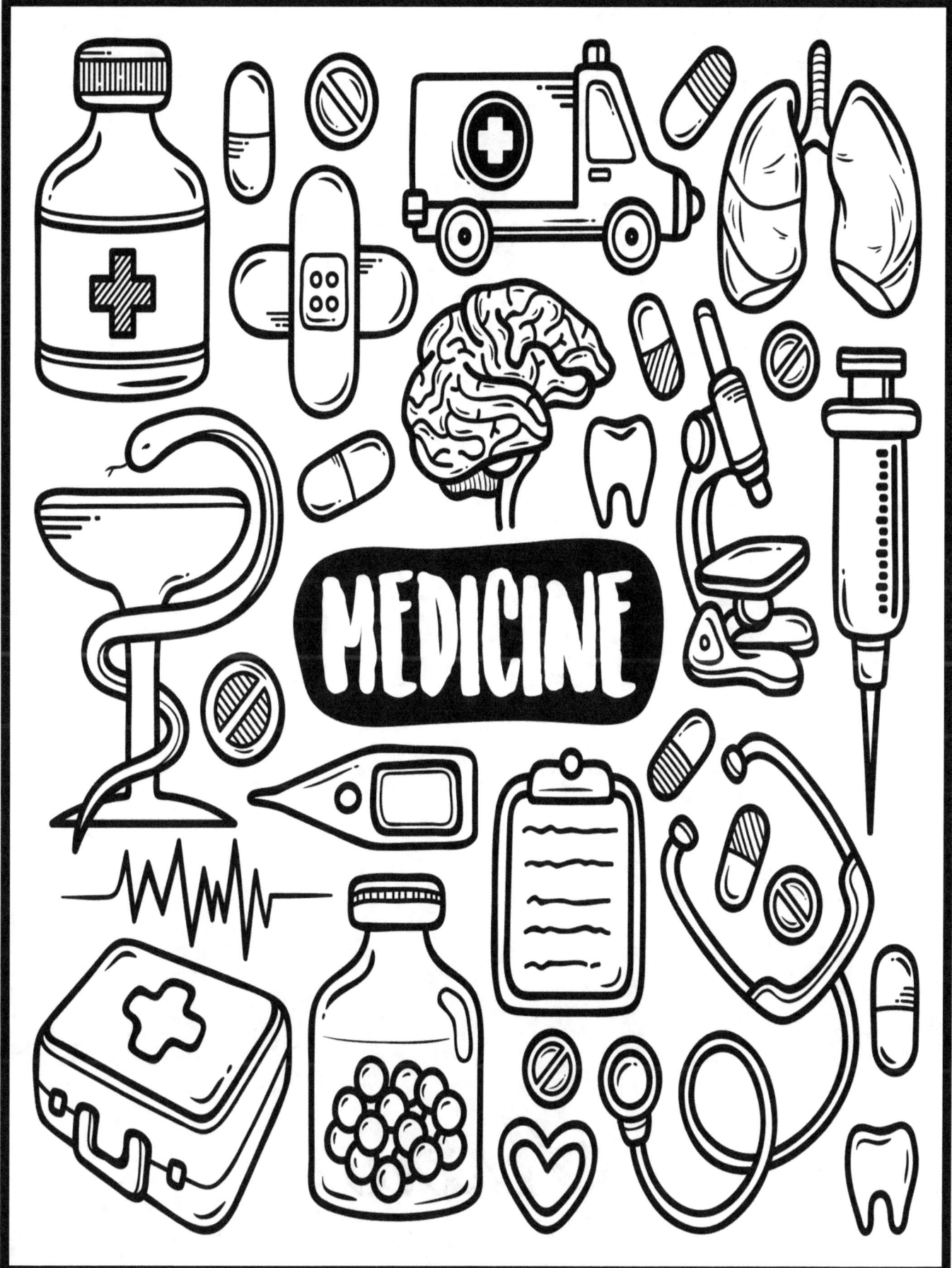

Astro

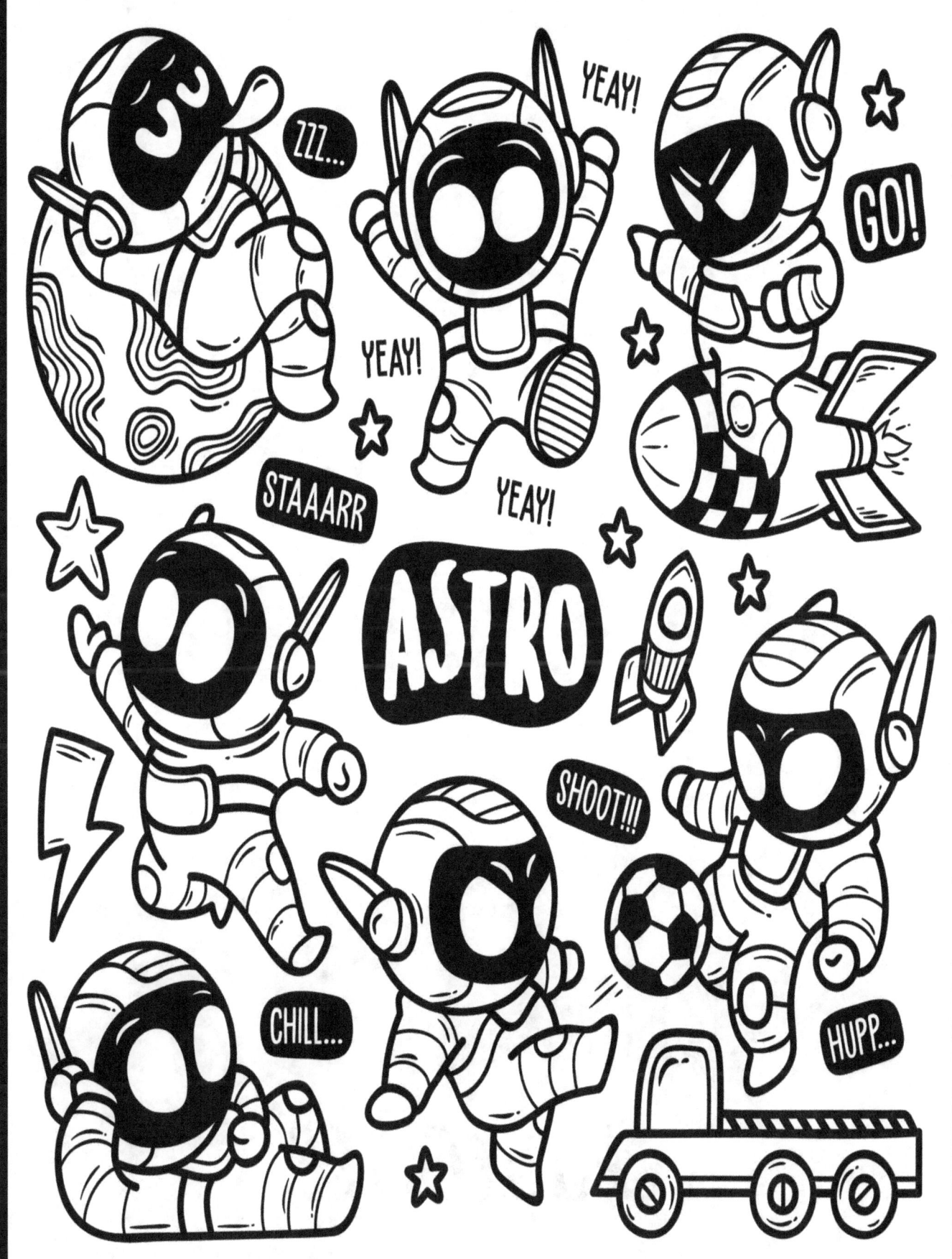

Football

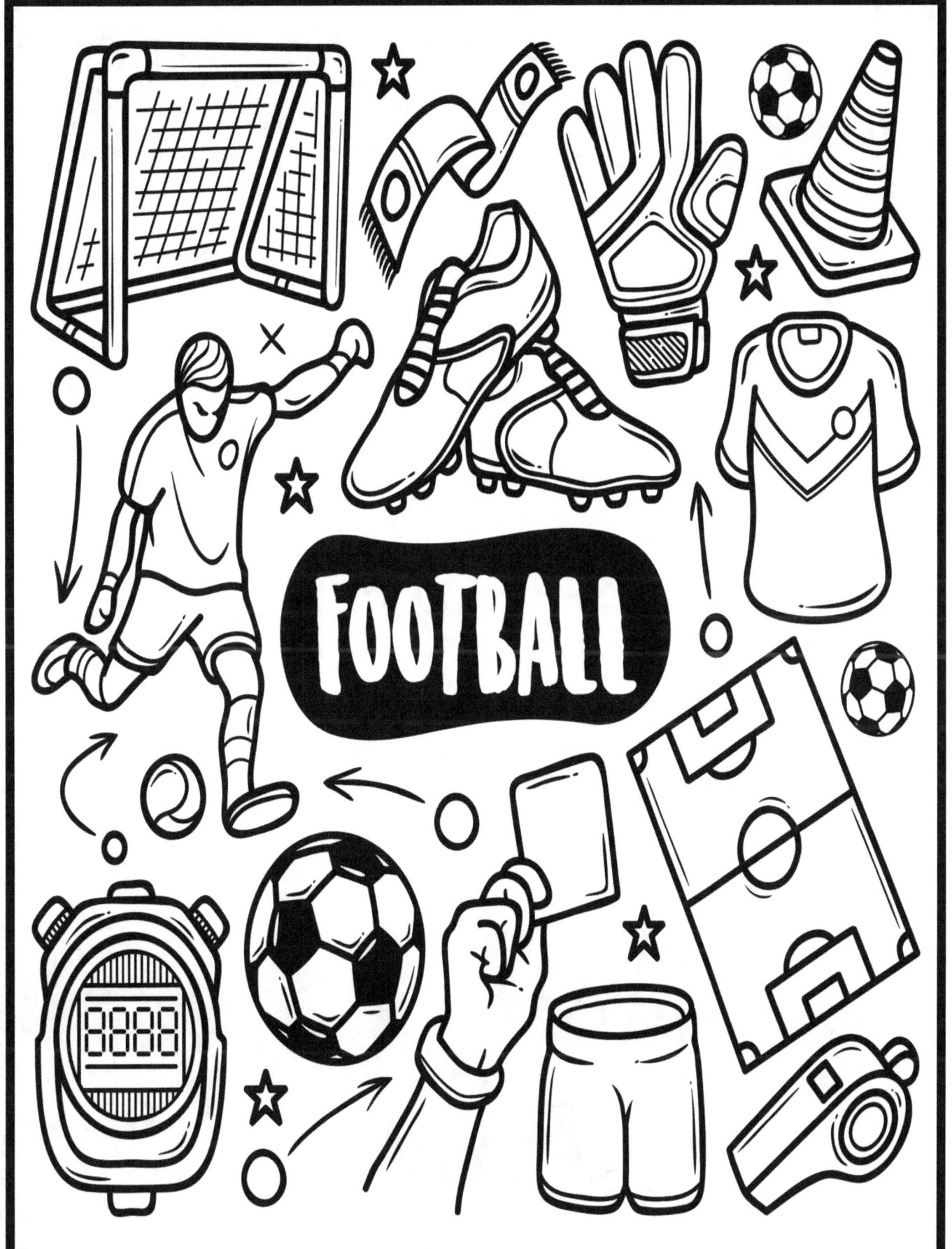

Pirate

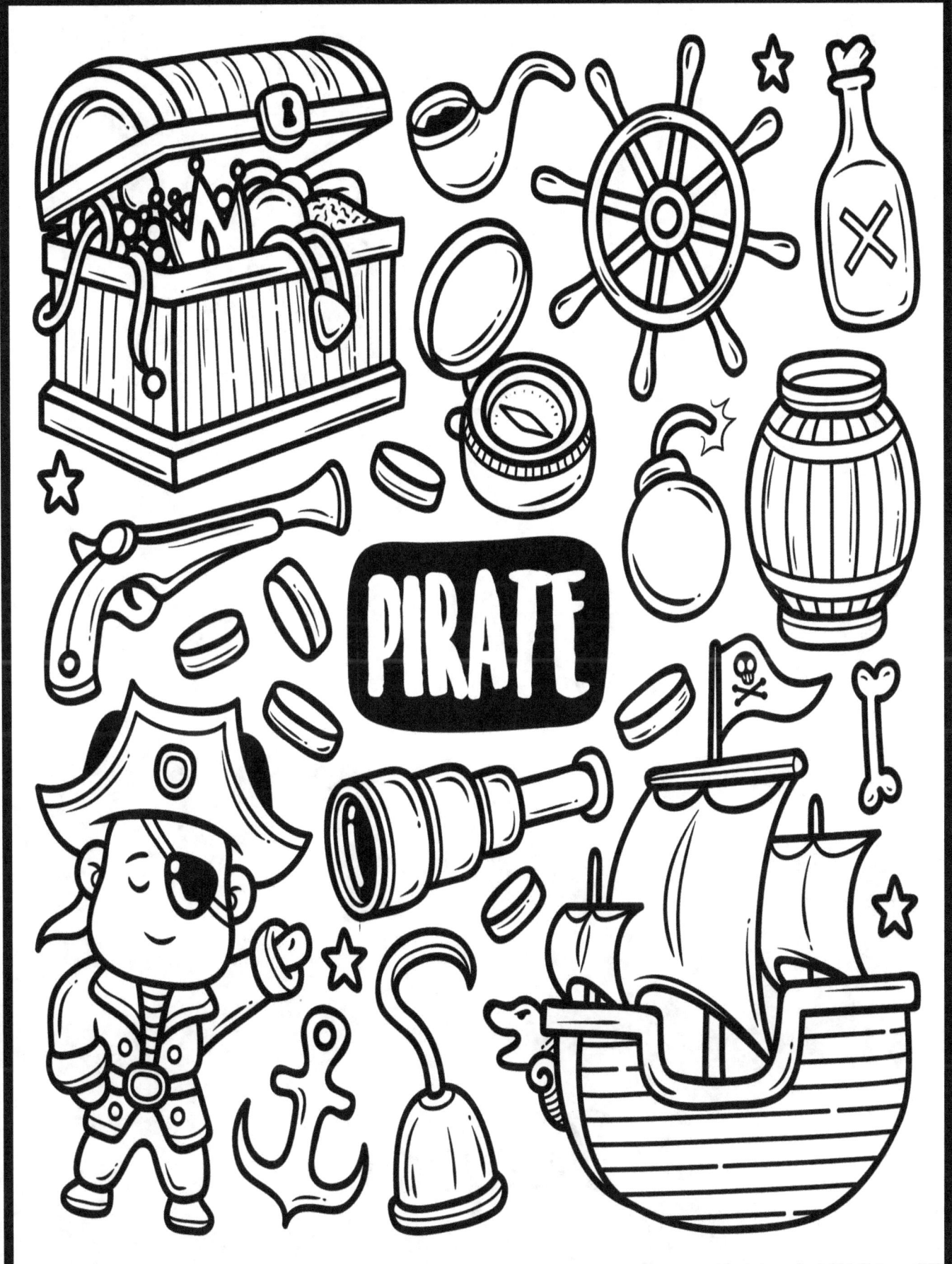

Teapot

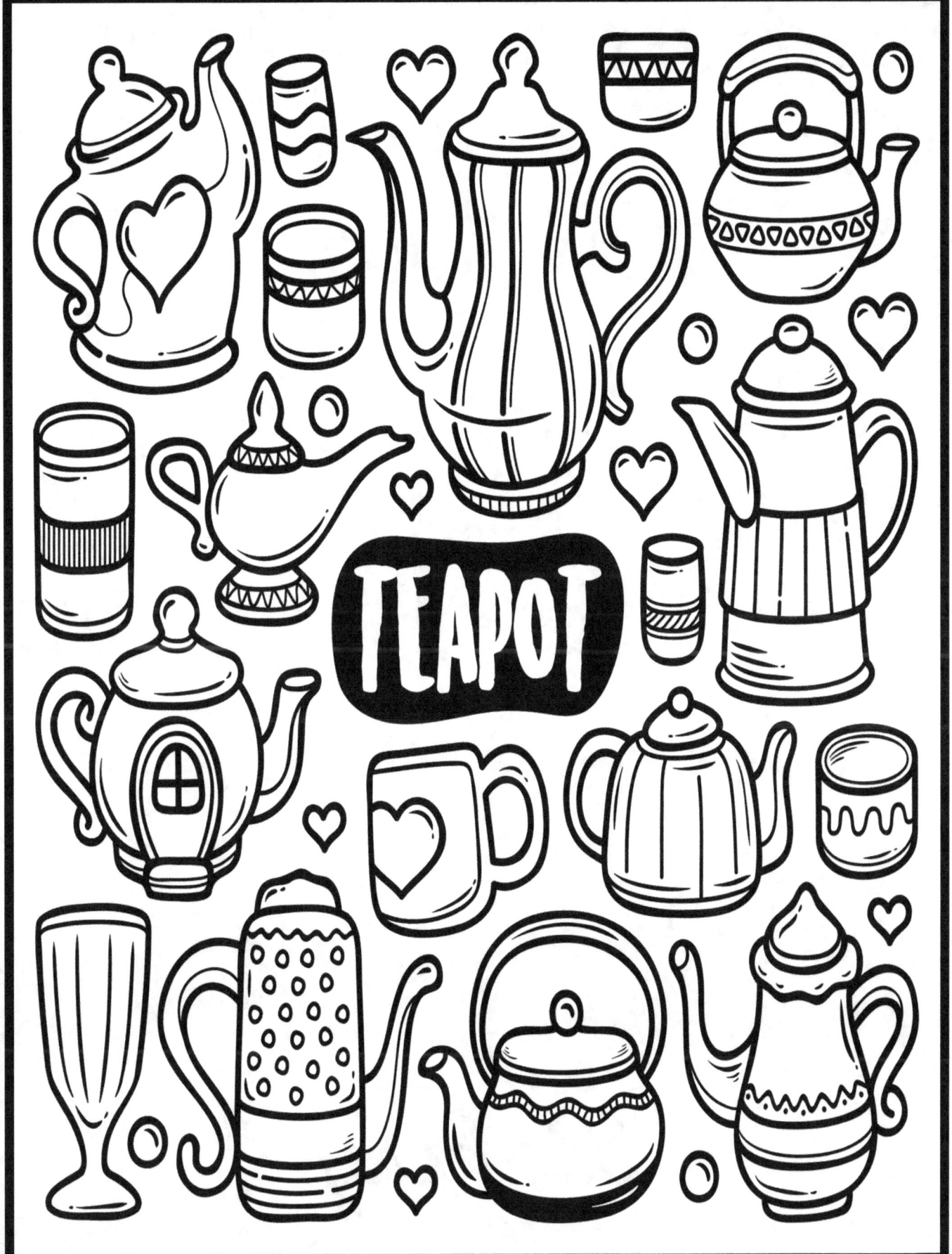

Bakery

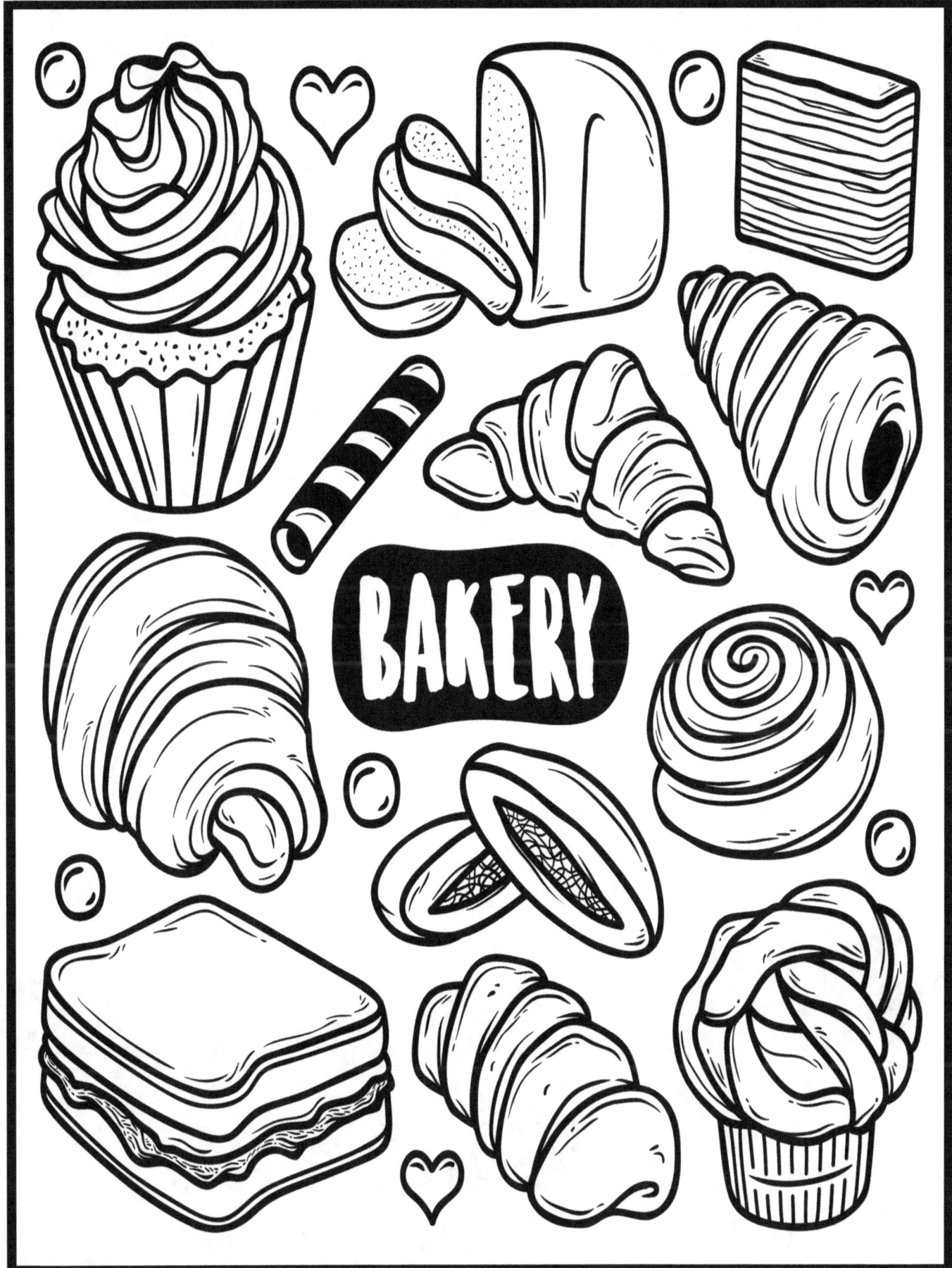

Book

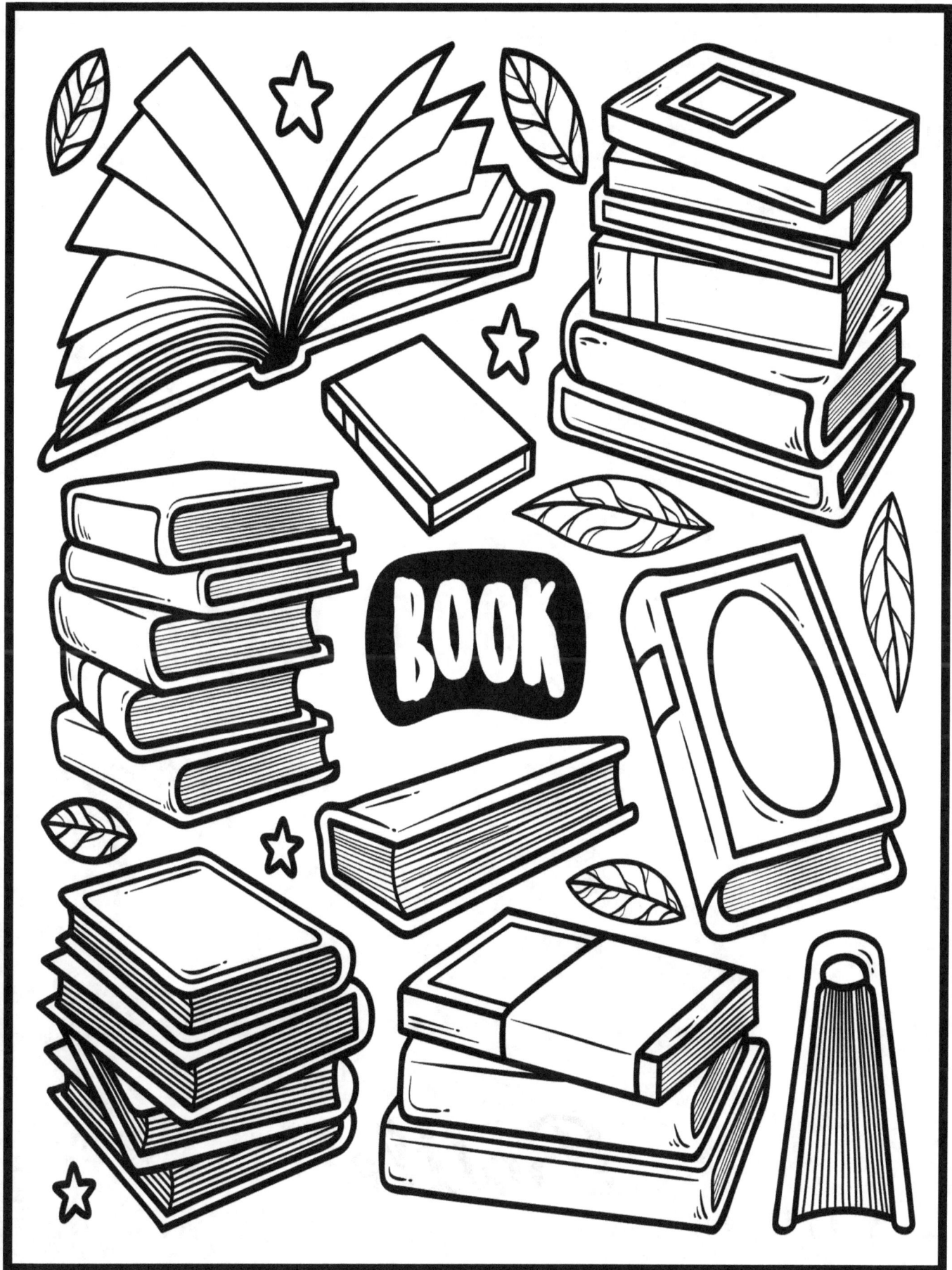

Bottle

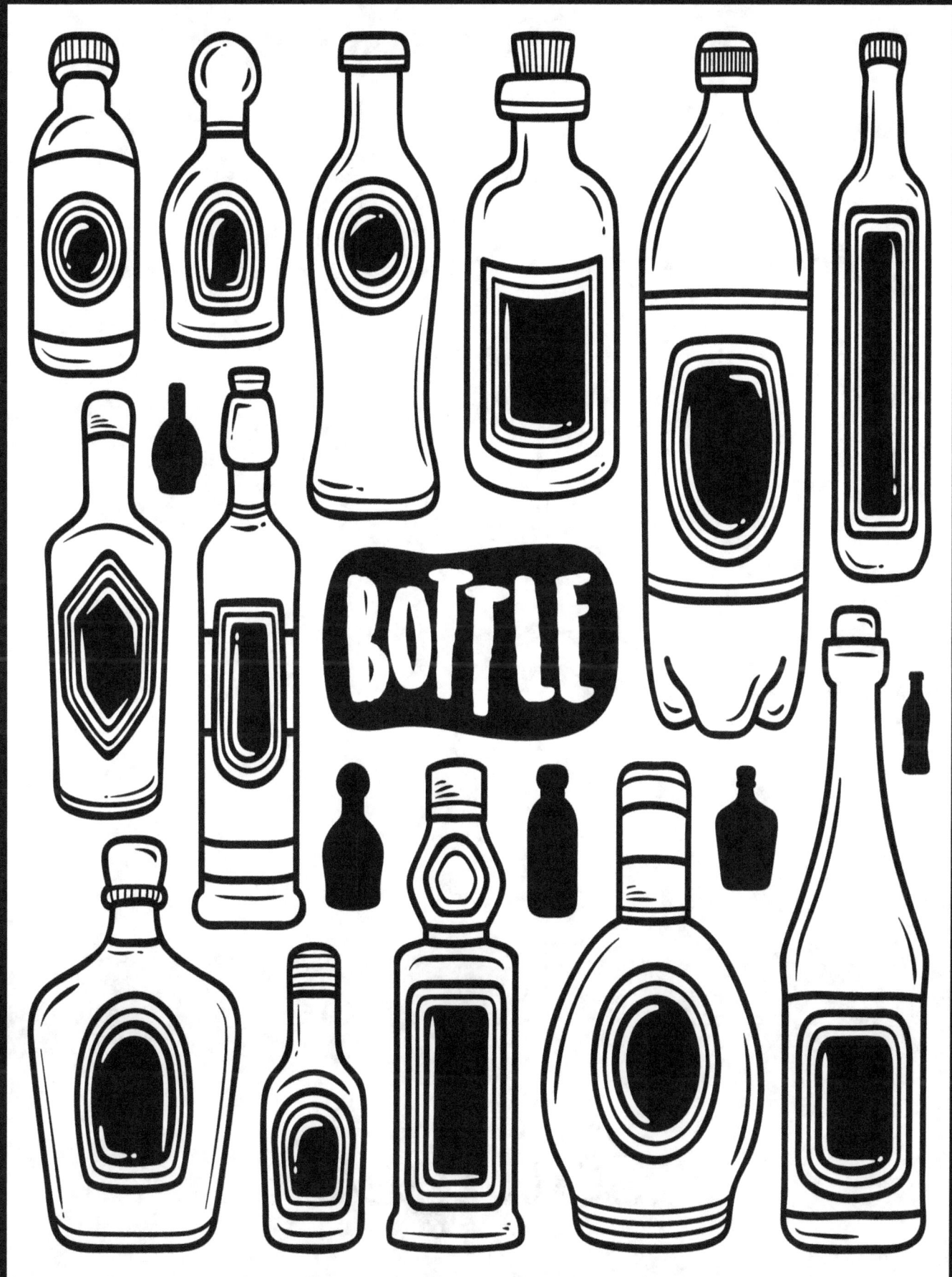

Burger

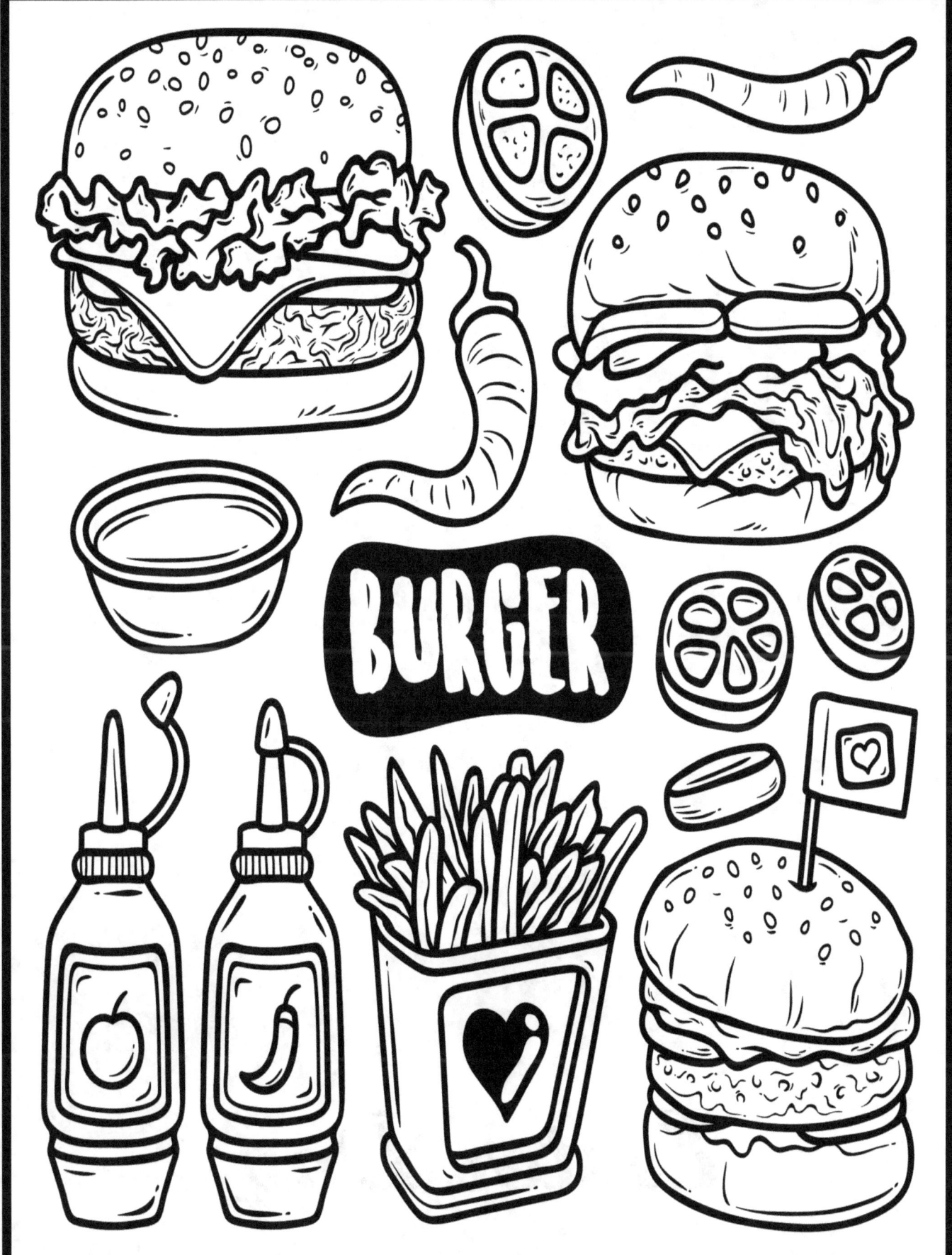

Easter Day

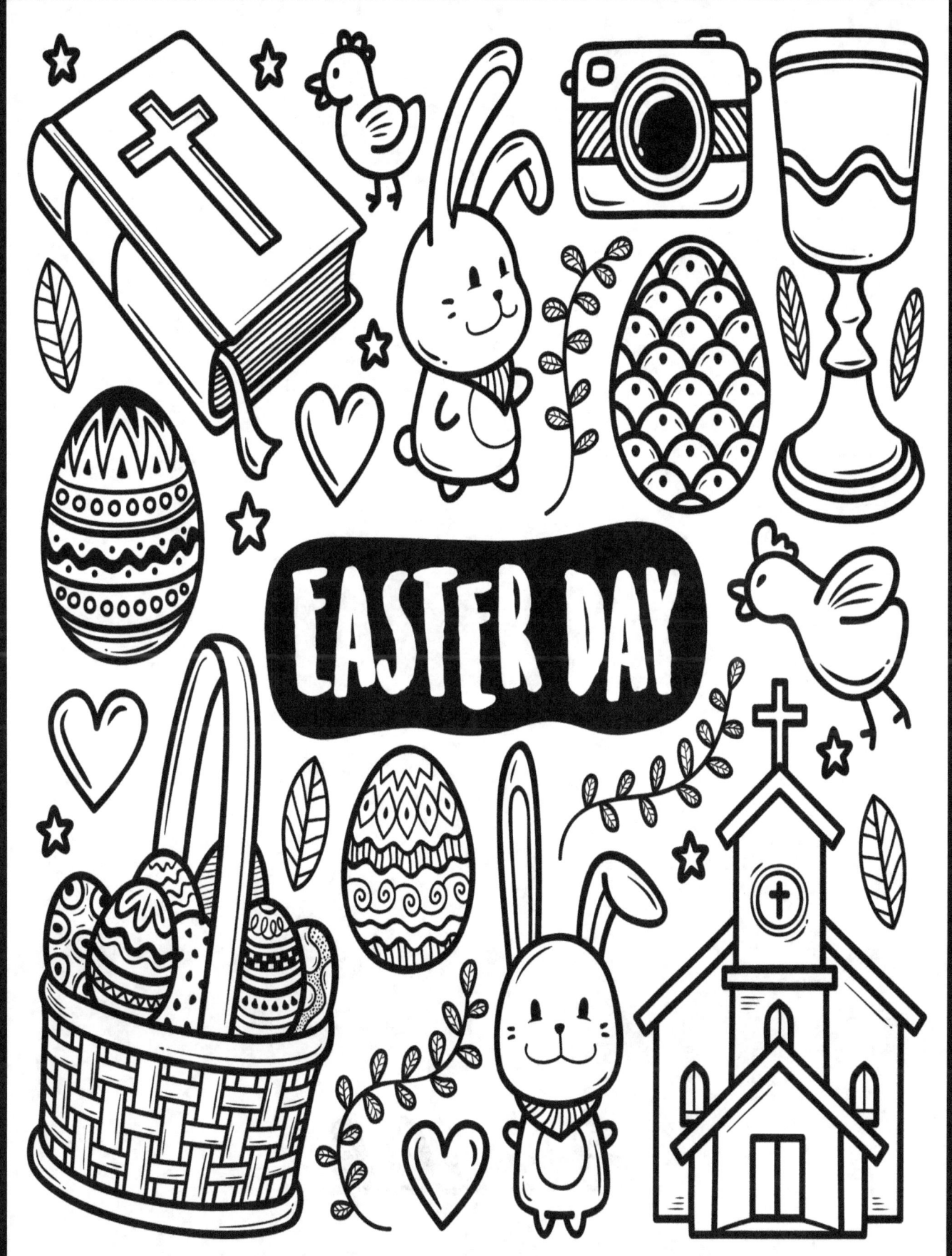

Health

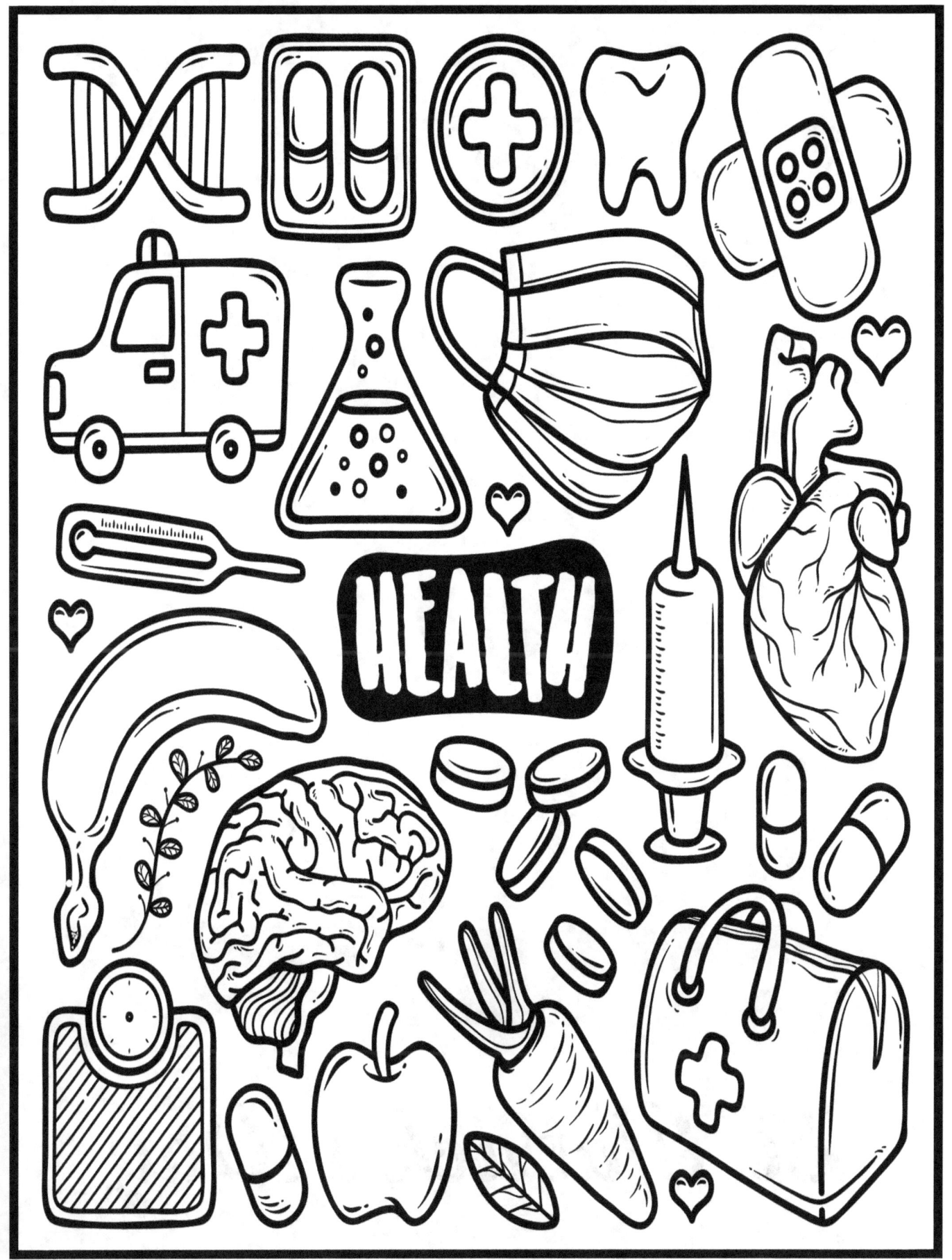

St. Patrick's Day

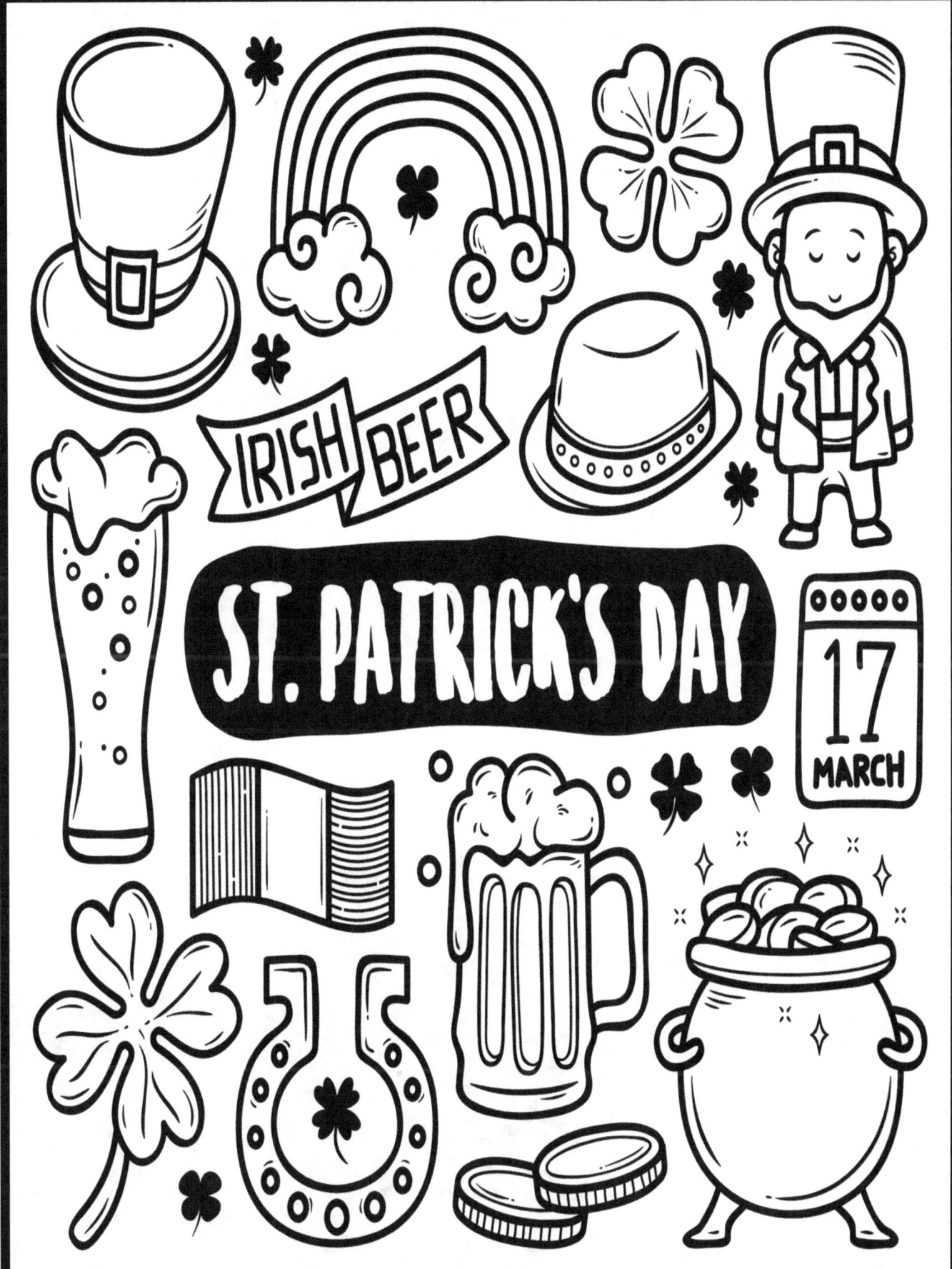

Plan

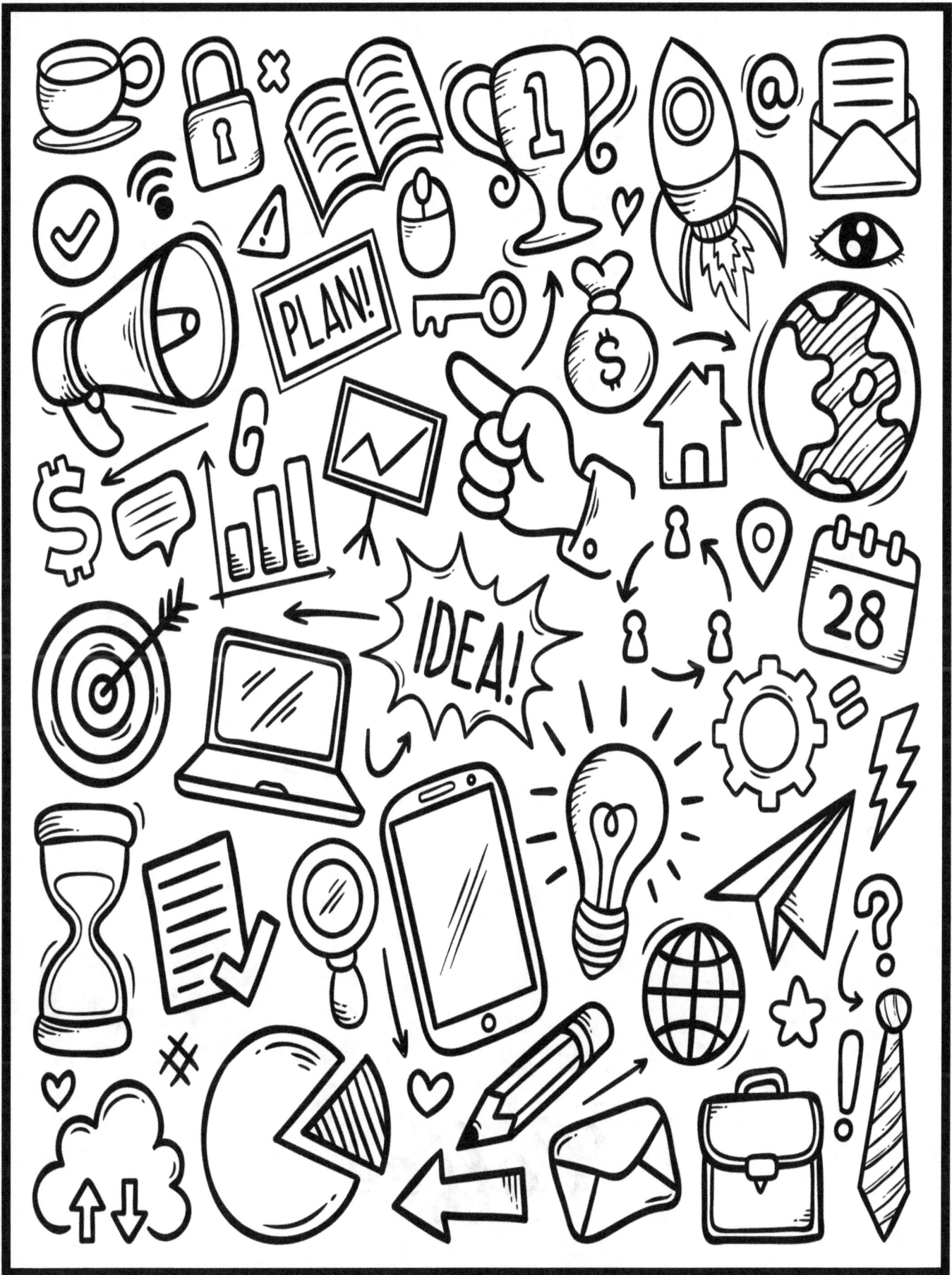

Coffee

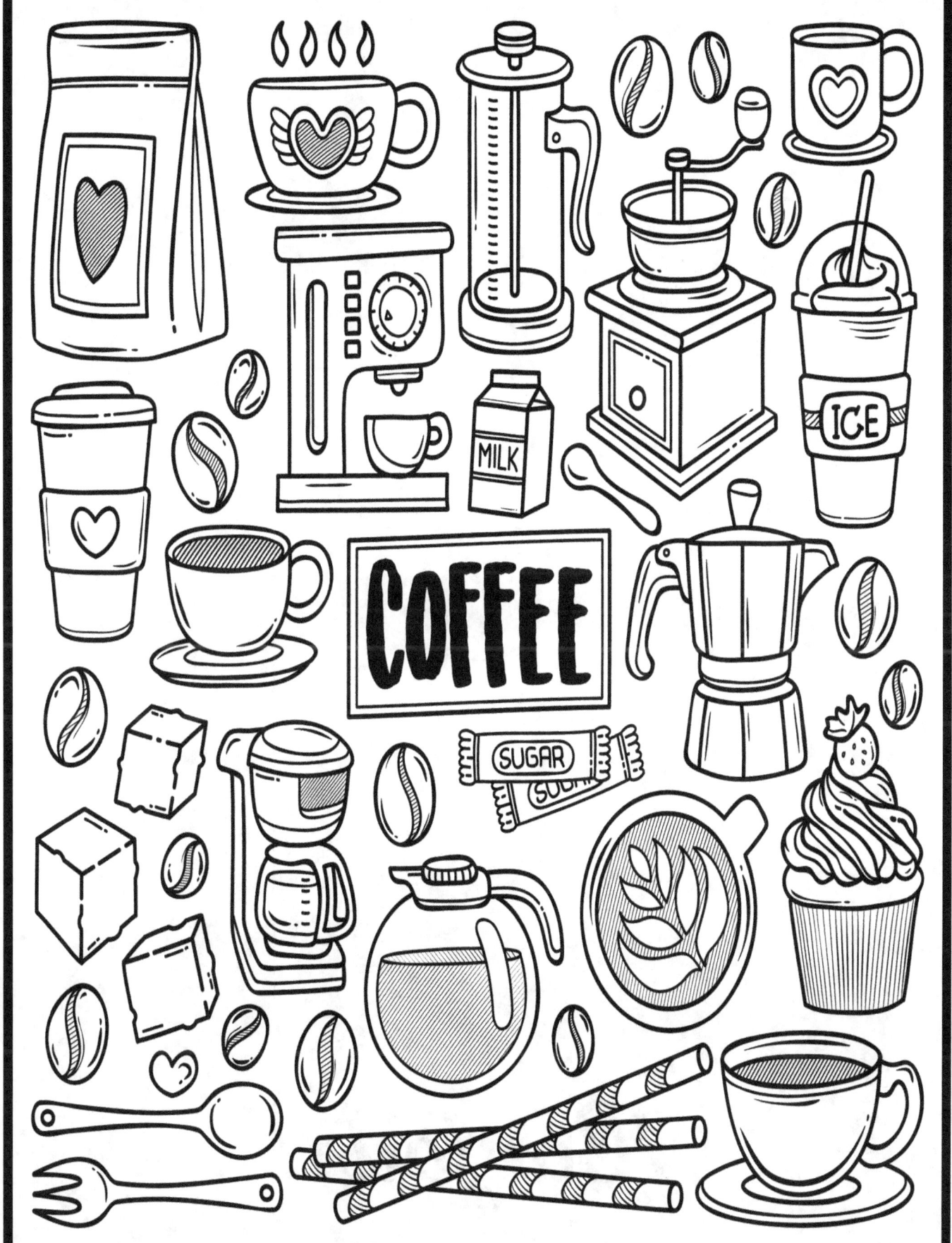

Bonjour!

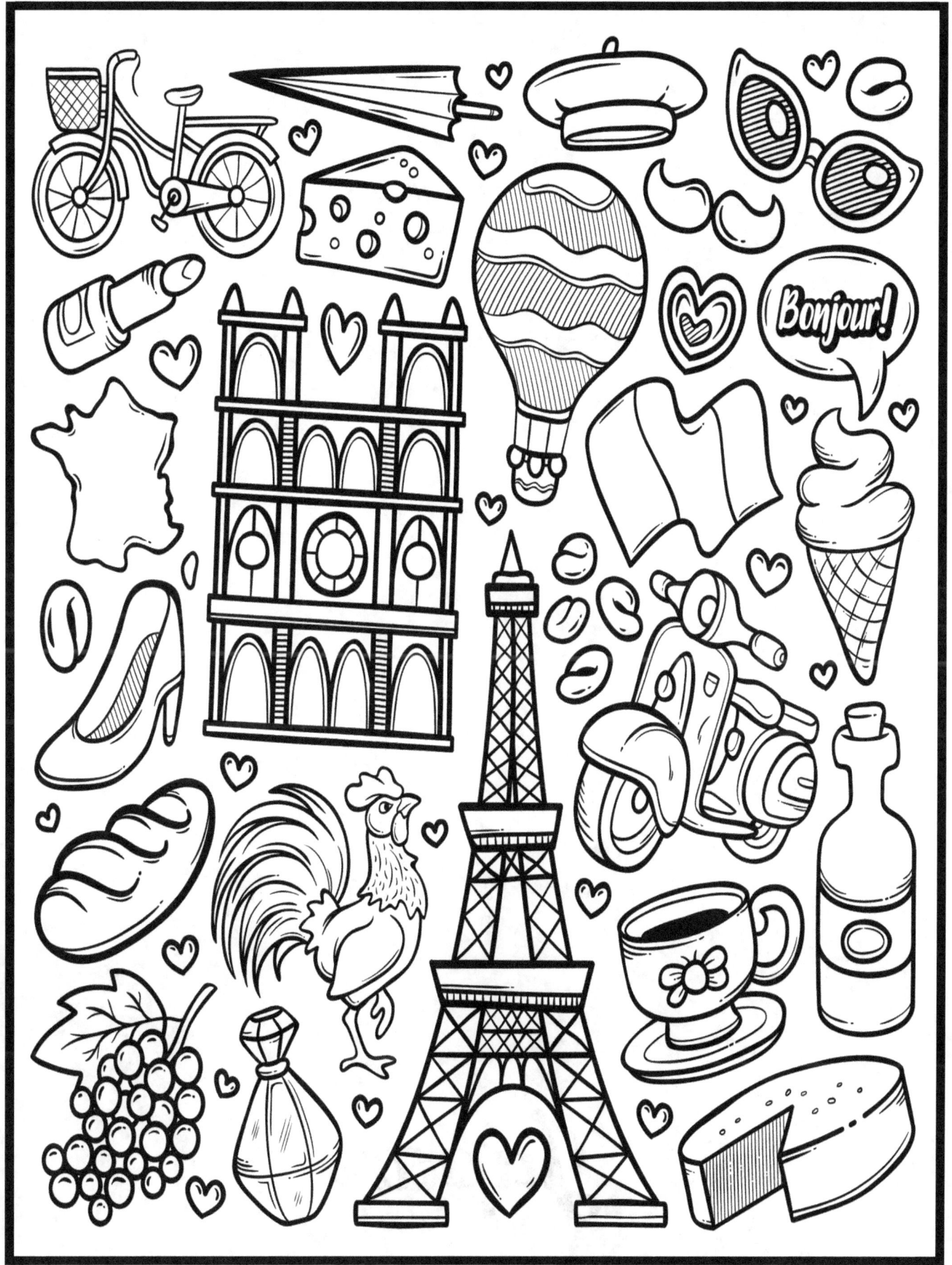

Japan

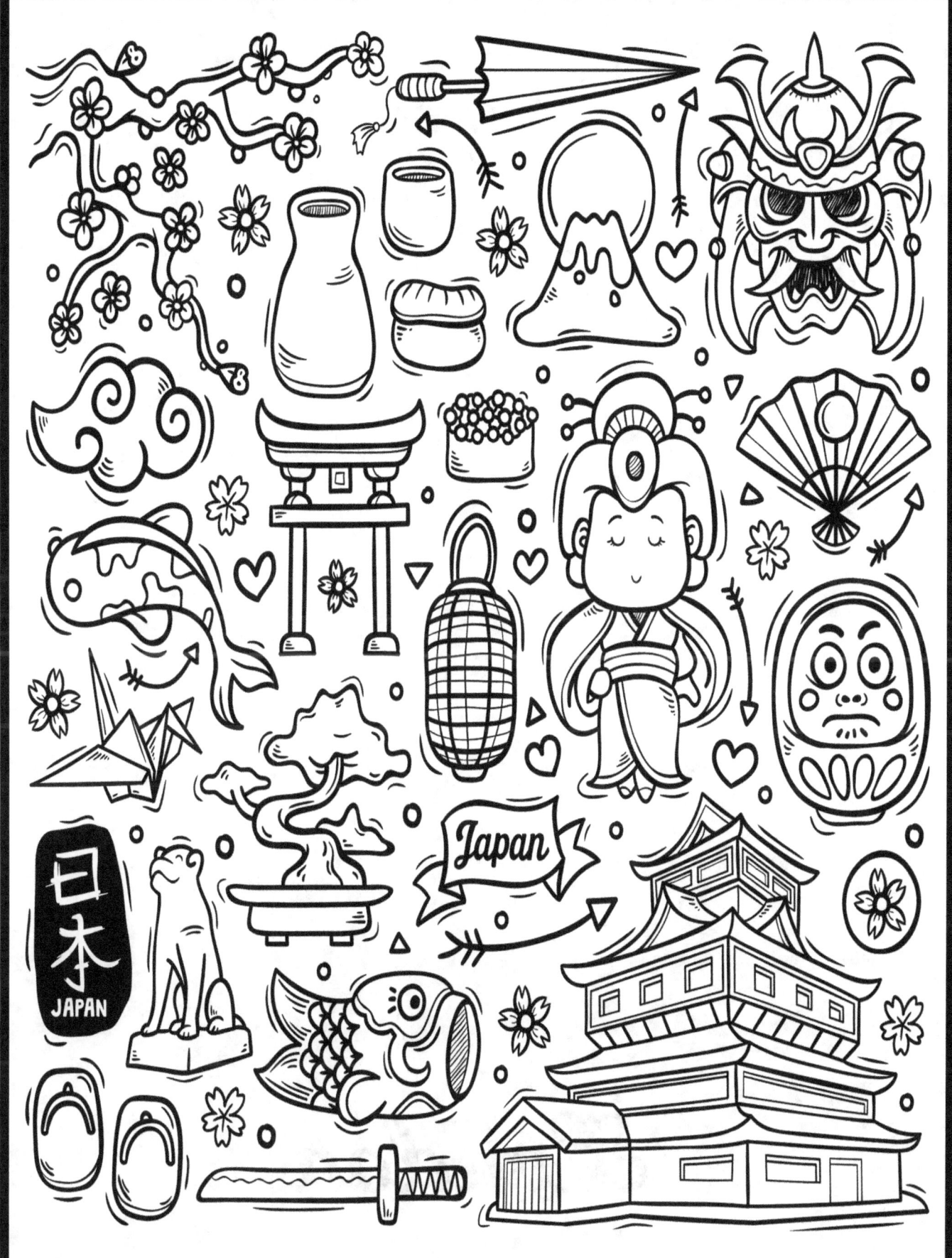

London

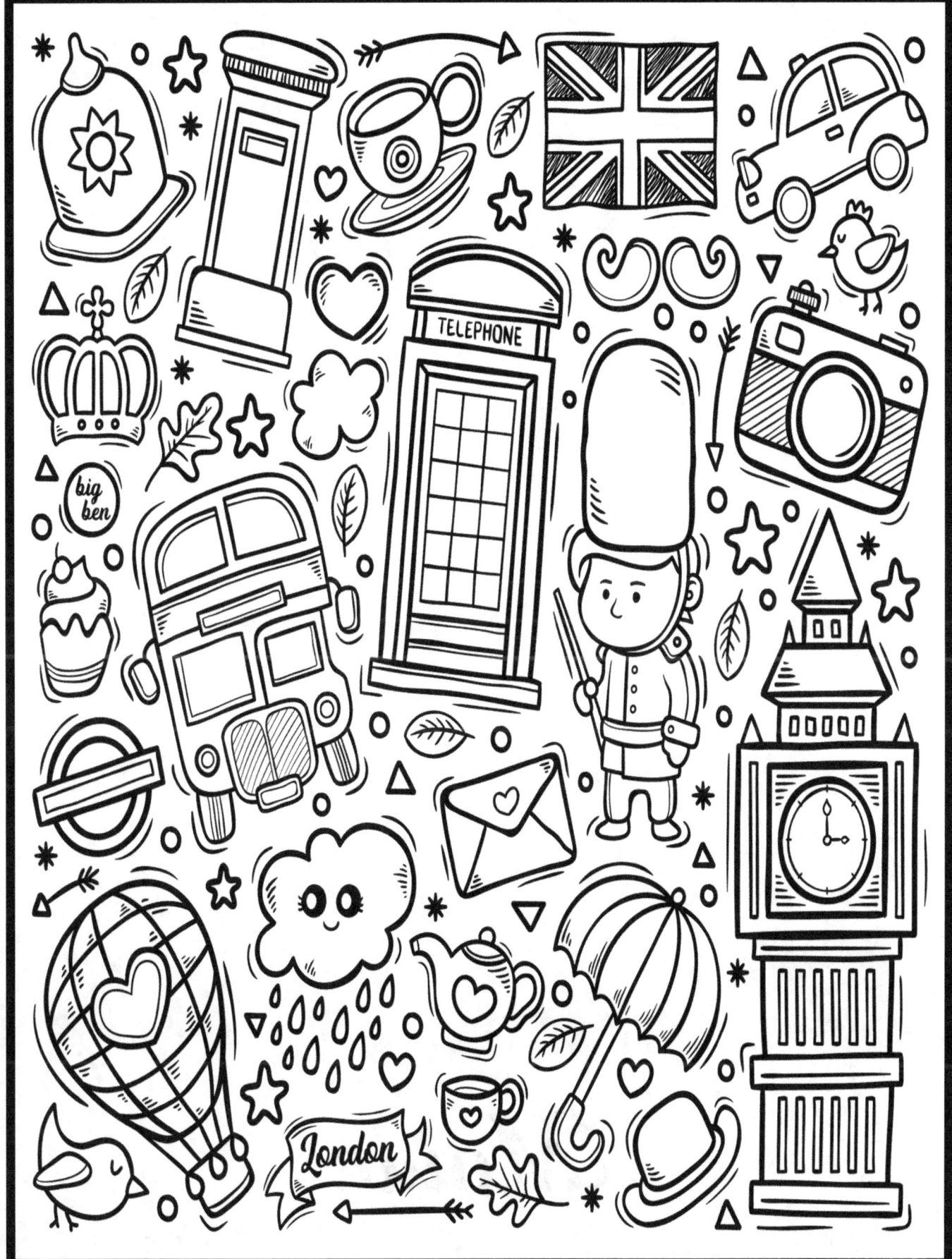

Movie

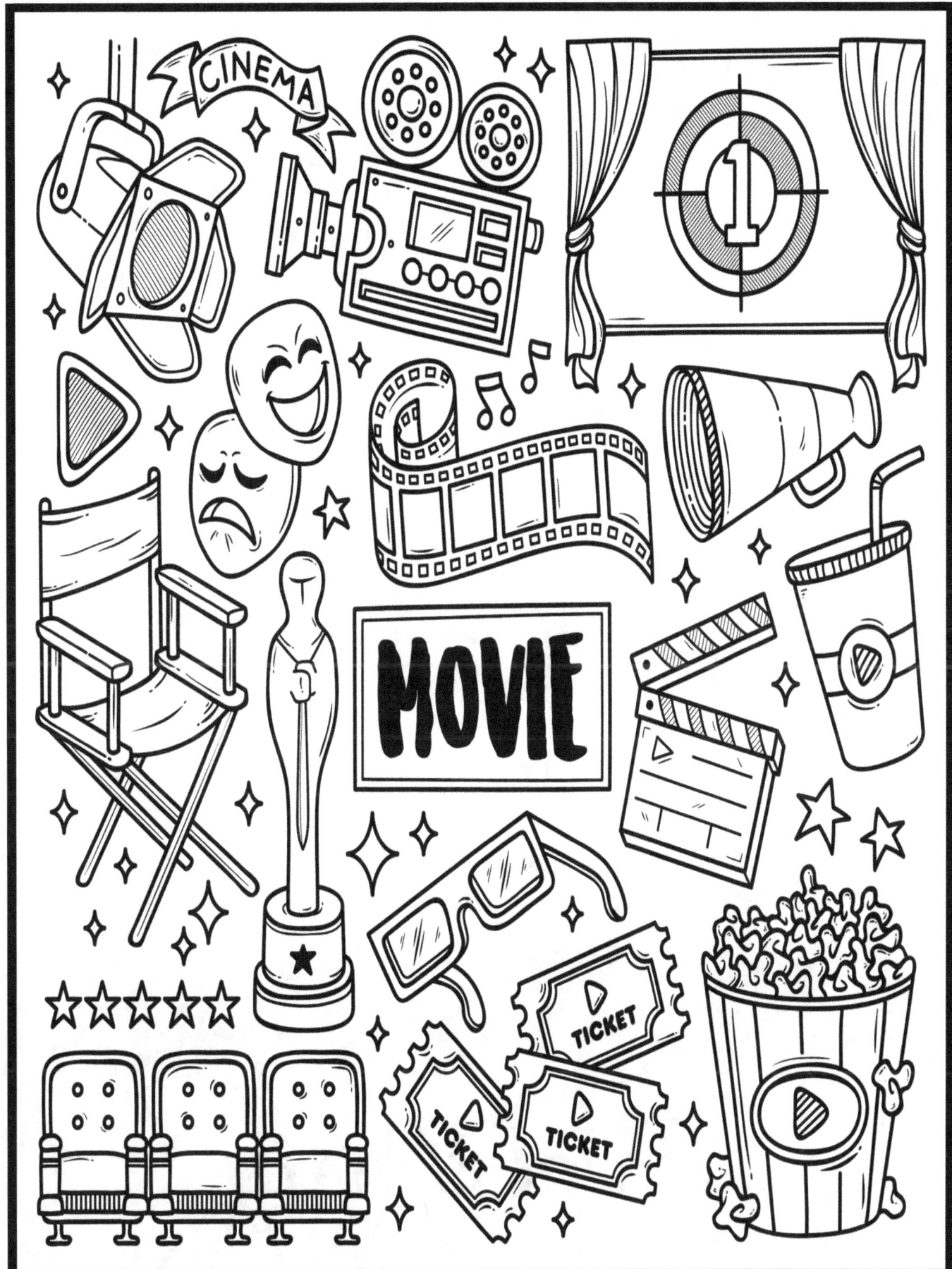

Pool Party

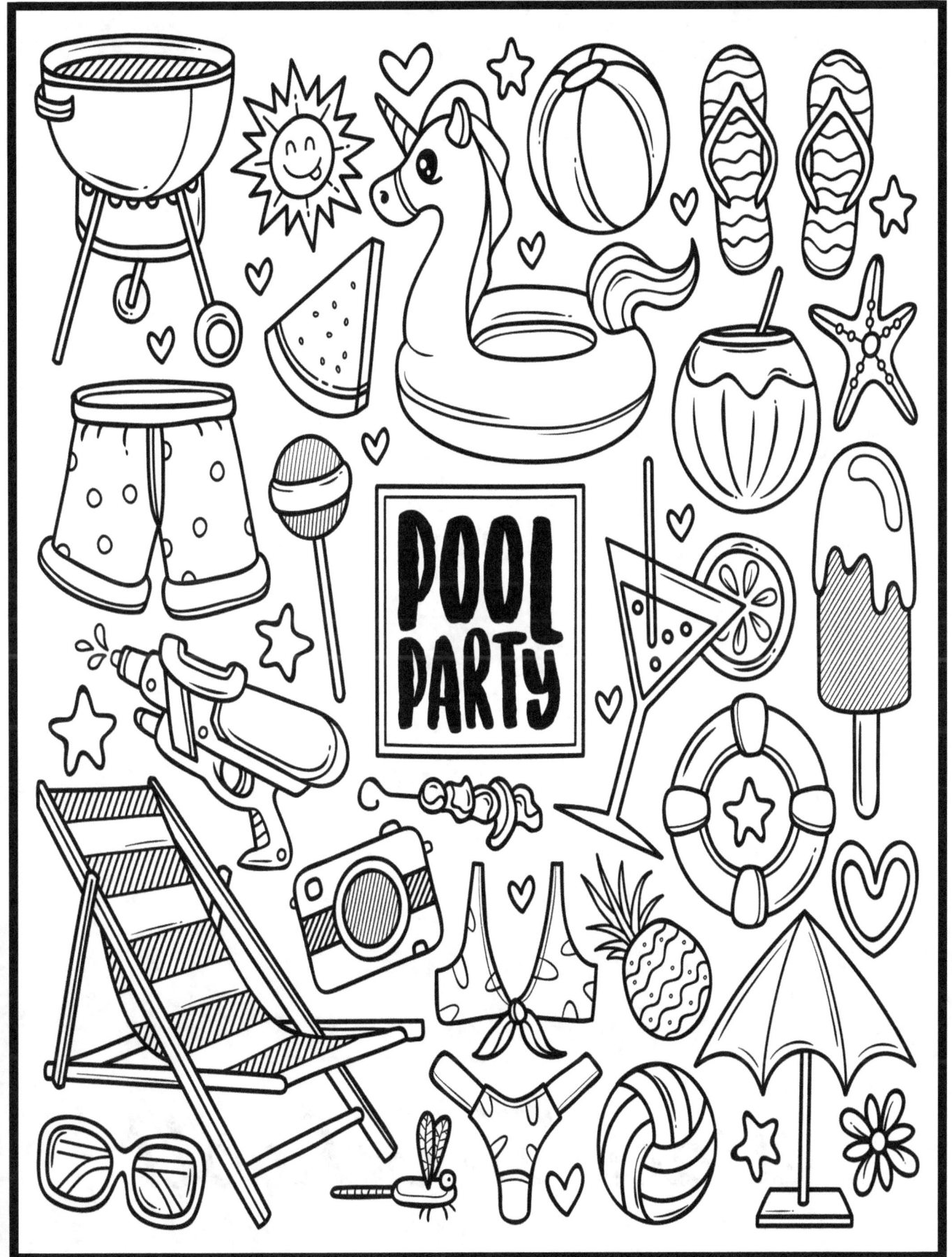

Back To School!

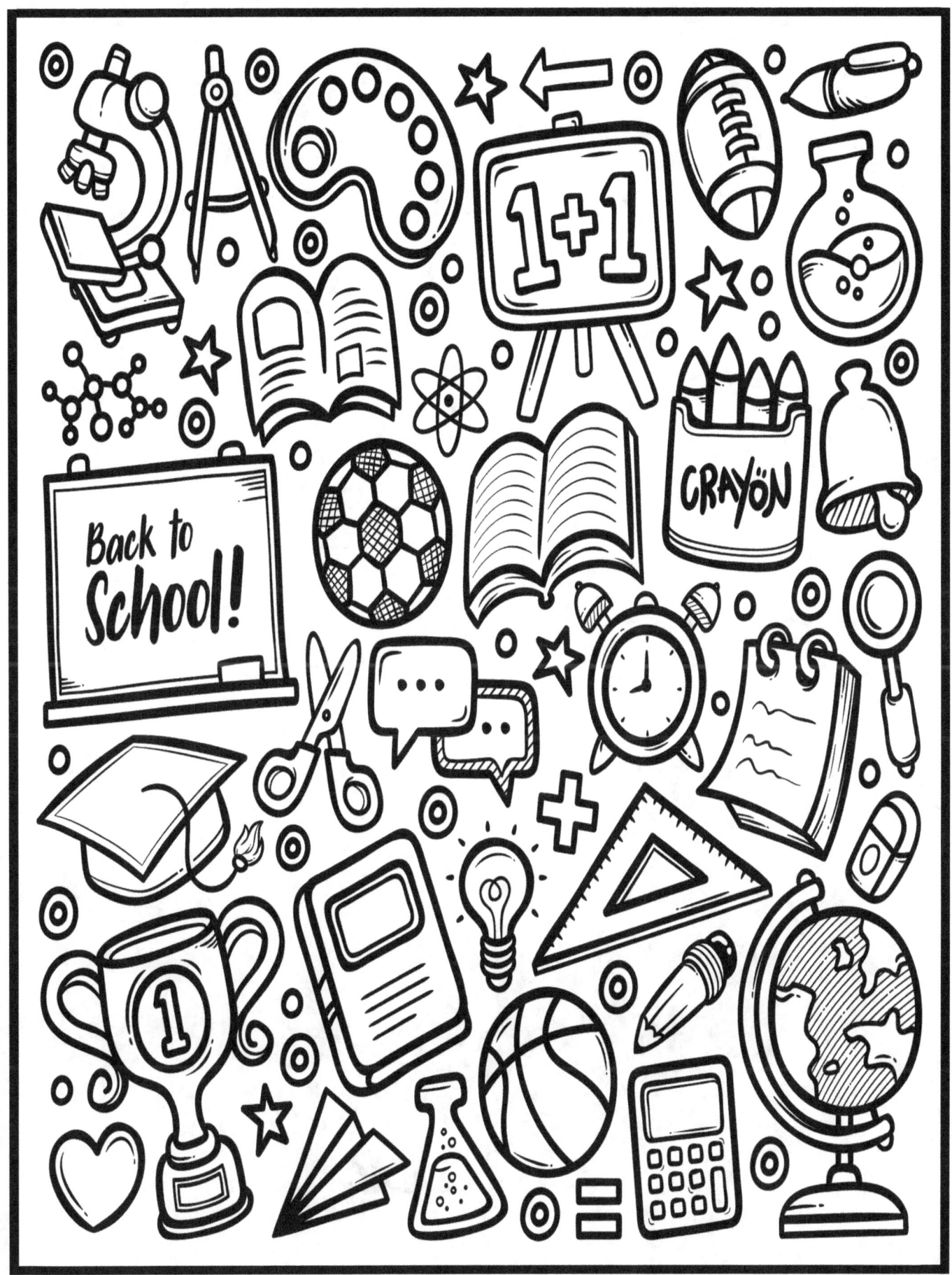

Space

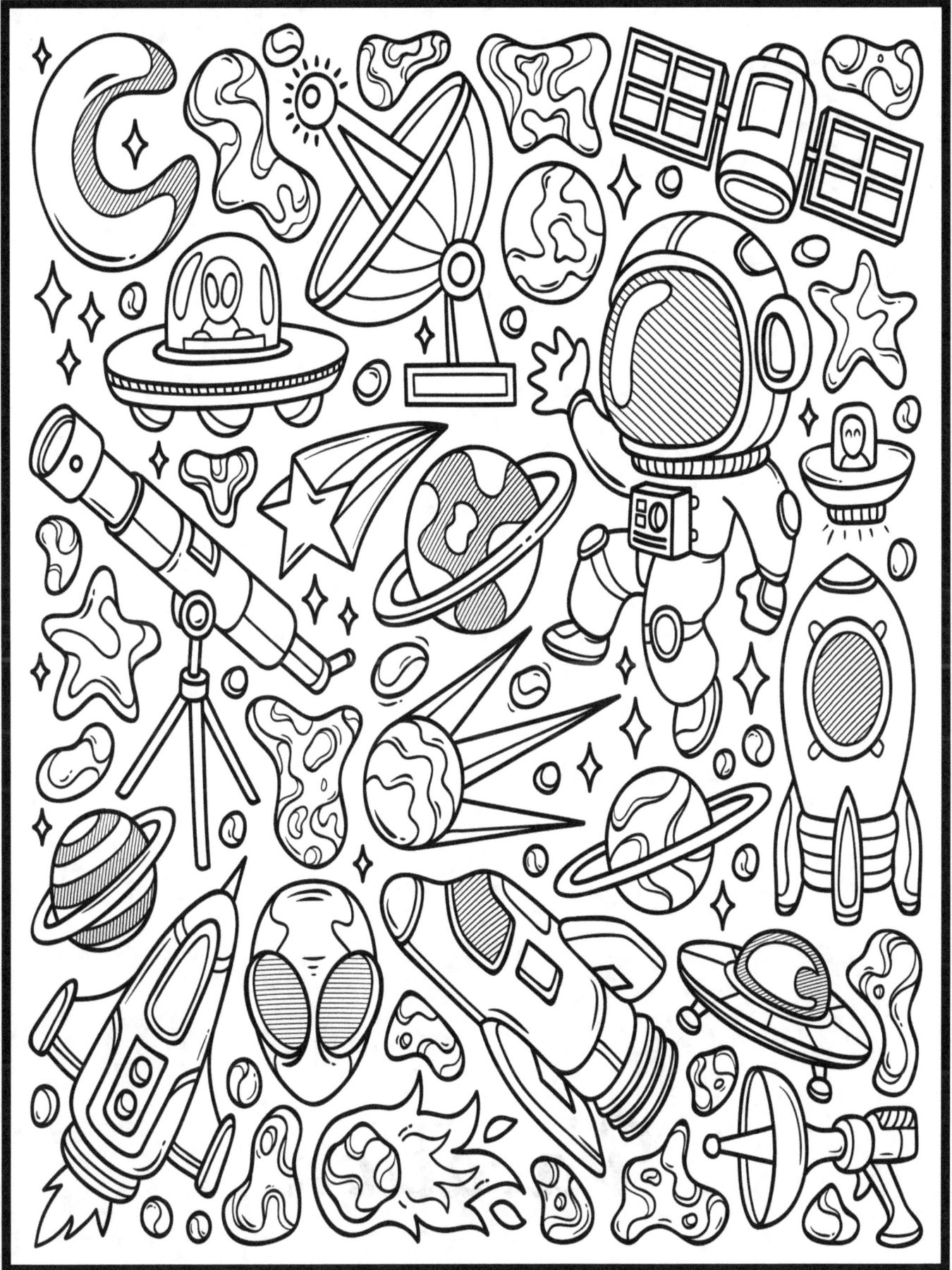

Vacation

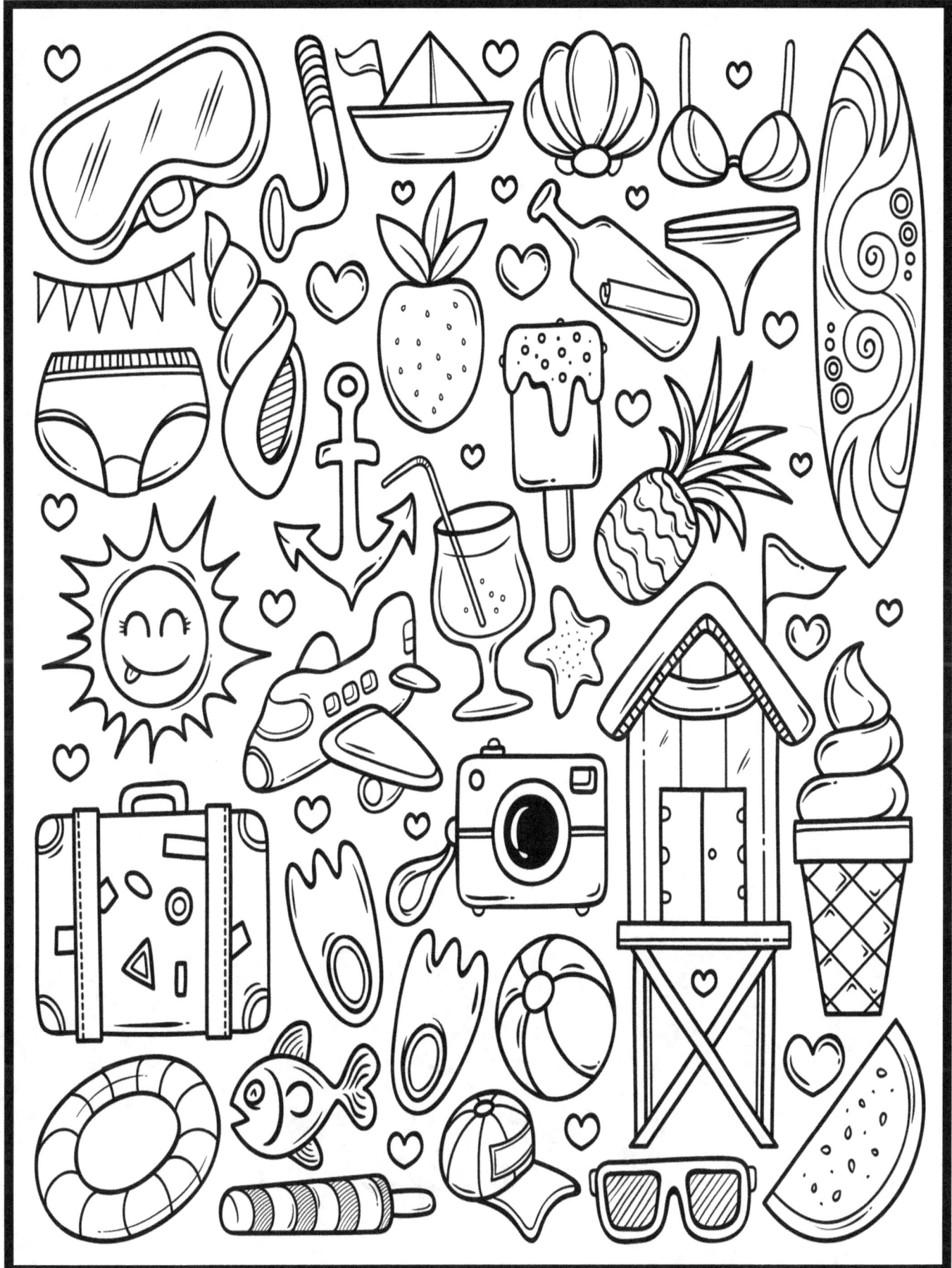

Jazz

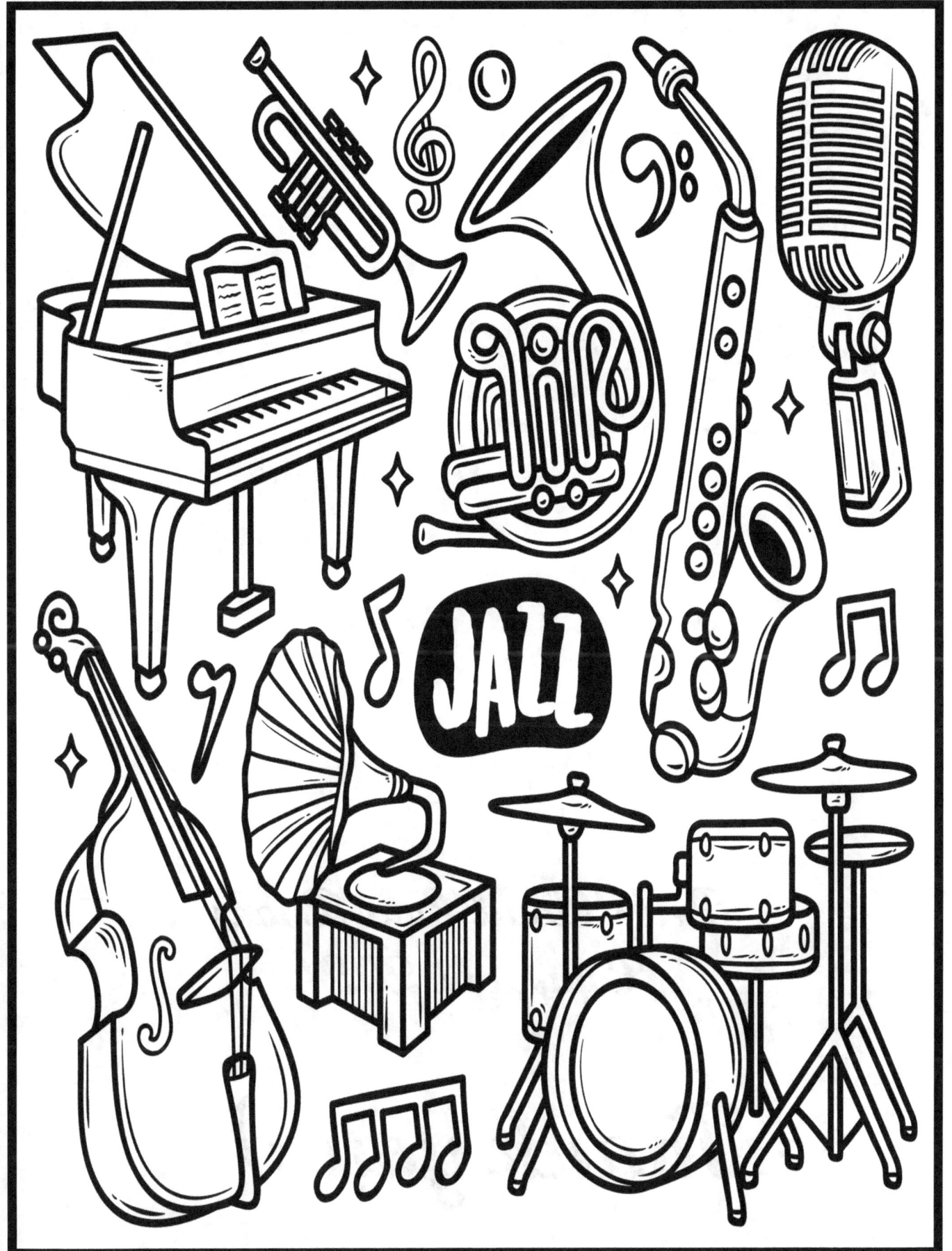

Thank you :)

www.ingramcontent.com/pod-product-compliance
Lightning Source LLC
Chambersburg PA
CBHW080826220526
45467CB00008B/2207